HYPERIMPROVISATION: COMPUTER-INTERACTIVE SOUND IMPROVISATION

THE COMPUTER MUSIC AND DIGITAL AUDIO SERIES

John Strawn, Founding Editor
James Zychowicz, Series Editor

DIGITAL AUDIO SIGNAL PROCESSING
Edited by John Strawn

COMPOSERS AND THE COMPUTER
Edited by Curtis Roads

DIGITAL AUDIO ENGINEERING
Edited by John Strawn

COMPUTER APPLICATIONS IN MUSIC:
A BIBLIOGRAPHY
Deta S. Davis

THE COMPACT DISC HANDBOOK
Ken C. Pohlman

COMPUTERS AND MUSICAL STYLE
David Cope

MIDI: A COMPREHENSIVE INTRODUCTION
Joseph Rothstein
William Eldridge, *Volume Editor*

SYNTHESIZER PERFORMANCE AND
REAL-TIME TECHNIQUES
Jeff Pressing
Chris Meyer, *Volume Editor*

MUSIC PROCESSING
Edited by Goffredo Haus

COMPUTER APPLICATIONS IN MUSIC:
A BIBLIOGRAPHY, SUPPLEMENT I
Deta S. Davis
Garrett Bowles, *Volume Editor*

GENERAL MIDI
Stanley Jungleib

EXPERIMENTS IN MUSICAL INTELLIGENCE
David Cope

KNOWLEDGE-BASED PROGRAMMING FOR
MUSIC RESEARCH
John W. Schaffer and Deron McGee

FUNDAMENTALS OF DIGITAL AUDIO
Alan P. Kefauver

THE DIGITAL AUDIO MUSIC LIST:
A CRITICAL GUIDE TO LISTENING
Howard W. Ferstler

THE ALGORITHMIC COMPOSER
David Cope

THE AUDIO RECORDING HANDBOOK
Alan P. Kefauver

COOKING WITH CSOUND
PART I: WOODWIND AND BRASS RECIPES
Andrew Horner and Lydia Ayers

HYPERIMPROVISATION: COMPUTER-
INTERACTIVE SOUND IMPROVISATION
Roger T. Dean

Volume 19 • THE COMPUTER MUSIC AND DIGITAL AUDIO SERIES

HYPERIMPROVISATION:
COMPUTER-INTERACTIVE SOUND IMPROVISATION

Roger T. Dean

■

A-R Editions, Inc.

Middleton, Wisconsin

ISBN 0-89579-508-6

A-R Editions, Inc., Middleton, Wisconsin 53562
  © 2003 All rights reserved.
  Printed in the United States of America
10 9 8 7 6 5 4 3 2 1

Contents

Preface and Abbreviations — ix

Introduction: Sound Improvisation and Computers — xi

Section 1: Environment and Antecedents — 1
- **Chapter 1 Computers as Cultural Forces** — 3
- **Chapter 2 Antecedents** — 11
  - Instruments and Software 11
  - Compositional Ideas 15
  - Early Interactive Electronic Ensembles 19

Section 2: Into the Interface: Instrument ⟷ Computer — 25
- **Chapter 3 Handling the Hardware** — 27
  - Digital Performance Instruments 27
  - Mixers and Beyond: Dedicated Digital Sound Processing Hardware 29
  - Hyperinstruments 31

- **Chapter 4 Entering the Interface** — 37
  - Interfaces for Sound Control 37
  - Properties of the Interface 41

After the Interface: The Sound Source(s) 43

The Computer as Semiotic Interface 44

Section 3: Sound Routes and MIDI Maps — 47

■ Chapter 5 Algorithmic Processing of Sound and Meta-Sound — 49

Analysis 52

Manipulation 53

Generation 56

Precision, Multiplicity, and Overlaying Features 57

Section 4: Hyperimprovisation: The Software Shoots — 59

■ Chapter 6 Software Media for Improvisation — 61

Historic Contributions 62

Improvisatory Software for MIDI-Stream Generation 65

Improvisatory Software for Audio Generation and Modification (DSP) 68

Improvisatory Looping 70

Generative Software for Sound 72

Specialized Functional Objectives of Generative and Other Software: Rhythm Engines and Other Mechanisms 74

A Case History: The Algorithmic and Interactive Production of Music Related to Drum 'n' Bass 76

■ Chapter 7 Speaking Locally — 79

A Conceptual Synopsis of Possibilities in Solo and Networked Computer Interactive Sound Improvisation 79

Three Case Studies of Networked Computer-Interactive Sound Improvisation 88

A Chronological Synopsis of Computer Interactive Sound Improvisation 96

Some Future Possibilities 99

■ Chapter 8 Mixing the Sounds — 103

The Timbres and Shapes of Sounds in Computer-Interactive Improvisation 103

        The Interaction of Sound with Words and Images   105

        Christopher Yavelow's "Music is the Message"   110

■ Chapter 9   Notes and Annotations: Into the Ear and Eye   113

        The Hub: Two Albums on Artifact   113

        Per Anders Nilsson: *Random Rhapsody*   115

        The austraLYSIS Electroband: Two Albums on Tall Poppies and Future Music Records   117

        Annotations on a Selection of Electroacoustic Improvisation, Some Antecedents to Computer Interactive Work   119

Section 5: Into the Ether   129

■ Chapter 10 Into the Memory and across the Ether   131

        CD-ROMs, DVD-ROMs, and Distribution of Materials for Computer-Interactive Sound Improvisation   131

        Improvisation across the Ether: Immersion   133

Section 6: Some Futures of Computer-Interactive Sound   139

■ Chapter 11 Evolving Futures   141

        Improvising Sound: Emergence   141

        Computers in the Analysis and Modeling of Sound Improvisation   146

        The Computer as Improviser   151

        Utility and Exploitation   152

        Evolution   156

Appendices   157

        Appendix 1: The Questionnaire and Selected Responses   157

        Appendix 2: The CD-ROM   183

References, Selected Bibliography, and Discography   185

Web and Software Resources 199

Index 201

Preface and Abbreviations

This book concerns the roles computers can fill within a real-time creative process—improvisation in sound. A computer can offer sensing, recording, analytical, and generation functions, all applicable to ongoing sound. The generative functions of the computer are of necessity algorithmic, and I indicate that in some important ways all music and sound art (with or without computers) is algorithmic. A compositional score is, in a sense, both an algorithm itself and the result of creation by an algorithmic process. Perhaps the most fundamental and exciting computer-interactive possibility within sound improvisation is that of real-time alteration of the active algorithm(s).

The distinction between the microprocessor in a digital synthesizer and that of a desktop computer is not absolute but rather falls on a continuum. Excellent books already exist on microprocessor instruments and their use (e.g., Pressing 1992). For simplicity, I have chosen mainly to focus on the use in sound improvisation of freestanding multifunctional desktop computers, but I will not hesitate to delve further into the continuum when it seems useful to do so. I also consider hypermedia work, in which sound is a part of a complex with text and image, to the extent that computer-interactive sound can be important. Again, the relationship between computer interaction and improvisation lies on a continuum, of which no fixed portion can be rigorously preferred in my discussion. I will present and analyze some algorithms, making use of the CD-ROM included with the book, often using MAX/MSP (and I confess to primary familiarity with the Macintosh computer); but my argument addresses fundamentals rather than specific programs or platforms. The CD-ROM also includes some interesting sound examples relevant to the text. The bibliography has been kept modest in extent by choosing general references mainly from the period since 1992; on the other hand, it aims to include a representative selection of the whole of the literature specifically relevant to the field of computers in sound improvisation, particularly since 1995. An exception to this is that several of the relevant conference presentations published in proceedings of the International Computer Music Conferences are not listed, since their material is often preliminary, and normally it is subsequently covered more fully elsewhere. This material can be located by means of RILM abstracts (available online), which list such presentations (furthermore, abstracts are often available in this database or elsewhere).

Part of the research for this book involved the use of a questionnaire that was sent to many of the active participants in the field. I would like to thank all the respondents for their useful comments and helpful input. Many of the responses are used in or have influenced the body of the text: quotations are attributed when they occur, and all respondents are acknowledged in an appendix to the book in which other aspects of the responses are briefly analyzed.

The computer can be a fellow-contributor in the performance process, or can extend the possible influence of an individual improviser or a group. It thereby permits "hyperimprovisation"—a new field, and the title of my book.

Roger Dean, austraLYSIS, Sydney

ABBREVIATIONS

aLEb: austraLYSIS Electroband [my computer-interactive improvisation ensemble]

CNMAT: Centre for New Music and Audio Technologies, University of California, Berkeley

EMF: Electronic Music Foundation

IRCAM: Institut de Recherche et de Coordination Acoustique / Musique [French research institution]

STEIM: Stichting Elektro-Instrumentale Muziek [Dutch research institution]

WELL: Whole Earth 'Lectronic Link [San Francisco-based mail net]

Introduction: Sound Improvisation and Computers

The acceptance of electronic instruments has made good music both easier to play and more powerful than ever before. Twenty years ago, only a handful of the most expert bands could hold the interest of a high school audience. Today, every school in the United States has its own group, who, with the aid of amplifiers, pickups, fuzz tones, and countless decibels, can mesmerize their classmates for hours. In a very real sense, the productivity of the group, measured by listener attention divided by the hours of practice and expertise of the performers, has vastly increased.

—*Max. V. Mathews, Frederic. R. Moore, and Jean-Claude Risset, "Computers and Future Music" (1974)*

Almost all existing music falls into one of two categories—completely prespecified pieces, in which each note is written in the score, or improvisational pieces, in which the performer must select the notes with little guidance from the composer. With the computer, there are there are many possibilities between these extremes. The composer may create a framework of relations that limit or direct the performer's choices. He may compose in terms of harmonic laws, rhythmic or metric groups, and gradual changes in overall dynamics or tempo. Some aspects of improvisational music such as jazz can be incorporated into the performance. . . . overall structures and precise interrelations between voices . . . can be retained.

—*Mathews, Moore, and Risset, "Computers and Future Music"*

Currently the rise of computerisation is having a major impact on social structure and human interaction. . . . Artistically there is a corresponding change of emphasis from live performance to studio events, which combine electronics and live performance. [This may be] called a combination of real time and reel time. Hence improvisation now often takes the form of interacting with a computer program rather than collaborating in live performance with another artist.

—*Hazel Smith and Roger T. Dean, Improvisation, Hypermedia, and the Arts since 1945 (1997)*

Technology aligned with the nature of clubbing to raise difficult contradictions of musicians still called upon to perform. How could a performance be meaningful in any traditional sense if the sound had been created through complex sample montage, laborious mathematical calculations and mouse clicks on a laptop computer? Fully immersed in the characteristics of the digital age . . . recording artists are the archaeologists of digitization and its glitches.

—*David Toop, "Just Look at That Sound" (2000)*

This book is as much about music as about sound, and the use of sound in its title is in part to make clear that no prejudicial discrimination between the two is to be expected. Douglas Kahn has emphasized the historical resistance of the sociocultural force known as (Western art) music to sound art (Kahn 1999). At the same time, he has indicated that the "idea of *the musicalization of sound* arose as a means to identify and supersede techniques in which sounds and noises were made significant by making them musical." As he also notes, adventurous music has at least since the 1980s tried to (re)assimilate many forms of sound art into its ambit, and in some spheres resistance now lies more with the sound artists and theorists than with the musicians. Kahn points to the importance of the phonograph, which "represented a new day in aurality through its ability to return virtually any sound back again and again into the sensorium and into the historical register" (5), and as Toop implies in the quotation above, the contemporary phonographs are the sampler and the computer. "Phonography did not simply produce sounds or ideas about sounds but produced audibility, it heard past physiological constraints to the imaginary realms of conceptual sounds, ancient and future sounds, voices of inner speech and the dead, subatomic vibrations, and so on" (Kahn 1999, 9). Kahn warns "against the tendency of subsuming techniques and technologies under technology alone when the two are encountered in the same setting" (15), as is often the case; the reader should bear this distinction in mind when the two are not distinguished in this book. I will aim not to separate sound art and music in the discussion that follows, but rather to emphasize that at least in their search for diversity and innovation, both can take benefit from computer-improvisatory techniques. Indeed, it may be that their mutual distinction will be of decreasing importance in the near future. As David Rosenboom comments, "All cultures seem to have something to which they refer with an utterance in their language that we translate into the word MUSIC" (Rosenboom 2000). Yet presently the same is probably not true of "sound art," and so a mutual acceptance may well be broadly beneficial.

Improvisation and composition in sound form a continuous spectrum, with mutual interfaces and slippages no more obvious than those between red and orange. However, improvisation is usually distinguished as involving substantial fresh input to the work at the time of each and every performance (Nettl and Russell 1998). Improvisation may be based on preexistent materials, such as the harmonic and metrical structure of a 12-bar blues or a popular song, or a series of arrhythmic pitch or sound structures. These materials are often called the "referent" of the improvisation; in the American usage in particular, referent-based improvisation is often termed comprovisation, emphasizing the continuity between composition (the referent) and improvisation (all other components of a performance). As a biochemist as well as musician, I am also tempted to think of the referent as a "substrate" for improvisation. This implies that, as in bodily metabolism, the substrate may undergo structural modifications that are functionally important, as well as simply providing a source of energy and material for the improvisation. Perhaps this is close to the reason that John Zorn has recently described the term comprovisation as "ludicrous" (Zorn 2000, v), though he does not elaborate, nor do other authors in his book.

The concept of improvisation is much more subtle and complex than this, and I have elaborated upon it in a previous book, particularly in a chapter entitled "Improv(is)ing the Definitions" (Smith and Dean 1997, 25–46). In this book I will focus on those aspects of improvisation that can be mediated by computers and only provide here a brief introductory discussion of theories of improvisation and its analysis as process that we have developed in the earlier book (unless otherwise attributed, quotations in the rest of this chapter are from this work). Improvisation has been neglected in the analytical study of Western music, especially in comparison with composition. The situation in the study of computer music is as yet little better, in relation both to the teaching of musical practice and to analysis. For example, even in a detailed taxonomy of computer music with 7 top-level divisions, 26 second-level and 583 third-level, computer-mediated improvisation does not receive its own entry; rather it is (presumably) sequestered under the heading "real-time interactive composition and performance systems" (Pope 1996). Although improvisation "engages with process and change rather than permanence" and exploits the "excitement and fluidity" of the present moment, it must not be viewed simply as spontaneous or lacking in expertise. For some in the 1960s particularly it was more a "mode of existence." Pure improvisation—that which occurred in public or for the purpose of recording—"1) takes place within a defined time frame; [and] 2) occurs continuously through time, at speed, and does not involve revision." Inevitably, choices made by an improviser are "influenced by past experience of improvising." Applied improvisation, in private, can be "a step towards producing a work which will eventually be displayed to audiences, perhaps on a canvas," more commonly in the theater. Most pure improvisation, but not applied improvisation, provides the opportunity for audience interaction. Computerized improvising does not always involve an audience; for example, "in hypermedia the improvisor collaborates not with other performers or the audience but with the computer program, making choices which may never be entirely fixed or reproducible" (as I will discuss further in chapter 8 of this book).

Consideration of improvisation requires emphasis on the relationship between process and product, in contrast to the current emphasis on mechanisms of reception of works of art. It can be useful to distinguish improvisation based on a "pre-arranged structure, procedure, theme or objective" (a referent) from those not so based, while recognizing that total nonreferentiality is almost impossible. "It is quite common for several co-improvisors to initiate a work with independent improvising-referent frames. The postmodern trend toward multiplicity of meaning, and self-deconstruction within works, is thus quite explicit within much group improvising." There can be interpersonal mediation between multiple referent frames, "by formation of continuity or magnification of discontinuity. . . . Thus a multiplicity of semiotic frames can be continually merging and disrupting during a 'free' (i.e., non referent) improvisation."

The improviser can take a stance anywhere between two extremes, "sensory" and "nonsensory," according to the degree of effort required to

> internalise and interpret all the materials provided in the improvisation, whether by him- or herself or by others, and to generate further materials related to those provided. In taking a non-sensory stance, the individual would not only make no response to external material, but would

attempt to avoid even perceiving it.... The sensory improvisor may create material ... intended primarily to affect [his or her own] semiotic field (the introvert attitude), or to affect the fields of the other participants (the extrovert attitude).... The terms introvert/extrovert can also refer to an individual's stance toward the audience,... but ... the audience/performer distinction need only be one of degree.

Techniques of association or nonassociation are central to the improvising process. "Individuals tend ... to develop their material by a transformative process, which necessarily entails that they generate self-associative tracks. These may at the same time be associative or non-associative with the other contributions within the improvising group." Such transformative processes include repetition, expansion and contraction, with the improviser concentrating on small elements. So "the improvising process ... tend[s] to be synecdochal (by which we refer to concentrating on parts) rather than totalising (concentrating upon the whole)." This associative/transformative dominance is probably the explanation for Ed Sarath's perception that "the improviser experiences time in an inner-directed, or 'vertical' manner, where the present is heightened and the past and future are perceptually subordinated" (Sarath 1996).

"To give oneself over to the process [of creativity by improvisation] is to be prepared to open oneself up to the unknown. Creativity as process also involves allowing the work of art to become self-generating, so that words, for example, suggest other words by sound or sense" (Smith and Dean 1997). As Rothenberg has pointed out, both "Janusian" and "homospatial" processes can be important—Janusian being those in which multiple antithetical objects are conceived simultaneously as equally valid though separate, and homospatial being those in which several objects are conceived as occupying the same space, thereby leading to the articulation of new objects (Rothenberg 1990).

Improvisation can be viewed as "a largely conscious procedure which may, because of speed and lack of revision, also access ideas from the unconscious.... A performer may control some process at the analytical level, and other more rapid processes solely at a motoric level.... This access to unconscious elements corresponds to a process of extending oneself, which is implicit in many improvisors' approaches." On the other hand,

> improvisation can be seen to be consistent with the theories of Derrida, Barthes and Foucault in challenging the notion of the creator as sole and immediate focus of meaning. The emphasis in much improvisation on

collaboration, or on the projection of multiple selves, radically interrogates traditional notions of subjectivity. Collaboration, for example, involves the merging of the self with another. . . . [Such factors] lead us to question generally the idea of the artist as the origin of meaning. Rather the artist is the site at which systems of meaning intersect. This helps us to understand that the source of an improvisation is not solely the personality of the creator: personality is an artificial and largely social construct. In addition there may be no such thing as completely spontaneous acts, since our actions move within semiotic systems and so are to some extent pre-conditioned. (Smith and Dean 1997)

In spite of this, it is common to view improvisation as a route to and expression of freedom. The two components of this view imply rather different relationships with both the techniques and the technologies of improvisation. Freedom is a concept that implies mutual acceptance by a community; thus, as a route to freedom, improvisation would require positive audience interaction. This can be seen as consistent with the "ecstasy feedback" model of improvisation, based particularly on Arabic musical ideas (as expounded, for example, by Ali Jihad Racy [Nettl and Russell 1998]), but having comparable relevance in free jazz and other movements. On the other hand, the expression of freedom might not be so bound. At present, computers are not efficient means of providing the ecstatic feedback of certain kinds of live audience; but they may be potent means of aiding the expression of freedom and freedom of ideas.

Improvisation may also be viewed as a means to provide the performers with a (cultural) environment of ambiguity, permitting them enhanced flexibility of expression. Chris Smith has argued this strongly, with particular reference to Miles Davis:

1) Miles's artistic interest was the creation and manipulation of a symbolic "ritual space."

2) Miles enacted this semiotic environment because he believed that certain musical . . . processes could only come out of a richly ambiguous symbolic experience.

3) Miles intentionally supplied, withheld, and distorted performance information because of a quality of attention that such an environment evoked from his players. . . .

4) . . . Miles acknowledged [with reference to Bitches Brew] ". . . I knew that what I wanted would come out of a process and not some prearranged stuff." (Smith 1998)

In this construct, a positive role for computer interaction can be readily envisaged. For example, unlike the well-trodden interface of an instrument in the hands or mouth of a player, the computer instrument can provide ambiguities, uncertainties, and variabilities galore. Similarly, as a meta-orchestra in front of a gesticulating and performing "conductor," the computer can avoid the staleness and the mechanical reproductiveness of a conventional orchestra, the members of which, paradoxically, can be amongst the most bored or negative of professional musical performers. Jon Rose, for example, recognizes his own fondness for such uncertain challenges:

> It's a challenge in the same way that playing with any resourceful improviser can be. The process maybe determined by the constituent parts of musician and technology but any definition would be quite reductive in trying to describe the quite beautiful psychological and physical states attained in this kind of music making. We all deal with the man and machine myth, even acoustic guitar players have to twiddle their machine heads. (Rose 1996)

Improvisation can thus be a sophisticated art, benefiting from experience, knowledge, experiment, and perhaps training (Dean 1989). However, it is desirable to offer entry to improvisational experiment to people untrained in music or sound performance. Computers offer special opportunities in this respect, since they can be used without the need for the ability to play a conventional musical instrument. Thus Morton Subotnick has provided, on the Web, a music-generating interface aimed at youthful people and a commercial CD-ROM counterpart (available from Voyager), while William Duckworth's ongoing Web project *Cathedral* involves interactive components in which less obvious compositional ideas, such as nonlinearity, can be expressed by the novice. While these and many related efforts are important and valuable, their essential provision to the user is one of interaction, rather than improvisation. Human-computer interaction obviously occurs whenever a computer is used, but interactive music mediated by computers involves offering choices to the user, which can influence the progression of the resultant music. Again, the point at which this interaction becomes sufficient to permit the user to improvise cannot be readily defined and probably depends on the individual as well as the software.

Perhaps what is most surprising is how rare it is for an audience at a sound-installation exhibition, or a screener on the Web, to be presented with any opportunity for interaction with the sound generation, in the sense of physical actions that permit changes in the soundstream, let alone opportunity for improvisation. For example, even in the diverse and fascinating major exhibition of sound-art installation work, Sonic Boom (in Hayward Gallery, London, in 2000, and curated by David Toop [Bell, Connellan, and Toop 2000]), an introductory statement displayed within the exhibition itself stated that the exhibition presents new works: "Some take the form of object, some are environmental. All actively involve the listener; they ask to be listened to, looked at, walked through, lingered among, joined in with, & even—in one case—played." "Even"! The playable piece was *If You Were Born in '33, You Would Have Been '45 in '78,* by Paul Burwell, and consisted of a record player "driven by an exercise bicycle" that the artist had modified to make playable by visitors. To be fair, there was also an interactive sound installation by GreyWorld, though unlike much of that group's work—such as the permanent *Playground* installation at the Yorkshire Sculpture Park—the relationship between the movements of the passerby and the expressed sound often went unnoticed. David Toop, musician and curator, provides a fascinating short history of sound art in the catalog. He considers sound art to be "sound combined with visual art practices" and emphasizes the role of a long stream of machines for sound generation, some interactive, as well as that of environmental sound: "The sounds themselves are mysterious for being unfamiliar, their source often uncertain. A sound may even be present by implication, without being heard. . . . [Sound art] offers a landscape of the imagination, transforming the perception of sound from peripheral sense or discrete spectated event to a total environment for the senses." It may be because of this distribution into larger sensory spaces that sound-causing (as opposed to sound-sensing) interaction is limited, but this is clearly not a universal necessity.

In contrast, it is possible to allow an enlargement of the interactive role of the exhibition visitor, and even sometimes its conversion into an improvisatory one. Michael Waisvicz describes how he has been making "playable exhibitions" since the 1970s (STEIM Web site; Wanderley and Battier 2000). These were often available for general users but form a continuum with his well-known development of gestural interfaces for his own performance work, such as Crackle, a range of gloves, and The Hands. Joel Chadabe early on used the term "interactive composing" for "a method for using performable, real-time computer music systems in composing and performing music" (Chadabe 1989). While his early software, such as Play, fits this description closely, he has devised "strategies for using the unexpected to advantage" while performing. Later software to which Chadabe contributed, such as Jam Factory and M, provided much wider opportunities for performer input of material and control of its processing, thus constituting true improvising platforms, to which I will return.

One of the relevant issues in distinguishing computer interaction from improvisation is, therefore, whether the computer response to a user interaction is or becomes predictable, or whether sufficient variability of response is programmed that users must in turn make unexpected responses to satisfy their own sense of musical kinetics. Robert Rowe has discussed computer-interactive music at length, with emphasis on its importance in the performance of composed electroacoustic music (Rowe 1993). The present book will not duplicate this discussion, but rather focus on those points at which improvisational opportunities become clear. However, it is important to note that computer interaction allows anyone access, and just as untrained musicians are among those successful in using computers to generate techno and dance-floor music, so they should be able to generate substantial improvisatory abilities.

One of the distinctions which I have elaborated previously is very pertinent to an archetype of computer music, techno: the distinction between applied and pure improvisation (Smith and Dean 1997). Applied improvisation occurs when a "soundsmith" works in private to establish the structure of a piece by real-time playing with an instrument or computer system, recording and codifying the results into acceptable choices and sequences. Pure improvisation, an analytical fiction, is that which occurs during public performance, particularly that part which is least predetermined. It can be argued that all composition is, or involves, applied improvisation, but the point in this book is to identify some cases and methods in which the improvisatory components seem particularly important. Surprisingly, relatively few techno or other commercial artists talk of their work in their "studio" (usually a room at home for the majority of their creative process) as involving the flexibility and freedom which would normally be available to an improviser (Rule 1999).

What, then, do computers offer to improvisers that may suffice to tempt them to interact? To approach this question, it is necessary to consider the psychological issues involved in improvisation and how computers might influence them. Jeff Pressing has codified the issues with great clarity, emphasizing the "constraints" on improvisational expertise, as well as investigating their impact (Pressing

1988; see discussion in Dean 1992 and Smith and Dean 1997). It is upon these constraints that computers might have most impact.

Pressing discusses improvisation as a system involving expertise, which can be cultivated, and may be only modestly dictated by an individual's "basic abilities." Individuals develop "domain-specific subskills." Improvisation is shaped by

> often rather severe constraints on human information-processing and action. . . . The improviser must effect real-time sensory and perceptual coding, optimal attention allocation, event interpretation, decision-making, prediction (of the actions of others), memory storage and recall, error correction, and movement control, and further, must integrate these processes into an optimally seamless set of musical statements that reflect both a personal perspective on musical organization and a capacity to affect listeners. Both speed and capacity constraints apply. (Pressing 1988)

Pressing then identifies a group of tools that are learned and used to circumvent, if not necessarily to overcome, these constraints. These include the use of referents (structural bases for improvisation), knowledge (a progressively enriching long-term memory of effective materials and responses), specialist memory (giving the example of chess masters remembering plausible positions, but not random positions, far better than novices), generative and evaluative processes, and cultural constraints (Pressing 1988). They filter input and output effort so as to focus most on the features the improviser deems (consciously or unconsciously) most pertinent, exploitable. Pressing also identifies two main "aids for improvisational coherence," one being the notational coding of referents, the other computer interaction. He indicates that these computer-interactive performance systems have been setting "new benchmarks in, if not fundamentally redefining, the improvisation/composition continuum. . . . Such systems have considerable potential for providing assisted musical competence, including improvisational competence, to those with mental or physical disabilities. The landscape of musical expertise will never be quite the same, and it remains to be seen to what extent such systems, even if only in an assisting role, can approach the capacity of the autonomous skilled human expert in terms of contextual fluency, interpersonal interaction, and emotional expression."

Computers, particularly neural nets (see chapters 1 and 9), can also provide a reduced memory representation of "important" previous and ongoing sonic events, so that systematic utilization of this representation can partly overcome some of the psychological constraints, such as the excess of data flux, that the human user experiences. It has been demonstrated that improvisers often select limited aspects of input musical material to use in their performance; computers could assist this, being trained by the performers to select features which they themselves might also select, or vice versa (see Palmer 1997).

This book will evidence throughout that the qualification "even if only" in the last quoted sentence might perhaps be removed, and that computers may well approach the denoted capacities, though without themselves necessarily requiring the connotation of interpersonal and emotional dealings. Their users, it is to be hoped, will retain these inquisitive and outgoing features. So to return to our question: What do computers offer? Computers can record, analyze, modify, and generate musical streams, either as audio sound itself or as MIDI codes (which define the instructions to permit an electronic instrument to generate the required sound). Since there are other codifying systems besides MIDI, some technically preferable such as ZIPI (see Dodge and Jerse 1997), I will often refer to such instructions generically as meta-sound for simplicity. These might include components of the instructions for digital signal processing—that is, modification—of incoming sound. This distinction between sound and meta-sound is sometimes described as data-as-signal versus data-as-event (e.g., Pressing 1997).

Within the limits of memory, data storage, and processor speed, computers can store long stretches of sound or meta-sound, store multiple modified versions of the sound, generate multiple sounds, and emit simultaneously multiple strands of sound. While the computer output is perhaps more obvious, at the input level a computer can also receive multiple simultaneous strands of sound or meta-sound. This has permitted the development of hyperinstruments, in which a novel or conventional instrument provides multiple separate streams of electronic data as a result of playing parameters. These parameters may be derived from body movements (for example, hand positions and rate and direction of movement) or from sensors on conventional instruments (for example, that detect not only pitch and volume, but also rate of airflow, bow or embouchure placements, etc).

Dodge and Jerse 1997 have categorized real-time computer music into a limited number of modes. The "electronic-organ mode" uses the computer just as a sophisticated and unusually flexible sound-generating machine, usually driven by the performer at a keyboard. When a live performer adds a part to a preprogrammed musical score realized by the computer, this is termed the "music-minus-one-mode." "Player-piano mode" is roughly the converse of electronic-organ mode, in that the computer drives another sound-generating module; it is the precision of the execution of the preformed musical instructions that exploits the capacity of the computer. "Conductor" mode is related to this, because the computer follows the performer's score but the performer influences the progression of the computer through the score. Max Mathews developed the first software, GROOVE, that permitted extensive "conducting" controls of computer-generated sound. "Synthetic-performer mode" (a term originated by Barry Vercoe) involves gestural control by a performer of a computer-synthesizer system. Dodge and Jerse happily go on to say that this mode also relates "to musical situations . . . for live and synthetic performers where at least some of the musical material itself is improvised by the computer in real time" (1997) and to refer to the work of Roger Dannenberg and Robert Rowe, which I will discuss. It is interesting to read their anthropomorphic description of computer as "improviser"; I will return later to the topic of computers as "personae." Rowe makes a related distinction, between the "instrument" and the "player" paradigms (Rowe 1993). The former paradigm is "concerned with constructing an extended musical instrument: performance gestures from a human player are analyzed by the computer and guide an elaborated output exceeding normal instrument response." The player paradigm, in contrast, seeks "to construct an artificial player, a musical presence with a personality and behavior of its own."

As pointed out in Smith and Dean 1997, computers also allow performers to network their efforts. Each performer may send information to any other, or to a central computer, and may control the processing of such information. Again, both sound and meta-sound can be exchanged and modified, though there are advantages of bandwidth and speed in restricting the exchange to meta-sound. For example, the Hub, a pioneering network improvisation band based in California's San Francisco Bay area, commonly used exchange of meta-sound, sometimes across the Web—in at least one instance set up such that each performer's computer had its own sound synthesis engine (identical in every case)—to act on the meta-sound information. Thus, what had to be transferred between computers was only the instruction set (meta-sound), usually quite compact in terms of data content, and not the information-intensive sound specification itself.

Superimposed on these possibilities related to direct sound input and output are those of improvisational or compositional algorithms. These may be constructed at any level of complexity and may be accessible to the user to a degree that permits substantial and instantaneous redesign of the algorithm. This is one of the most fascinating possibilities of computer-interactive improvisation, permitting what can be considered "hyperimprovisation." As yet, only a few of the possibilities of hyperimprovisation have been exploited, and this book is probably the first attempt to propose a rational framework for their artistic development.

Surprisingly, while the related idea of hypermedia art has become important in visual work, and to a lesser degree in texts, it has yet to be much exploited in sound work. An essential feature of a hypermedia work is the capacity for nonlinear progression on the part of the user, who may jump from one segment to another disjunct from the previous one to any degree the artist permits. The components of the work form what can seem like a three-dimensional web, as opposed to a linear progression in a movie or a book. A consequence of this for the artist can be the opportunity of dissociating concordant materials from each other, rather presenting disjunction, since multiple jumping strands may be activated simultaneously (see for example, *Sympathetic Strings,* a Web piece by the author included on the CD-ROM). But how often have you seen and heard a Web or CD-ROM piece in which the sound does challenge the image? Partly this is a consequence of technical restrictions on the Web, but this excuse is not valid for CD-ROM works; probably it reflects a technical reticence. I will develop the implied idea of the musical hypertext and its use for improvisers and for less expert interactive users as the book progresses.

Improvisation often breaks boundaries, assuming it recognizes them in the first place. In certain style-bound traditions, such as those of Karnatic or Arabian music, or of "modern jazz," the breakages are modest, but they contribute frissons of extra excitement shared by the improvisers and the cognoscenti of the audience. In some improvisation, however, no preexisting concept of style is envisaged, though references to such styles may veer in and out of view. Derek Bailey has described this approach as "non-idiomatic" improvisation (Bailey 1992), and Anthony Braxton proposes a related dichotomy between "stylist" and "re-structuralist" work (Braxton 1985). David Rosenboom has elaborated on this concept of separation from prior style(s), developing his own term, "propositional music." He writes in an erudite and sophisticated article:

> Propositional music . . . refers to a . . . mindset about music. It assumes that prior to engaging in a compositional act, the composer asks and

then answers the question "WHAT IS MUSIC." Furthermore, propositional music may involve inventing a definition of music and then proceeding to operate within that definition. We may invoke the concept of COGNITIVE MODEL here and say that the composer of propositional music works by first creating a cognitive model of music and then proceeding to make music that is consistent with that model. (Rosenboom 2000)

Rosenboom is a composer and improviser, and his use here of the term *composition* does not exclude improvisation. Thus it is a very broad exhortation toward stylistic slippage, even rupture of prior bonds, in spite of the fact that it invokes a (new) "definition." A computer algorithm, whether for a composer or for improvisers, could readily embody an example (or a component) of such propositional music. Indeed, if we take seriously Rosenboom's suggestion that a musician might first develop a "cognitive model of music" (even an "invented" one) and then use it, then computers are excellent vehicles for embodying such a model and applying it consistently to the musical process. However tempting the general idea here—and I will return to it later in discussing cognitively based improvisation programs—there are some questions. A cognitive model implies a model of some other cognitive entity, perhaps the human mind. At any one time there may only be a limited range of models that retain scientific plausibility, yet it would seem that Rosenboom's purpose in invoking such models is to imply that they might facilitate cognition on the part of listeners. He has considered this: "The mind cannot study itself without affecting itself. Ergo, a composer's mind is changed by the act of studying its own representations for music. Consequently, attempting to derive a mental model of musical representation may, in fact, bring that model into a functional existence" (Rosenboom 2000).

Another general solution to this issue is to think rather of cognitive schema, which might be purely conjectural, and not envisaged as seeking to meet any test of conformance with any other cognitive entity. Taking such an approach in conjunction with the idea that cognition of music by any individual is ever changing (and in that sense not susceptible to a conventional scientific method, which studies invariant physical properties), then a mutual molding of cognitive approaches by improviser and responder becomes plausible. Such a view permits the maximum flexibility in the "propositional music" approach, as Rosenboom no doubt envisaged. It also complements the current emphasis on "embodied cognition." Here cognition is not considered separate from bodily sensation or interpersonal interaction, not a "disembodied," but instead a more subtle interaction of the physical, the bodily, and the sociocultural. From this perspective, the computer can again provide a "disembodied" assistant and/or a pseudo-persona.

I aim to survey both possibilities and achievements in computer-interactive sound improvisation, with regular forays into composition and into the other arts. I will emphasize commercial and dance music, as well as more experimental musics. The book proposes as much as it surveys, since several areas remain relatively unexplored. If it encourages further exploration, it will have succeeded.

SECTION 1

Environment and Antecedents

ONE

Computers as Cultural Forces

> If there comes into being a medium in which a composer writes a program, in which one or perhaps many performer-listeners execute the program on a computer synthesizer, in which the performer-listeners can interact with the program in complex ways to influence the course of the sound, in which there may be no audience, either by choice of the performers or because the potential audience prefers to do its "own thing," should the medium be called music?
> —M. V. Mathews, F. R. Moore, and J. C. Risset, *"Computers and Future Music"* (1974)

> The composer's freedom to explore the data world should not be limited by the audience's level of musical/aural perception.
> —R. Povall, *"Compositional Methods in Interactive Performance Environments"* (1995)

Since this is a book about the use of computers in sound and musical improvisation, it does not deal with computers alone. However, the broader impact of computers necessarily influences their use, and the perception of their use in the arts in general and improvisation in particular. Computers are now orders of magnitude smaller, faster, and cheaper per unit processing power than ever before. They are also distributed throughout the community more and more widely, and there are many public access points, particularly to their use as nodes on the Internet. Thus, unlike many nonelectronic commodities, computers are increasingly accessible economically and practically. For most people, a computer is primarily a vehicle for recording, analyzing, and processing practical and business data efficiently. This functional aspect desensitizes users to the creative uses of computers and may even polarize them against computer art and computer performance.

Katherine Hayles argues (Lunenfeld 1999, 69ff.) that "virtuality is the condition millions of people now inhabit.... Virtuality is the cultural perception that material objects are interpenetrated by information patterns." The virtual subject is "formed through dynamical interfaces with computers" (p. 93). Body boundaries are "extended or disrupted through proprioceptive coherence formed in conjunction with computer interfaces" such that ultimately they constitute a cyborg, a body that is partly or wholly dependent on computers. "What this interpenetration means and how it is to be understood will be our collective invention. The choices we make are consequential, for it is in the complex, doubly figured, and intensely ambiguous conditions of virtuality that our futures lie" (p. 94).

Using computers across the Internet affords many people access to a myriad of information and contacts that would formerly have been inaccessible, or at least not available on demand without great effort. The contrast between the externally imposed choices of television, on the one hand, and the user-responsive, user-created choices of the Internet, on the other, is substantial. Optimists can view the Internet as a force both toward equalization (most people can enter the same vast terrain at little cost) and decommodification (material formerly only available commercially, and in an elitist market, becomes more generally available and often free).

On the other hand, there is plenty of evidence that computers do not (at present at least) sustain a utopia, in spite of the optimism for the future ("an inexorable emergence") embodied in Ray Kurzweil's 1999 book *The Age of Spiritual Machines*. For example, computer use by women lags behind that by men, in spite of the universality of computers in business environments. Cultural association with male dominance and/or "geekiness" remains. This is reflected statistically in the subjects of this book: as Mary Simoni has argued, a male coterie has, whatever its motivation, tended to exclude women from computer music at large. In computer-interactive sound performance, Laurie Anderson is preeminent, but in its improvisatory counterpart, relatively few women are evident (cf. the discussion of Kaffe Mathews in a later chapter of this book).

There has also been a somewhat uncritical acceptance of computer technologies in the arts by those active in their exploitation. Tim Perkis, cofounder of the Hub, has analyzed this:

> [A]rtists who embrace complex technologies have largely abandoned their critical function and have been co-opted, becoming unwitting (or witting) servants of other social and commercial projects that have little to do with art. As a result in music, there has been a shift in emphasis

away from the development of a personal spiritual power, and away from the inherently social aspect of music making. (Perkis 1993)

Perkis points out that computer artists have become consumers of high-tech gear which they have to update continually, and that in the process they become "marketers" and "researchers . . . for industry." But he also notes that "music is social" and "instruments are personal": the backdrop of his work with the Hub involves personal programs, interfaces, and "social" exchanges across the network and outside performance:

> I think that in a techno-capitalist world, where all community and spiritual needs are supposed to be taken care of as a "side-effect" of market forces, it isn't surprising that art would eventually share the same off-center emphasis, marginalizing spirituality and community in the pursuit of technical wizardry. But rather than becoming a cheerleader for industrial technology, the artist has a duty to try to define another way of seeing the world. I'm trying to hold to what may be an old-fashioned view of art: that the artist's job is to be directly involved in developing the spiritual power of individuals, and the power of our communities to deal with what we must: in this case, rapid technological change. (Perkis 1993)

It seems that Perkis still supports similarly positive conclusions in 2000, as evidenced by the continued presence of the text of this talk on his Web site and my personal communications with him.

While the Internet may encourage an inquisitive approach to the world and expand its reality, it also creates its own virtual reality and cyberspace. Until now, much virtual reality (VR) offered by computers and through the Internet has been simply an incomplete reality: in other words, VR, however immersive, has often sought to represent or re-create reality as it is directly perceived. The cyborgs that inhabit such worlds have usually been humanoid, and with luck have possessed *qualia,* feelings and responses like our own, which can be seen as such by an immersed user. However, the possibilities are much broader, as foreshadowed by William Gibson and first analyzed eloquently by Michael Benedikt in his classic *Cyberspace: First Steps* (1991). VR entities can have their own nonphysical yet consistent properties, which may ultimately become predictable to the user.

Such entities have been central in the development of several visual arts movements, such as A-life (artificial life), in which biomorphs or other reproducing entities evolve as the work progresses, be it in private composition or in real-time public performance. I will return to their as-yet limited use in the sound arts; as an introductory example, I note that whereas nearly all musical and other sounds are physically asymmetrical, having an attack which is very different from the decay, an algorithm could readily be written that reproduces sounds but converts every incoming sound into a symmetrical one.

Reproducing VR entities are specialized cases of artificial intelligence (AI) algorithms. In AI the "properties" of the intrinsic entities within the software are more often thought of as algorithms themselves, and most commonly they are still rule based. Thus rules can be devised that, for example, allow a computer to generate a stream of works each bearing a reasonable semblance to a Mozart minuet (Löthe 2000) or to a poem from a particular period of Spanish poetry (Gervas 2000). More fundamental applications of AI seek to use it to develop new theories, often by recombining previous theories, or to write software from scratch that is directed toward some desired function. Genetic algorithms and genetic programming allow the evolution of new functions and properties for components of the software.

The evolution may either be guided by the user (by direct or indirect selection) or exploit criteria built into the software. Both these possibilities can contribute to the ongoing *process* of an improvisation (just as they may be used for generation of software entities that will be used only later). This capacity of computers to influence ongoing processes, together with the possibility that any (non-evolutionary) algorithm may be designed with an interface that permits real-time user interaction to modify the whole basis of the program, rather than simply its parameters, is central to my analysis. Such flexibility of an algorithm allows a precomposed musical score to be drastically varied during the process of performance. This permits improvisation on structural levels that previously were probably not accessible to group and hardly so to solo improvisers.

Networking of computers has other novel implications for information exchange among improvisers, as we have pointed out previously (Smith and Dean 1997) and as will also be analyzed in greater detail later in this book. Computer interaction must be distinguished from improvisation (as mentioned in the introduction), though it may contribute to it. I distinguish between computer interaction in which a user simply explores the material of a program (for example, a hypermedia information display) and generative interaction, in which the program creates a new output in response to the user input. The latter permits the user to employ a process close to improvisation, though if they have any control at all it is usually much less extensive than that which a proficient improviser would exploit.

Earlier I pointed out that improvisation in the arts and more broadly may be a means of liberation from behavioral and stylistic conventions. This can be critical both in applied and pure improvisation—in other words, in devising a work for later presentation or in the process of performance. Computers offer further freedoms. The person who only exists as or "feels" like a cyborg avatar may ultimately have social problems outside virtual reality. But their cyborg incarnation may be able to improvise in ways even beyond those they can effect in person. Similarly, the composer of a computer algorithm for music generation may establish within it variability mechanisms that go beyond those they can use when performing alone or in a non-computer ensemble.

The production of an AI algorithm that responds to certain ranges, however wide, of inputs as a human would respond is not to be equated with the creation of a conscious being. But even much simpler sound-manipulating algorithms may take on the impression of a "personality," or individuality, sometimes quite distinct from that of its author. It is interesting that, in contrast, Jonathan Impett (Impett, in press) has referred to "George Lewis's improvising companion—a computer program in his own self-image"; we will return to a discussion of Lewis's own perspective on the "personalities" of his software. Similarly, Mari Kimura, a violinist expert in performance with computers, has written of performing Zeta violin with Robert Rowe's software Cypher in his piece *Maritime:* after numerous performances "I also learned the personality of Cypher which interacts with my playing."

The "psychological" possibilities of the computer from which a human performer can choose when interacting with such software are powerful. For example, the computer might be left to function completely autonomously, free from algorithmic interference from a user. It might just receive the same range of sonic (or MIDI) inputs as are available to the human performers and evolve its response(s) with time under its own influence alone. While the algorithms used must ultimately have originated from a user, they may be sufficiently complex that even the user can predict little regarding their response. Additionally, the algorithms may have undergone subsequent evolution since their initial construction. A combination of predictability and unpredictability in an algorithm can thus construct a musical persona along with which it is fascinating to improvise.

For the audience, the psychology of interaction with computer music and computer-interactive performance can still be tinged with the impression of the computer as purely utilitarian and lacking in characterful features. In an even more extreme response, music journalists tend to emphasize the visual appearance of an event and the jungle of text that surrounds it. They stereotypically applaud "dynamic performance" or "high energy" when they often mean extensive movement; they salute the "flying fingers" of a brilliant player. Apart from being a mechanism to avoid commenting on the music per se, and even to avoid reading the score of a new composed work, this also reflects a modernist view, centered on the creator and the performer, of the import of a musical event. The focus is on what can be seen, more than on what can be heard. And a single creative mind is assumed to be behind it all. But how interesting is it to watch body parts articulating with the instrument(al)/machine in use?

Clearly this depends on the nature of the articulation, and Schloss and Jaffe describe an amusing instance (Schloss and Jaffe 1993). On occasion, the Flying Karamazov Brothers wore wireless MIDI transmitters in hockey helmets to play music as they juggled and repeatedly bashed each other with juggling clubs. Apparently the audience thought that they were "juggling to a tape." "They had reached the threshold of 'magic' and were doing a lot of work for nothing."

Terre Thaemlitz (dance and electronica artist) has spoken of "getting away from the hyperindividualist thing" in his creative work and of making music "as a way of finding [my] fellow audience . . . an elaborate extension of consuming music" (Thaemlitz 2000). While much of his music is a studio construct, he also has several performance set-ups, one involving a keyboard and a computer and normally done in drag. Thaemlitz commonly establishes an "ambiguous" relationship to the keyboard—for example, perhaps having "frenetic" keyboard playing accompany the sound of restrained and sad music. For him, this requires the audience to "perform" the music by questioning and interpreting. He sees a need for the audience to renegotiate its position in relation to such performance.

In contrast, the audience for the electronica of the dance floor and of the undergound sound event has often achieved this renegotiation and is just as likely to focus its attention (visual and otherwise) uniformly in the physical direction of a spot in which no person is visible, no sound initiation obvious, other than some of the speakers which project the sound. The event may be accompanied by computer-controlled lighting, but this also rarely has a single focus, rather a continuously changing multiplicity of foci. An intermediate event features a DJ (disc jockey) or two who resonate with the musical pulse and listen to new segments on headphones before crossing to them with various degrees of abruptness. Unless the DJ is also a turntable artist who uses the turntable as an instrument, then he or she is usually little or not at all responsible for real-time generation of the sound (though perhaps having pre-recorded it). The element of performance is limited in most of these circumstances.

Theories of deconstruction and postmodernism have downplayed the modernist central role of the creative individual in the production of a work and foregrounded the importance of its variable reception, as in the concept of the writerly text. There is thus a clear convergence between these theoretical views and the behavior of the electronica audience. David Toop provides a relevant description of a partially decentered laptop performance in Tokyo in January 2000, with not an instrument in sight:

> Three men—one Swedish, one German, one Japanese-American—sat bookishly hunched over laptop computers in the centre of the performance area. Perched on a bench within the audience was a Frenchman, also perusing a laptop display that apparently generated sound. Secreted elsewhere among the paying guests were two Japanese longhairs playing mixing desks. In other words, not a musical instrument in sight and even less animation than at a typical Oasis gig. So what did it sound like? Something like eavesdropping on the circulating murmur of an android coffee morning, a pleasantly relaxing detox in the brave new digital steam room. (Toop 2000)

Because computers do not usually move or even readily display direct evidence of the myriad of actions they are undertaking during a musical performance, such events do not readily meet the modernist expectations of a traditional critic, or of a few of their fellow audience members. However, they are directly in tune with postmodernism and beyond. Some audiences are already adjusted to the idea of focusing on sound rather than action; others will simply have to catch up. It is fatuous for them to suggest, as some do, that computer musicians create a direct visual analogue of the computer performance, such as projecting the computer console or a graph of its calculations, to display to the audience, simply to give them something distracting to look at—and to save them from having to listen. Unless such a visual component is a constructive complement to the sound component, as in an intermedia work, it is redundant.

> The common denominator for most [sound] artists is their frustration with traditional music performance. Sitting quietly in rows of chairs, listening to a group of musicians pluck, bang and scrape for a designated

time is a fairly recent notion in the history of music. . . . Then disco, followed by hip-hop, replaced musical instruments with record decks and lifted the audience off its collective backside and on to the dance-floor so rushing the obsolescence of the gig towards its final conclusion. (Toop 2000)

Computer improvisation flourishes in both the obsolescing and future environments, as we will see.

TWO

Antecedents

Many of the possibilities that became widely available to musicians only after computers became digital and desktop had nevertheless been explored in earlier eras. There were prototype interactive electronic instruments and ensembles (Chadabe 1997), and certain composers theorized or wrote scores whose realization was unlikely without the development of such instruments. Since Joel Chadabe, an early electronic practitioner-composer, has quite recently published an entertaining and detailed book on the development of such electronic instruments and ensembles, I will here only survey the important ideas, rather than providing detailed documentation, and emphasize the improvisatory applications.

Excellent information on the early period of electronic music from a more contemporaneous viewpoint is also available (Appleton and Perera 1975; Ernst 1977; Holmes 1985). Pressing provides a very useful chronological "Outline of Developments in Electronic Music" (Pressing 1992). Appleton essentially divides early electronic music into "tape music" and that using voltage-controlled synthesizers; the latter is closer to the interests of this book.

■ INSTRUMENTS AND SOFTWARE

An archetypical interactive electronic instrument is the theremin, which detects hand position and movement in relation to the instrument by capacitance measurement and translates it into pitch and its fluctuations and dynamic. Some performers such as Clara Rockwell (Anonymous 1998) achieved considerable virtuosity on the instrument, which nevertheless has a limited timbral range. However, it was very important in revealing that gesture in space could be the indirect source of musical sound: neither physical origination of sound, as on most string and wind instruments, nor keyboard attacks are necessary for performance. For some listener-viewers this remains a problem in the appreciation of computer music, even almost a century after the theremin's invention. Paradiso has recently reviewed other applications of "electric field sensing" in instruments such as the hypercello and its viola counterpart (see chapter 3) as well as sensing mannequins and chairs (Paradiso and Gershenfeld 1997).

Mumma 1975 gives a fascinating discussion of some other early electronic instruments, commencing with a patent granted to Ernst Lorenz in 1885 for "an electromagnetic resonator controlled by a vibrating metal bar and a hammer," and continuing with the "incredible Thaddeus Cahill," an American lawyer who between 1892 and 1907 built the telharmonium, an electronic music synthesizer that "could be performed live over the telephone system." He also discusses the ondes martenot, an early electronic instrument that even more than the theremin has established and maintained a position in concert music, by virtue of the dedication of a series of performers and composers.

By 1970, according to Chadabe (cited in Appleton and Perera 1975), there were already "several hundred" voltage-controlled (i.e., analog) synthesizers in U.S. colleges and other institutions. In this context Ciamaga (pp. 68–137 in Appleton and Perera 1975) states that "exact repetition of programmed information is restricted by the stability of the oscillator and timing generators, and so forth. The composer who understands these limitations and can tame the abundant sound material offered by the synthesizer through the meeting of improvisation and simple programming will not be disappointed." He clearly refers to applied improvisation, in my typology. Martin Bartlett (1985) was among those who used microcomputers to control synthesizers in performance from 1977 onward using the KIM-1 computer, a choice he shared with the members of the League of Automatic Composers (see below). The KIM-1 controlled a "personal analog synthesis system," the Black Box. Bartlett used it solo and as part of the Networks Orchestra, an electronic-instrument improvisation ensemble. Bartlett says, "I am impressed at the complexity and diversity of the music I can make with it. The countless hours [of construction of the system] have been rewarded by the partial realization of a long-term goal: to perform a lively and intricate music full of timbral, tonal, temporal and spatial variety, and to do so with my own resources wherever I may happen to be."

Several exceptional "instruments" are discussed in Mumma 1975. Stanley Lunetta's "Moosak Machine" used light, temperature, and proximity sensors. It "produces, mixes and processes [sound]. . . . [It is a cross] between an automaton and an artificial intelligence. In this sense it is a candidate for the category of live electronic music because it so closely mimics the attributes of live performance." Ramon Sender, in his 1964 piece *Desert Ambulance,* used an instrument called the chamberlain: "probably the most unusual live performance invention . . . a series of magnetic tape loops, with each loop activated by a corresponding key on a traditional keyboard. The sounds . . . are from any sources, and are recorded by the performer in advance." In other words, a prototype sampler player!

John Rogers (pp. 189–285 in Appleton and Perera 1975) discusses early uses of digital computers in electronic music creation, noting that the first endeavors in computer sound synthesis occurred in the late 1950s at Bell Telephone Labs in New Jersey. Early practitioners, some of whom were perhaps as much experimentalists and computer scientists as composers, included Lejaren Hiller (Hiller and Isaacson 1959) and Max Mathews (Mathews 1969). Mathews, who initiated the well-known series of Music N synthesis languages, was a forward-thinking scientist (Mathews et al. 1974) later saluted in the naming of the interactive software platform MAX, which will be discussed frequently in this book. Mathews, together with Moore and Risset, also developed Groove: "our first realization of a realtime system is called Groove (generated real-time operations on voltage controlled equipment). Groove is a hybrid system that interposes a digital computer between a human composer-performer and an electronic sound synthesizer" (Mathews et al. 1974). This involved the "conductor concept": "that the relation between the performer and the computer is not that between a player and his instrument, but rather that between a conductor and an orchestra." Even in 1974, they could go on to write: "Although Groove has been in existence for only a little more than 3 years, many hours of music have been composed and, even more encouraging, the musicians who have tried it are highly enthusiastic. . . . Within the next few years, a Groove-like system consisting of composer, computer, and digital sound synthesizer, will allow the interactive generation of virtually any sound that can come from a loudspeaker in real-time" (Mathews et al. 1974). Among the excited musicians was Laurie Spiegel, to whom we will return later.

The Fairlight computer music instrument (CMI) was a pioneering machine from the early 1980s and is discussed in some detail in Chadabe 1997. While there were other competing contemporary machines, some of the attitudes toward CMIs are interestingly revealed in relation to this then highly expensive machine.

Martin Wesley-Smith, a leading Australian composer and video artist who has also participated in improvisation, stated in his response to my questionnaire:

> We're talking here about the 8-bit Fairlight II, which was being phased outin 1986 or so. . . . I wasn't very interested in it as a conventional live keyboard instrument, though it was used extensively in the early days in that capacity by pop artists such as Stevie Wonder. Apart from being cumbersome (physically large and heavy, and voices took a long time to load), it was the greatest thing since sliced bread, mainly because its sounds were so good. Like a lot of analog instruments back then, it seemed to have its own particular sound, one that attracted a lot of players and composers (it largely lost that sound, IMHO, when it moved to 16 bits. . . . Users [could] sample then work on their own sounds and thus develop their own distinctive set of voices (it also allowed the creation of voices through additive synthesis). Users could also swap voices on disk, and Fairlight would collect good voices from users and send them around to others. . . .
>
> My main use of the Series II as a non-conventional real-time instrument was the stuff I did with Jon Rose (several concerts and the LP). It was not designed for this use, of course, so it had to be encouraged to produce unconventional sounds and effects. The usual limitation of sampled voices (play them higher or lower and they read the samples faster or slower) was a blessing here, for it enabled some very interesting sounds to be produced. The 8-bit sampling was also a limitation in terms of sound quality, of course, but it didn't seem so at the time (we hadn't yet been seduced by the cleanliness of 16-bit sampling)—in fact, looking back it was another blessing, for the sounds were often dirty but rich, with compelling grunginess. Other limitations, such as a maximum polyphony of eight voices, were limitations to be worked around (e.g., sample chords, or learn how to produce maximum effect with just 8 voices). Fairlight's unique MIDI sequencer, Page R, which cycled one bar ad infinitum, or until the user kicked off a pre-defined sequence, was useful for building up repetitive patterns. Being a computer musical instrument, it did not, ridiculously, though in common with most other computer instruments produced since, enable the real-time user to exploit pseudo-randomness as one could using control voltages: you pressed a key and got back the same sound every time (you could vary vibrato, reverb etc with faders, but the effects produced were relatively minimal). It was a challenge to use, but it was reliable and one could do some great things with it. . . .
>
> "[H]ow it seemed psychologically"? I felt very comfortable with that machine, for I knew it pretty well (its strengths and its weaknesses). In its day it was the most advanced machine of its kind anywhere (Synclavier users might dispute that), and I was constantly, throughout its life, discovering new things I could do with it. Thus while I was challenged by it I was excited by it. More than that, it became a reliable

friend, a companion on Life's journey through the sonic maze. I was devastated, looking back, by its early demise, and never felt as comfortable with the new-fangled modular MIDI systems, with their computer sequencers etc., that replaced it. They might have been smaller, and cheaper, and technically better, and more powerful, but they lacked character!

■ COMPOSITIONAL IDEAS

Early in the century many composers proposed that synesthetic relationships between sound and image could be established and important (for example, Scriabin). This was an anticipation of the current trend for hyper- or intermedia work, especially in that the early composers envisaged that there might be perceptually or cognitively prioritized relationships between sounds and certain images or colors: a conventionalized association between kinds of images and subordinated stereotypes of music is often still claimed. On the other hand, current intermedia work has also opened up the possibility of mutual interrogation by sound and image.

Certain composers, notably Percy Grainger and subsequently Karlheinz Stockhausen and Iannis Xenakis, advocated ideas of sound composition that almost inevitably required the participation of electronic instruments, or at least instruments capable of control of timbre and pitch in ways rather different from those of most acoustic instruments. For example, Grainger's *Free Music* envisaged a complex of sliding tones that could readily be played on string instruments, and with more difficulty on wind, and that he best envisaged on the theremin (Kahn 1999, 89ff.). According to Grainger, "Machines (if properly constructed and properly written for) are capable of niceties of emotional expression impossible to a human performer. That is why I write my Free Music for Theremins—the most perfect tonal instruments I know." The notations often involve a multidimensional grid, which gives the impression of being a graph such as is generated and interpreted by computer. With the assistance of Burnett Cross, Grainger designed many instruments using other mechanical objects. Recent realizations of his pieces have naturally taken advantage of other electronic aids, as well as using acoustic instruments.

There are many ways in which the modernist work of Stockhausen, Boulez, and their contemporaries foreshadowed the potential of digital computers. On one hand, the total serialism in which they both participated at certain times predicated a score whose depth of information is so great that a human performer has considerable difficulty in achieving a totally precise realization; a computer performer is an implied surrogate. On the other hand, Stockhausen in particular pioneered electronic music techniques using tape editing and analog studio techniques whose digital counterparts became necessary parts of digital electronic technology once it developed. Stockhausen was unusual among his total-serialist colleagues in soon afterward writing scores for "intuitive" music that are largely text-based referents for improvisation. The text may be a music-procedural instruction, or it may be an exhortation to achieve a particular psychological state through the process of improvising.

Xenakis, in his exciting book *Formalized Music* (1971) proselytizes for a range of stochastic (chance-driven) computer approaches to generating scores, be they for instruments or electronics. In some cases these generate the microdetail of pieces whose higher-level structure is dictated more conventionally. In others, the computer algorithms are the higher-level structure and dictate every aspect of the resultant piece. In all these cases, the approach that Xenakis used to compose is now accessible in real time to a computer-interactive improviser who is prepared to write the appropriate algorithms into a performing platform.

David Cope (1991) discusses some of the compositional background in his stimulating book about computer-algorithmic composition, which focuses particularly on the re-creation of earlier musical styles, such as those of certain keyboard works of J. S. Bach and W. A. Mozart. Augmented transition network (ATN) parsing (which exploits recursive possibilities in the programming language LISP) was central to Cope's own approach. ATNs use variation processes akin to those of natural language processing. For example, a musical phrase analyzed into Statement, Preparation, Extension, Antecedent, and Consequent (Cope's SPEAC system) can be used as the basis for generation of further phrases of the same structure with substitute components—$A_{1->n}$ for A, new $E_{1->n}$ for E, and so on, or new $S_{1->n}$ for P, E, A or C; the former results in modest or no durational expansion, while the latter results in substantial expansion. What is required for such an approach is akin to requirements of natural language: for example, a dictionary of nouns is needed, so that nouns can be replaced with new nouns in a sentence generated from a source sentence. Such devices are commonly used in automated question-answer systems. Cope points out the relationships between SPEAC analysis and that of Heinrich Schenker, in so doing emphasizing the possibility of top-down construction, in which a single large-scale rule and description is progressively broken down into component rules, descriptions, and attendant ATNs, to a degree that ultimately permits note-by-note realization.

By extension from natural-language analysis, analyses of works of literature can provide rules that reflect particular writing styles, and those of music can reflect particular composing styles. Cope states that "a 'transition network' consists of interconnecting states that end subphrases of sentences, initiate correct new phrase subsections, or do both . . . the success or failure of efforts to generate grammatically correct music depends on . . . appropriately constructed dictionaries of harmonies (notes—word equivalents) and motives (signatures—phrase equivalents)." A higher-level component is the "signature . . . a set of contiguous intervals (i.e., exempt from key differences) found in more than one work by the same composer. Signatures typically contain two to nine notes melodically and more if combined with harmonies. They are generally divorced from rhythm, though rhythmic ratios often remain intact." Such dictionaries and signatures are stored in his "Experiments in Musical Intelligence" system in relation to the styles of several composers, from Bach and Mozart to Bartók, Prokofiev, Stravinsky, and himself. "Using function equivalents similar to Chomsky's . . . transformational grammar, entrances and exits to these ATN matches are made logical and made to conform to the musical parsing of the original style in the database." Although Cope's description is laced with terms of constraint such as "correct" and "appropriate," he also notes: "Constraints are better presented as lists of desired results rather than as lists of what should not take place." It is notable that the overall program structure does not require substantial changing when moving from one style to another, just the database of grammars and signatures. Decisions about tonality versus atonality are in the main category of possible exceptions to this rule.

Besides composers from the mainstream of classical concert music, Cope also automated versions of one style of George Gershwin and of the rags of Scott Joplin, with, in his own view reasonable success. He was perhaps less optimistic about his efforts with a Balinese gamelan style: "As with their Western counterparts, Balinese listeners differ in whether machine-composed gamelan music imitates the genre successfully. So much depends on the performers' style of improvisation, which will vary from performance to performance." Cope thus seems not to anticipate that improvisatory styles will be as susceptible to the experiments-in-musical-intelligence approach as composition, though he does not discuss this. In principle, it would seem that idiomatic improvisation in particular, coherent with a particular genre and musician or period (e.g., hard bop jazz or the meditative music of John Coltrane), would also present signatures and grammars that might be analyzed and parsed.

Accordingly, the Flavors Band is a language developed as a rule-based method "for specifying jazz and popular musical styles procedurally" and has been used with modest success, according to the author, in generating the bass line and a solo line for John Coltrane's *Giant Steps:* "except for the unnatural sound of the Chroma synthesizer, it is conceivable that the piece could have been performed by a human jazz band" (Fry 1989). More recently, Assayag and colleagues have tried to develop a "universal prediction algorithm that provides a very general and flexible approach to machine learning in the domain of musical style," claiming that "improvisation or assistance to composition can be realized on the resulting representations" (Assayag et al. 1999). A degree of success with the generation of Bach such as the two-part inventions (based on the input of a set of his inventions) and in the generation of jazz parts for the Orchestre National de Jazz in a piece by Jean-Remy Guerdon, MiniX (material used as input is not specified) is claimed.

Another idea has also been influential in the computer modeling of improvisation: that of conversation between several individuals. This uses an analogy with natural language in which the variants are the result of successive input by different individuals. Bill Walker has written his quite effective "ImprovisationBuilder" software in part on this basis, and it can participate in real-time performance, rather as if it were an individual improviser. To quote Walker's thesis (available on the Web at the time of writing): "ImprovisationBuilder (IB) addresses three central problems for human-computer interaction in music—generation, interaction, and re-use. IB has been applied to two musical domains—the free-form improvisation . . . , and the small jazz ensemble of the 1940's and 50's. IB proved quite appropriate to the two musical domains" (Walker et al. 1992).

I will return next in Chapter 5 to a discussion of such algorithmic improvisation efforts. A separate difficulty faced in some later algorithmic adjuncts to improvisation is that of supporting nonidiomatic improvisation, as mentioned in the introduction. In such contexts, an improviser might not wish to be bounded by invariant constraints, or even by any preconceived constraints.

■ EARLY INTERACTIVE ELECTRONIC ENSEMBLES

Stockhausen opened up many new avenues in electronic music in the 1950s. Before and alongside his own "intuitive" music, some performing musicians with access to electronic instruments began to develop ensembles in which group interactive improvisation with electronics was a focus. Well-known examples in electronic music that were related partly to contemporary classical music and partly to improvisation were Gruppo Nuova Consonanza (GNC; founded in Rome in 1964 and also known as the Gruppo di Improvisazione Nuova Consonanza) and Musica Elettronica Viva (MEV; founded in Rome in 1966 and also known as Musica Elettronica Viva) in Italy, and Sonic Arts Union in the United States. Both GNC and MEV were concerned in part with music as social therapy, as tangentially evidenced in Rzewski's description of MEV's *Spacecraft,* an improvisatory group composition (1967–68): it involved interactions to lead each player from his "occupied space" of personal inclination to a "new space which was neither his nor another's, but everybody's" (Griffiths 1979).

Tim Perkis has commented on a more recent (1994) MEV concert in Oakland, California, involving Frederic Rzewski (piano), Alvin Curran (piano and sampler), Richard Teitelbaum (electronic keyboards), and George Lewis (trombone and live electronics):

> The musical performance was one continuous improvisation lasting for nearly an hour. An unforeseen circumstance enhanced the air of improvisation: Teitelbaum was snowed in in upstate New York and was unable to attend, so at the last minute a modem link was made between his keyboard synthesizer in New York and an identical one on the stage. So Teitelbaum was present in an eerie invisible way, the keyboard sitting center stage before an empty chair. . . .
>
> MEV has embodied and carried forward several of the main avantgarde currents that arose in the sixties: an interest in using cheap, homebuilt electronics in the context of live performance; improvisation as an extension to written composition, and an emphasis on the collective and spontaneous aspect of music making. While the means are no longer rough homebuilt electronics—MIDI has hit MEV as it has many others—these newer tools are handled in an almost naive and spontaneous way. (Perkis 1999)

Teitelbaum's remote-control performance on this occasion was perhaps fitting for someone who had also been an early participant in the biofeedback endeavors associated with David Rosenboom (Teitelbaum 1976). Gentle Fire (1968–76; including Richard Bernas,

Hugh Davies, and others) and Intermodulation (1969–76; including Roger Smaller, Tim Souster, and others) were some of his counterparts in the United Kingdom that developed in part as a result of direct interaction with Stockhausen (Griffiths 1979) and were invited by him to perform some of his electronic music. Teletopa (initially with David Ahern, Roger Frampton, and Peter Evans) was active in Australia in the early 1970s. Mother Mallard's Portable Masterpiece Company in the United States had a very clear-cut and achievable agenda: to create "improvisation situations that foster innovation" (Mumma 1975). In music more closely related to the jazz tradition, at least in origins, we might consider Sun Ra and his barrage of analog (and later digital) synthesizer sounds, and AMM and their unique European contribution (Toop 1995).

Alvin Lucier, a member of Sonic Arts Union, provided an early electronic group comprovisation, "North American Time Capsule 1967." The sleeve notes to the recording (Odyssey 321 60156), as quoted by Ciamaga (Appleton and Perera 1975), state: "The performers are asked to prepare material using any sounds at all that would describe . . . the . . . situation in which we currently find ourselves. The performers' sounds are fed into the vocoder and are modified during the performance both by the sounds acting as control signals and by the manual alteration of the vocoder components."

Although performers in electronic contexts commonly used analog synthesizers, and sometimes analog sequencers, it was unusual for a multipurpose analog computer to be used, and my research has not revealed detailed documentation of such applications. However, once computers made the transition from analog and/or mainframe to digital and desktop, beginning in the late 1970s, there was an accelerating interest in their use as core to the interactive component of electronic sound improvisation. Gordon Mumma was prescient (Mumma 1975), particularly in the fascinating section of his article "Astro-Bio-Geo-Physical Application." He discusses David Rosenboom's 1970 piece *Ecology of the Skin,* in which "α,β,θ currents of several people were applied to control inputs of an electronic-music synthesizer. . . . members of the audience could have their own private light show by applying phosgene-stimulating electrodes to their temporal lobes." Rosenboom pioneered the use of "biofeedback" and novel instruments and computer languages for their control or interpretation, such as the appropriately named FOIL (Far Out Instrument Language) (Polansky 1989; Rosenboom 1989). He sought "performance of a musical structure in response to shifts in selective attention, as evinced by phenomena detected in the EEG" (Rosenboom 1990). Later Californian developments included Kiva, an improvisation group active at the University of California at San Diego, of whose activities in the mid-1980s one of the participants, Xavier Chabot, has said:

> In the context of Kiva, I began to use electronics because electronics allowed me to deal with the problems of finding a rapport between making a gesture and hearing a sound. . . . We tried all sorts of things. We experimented with fuzzy logic. We used electronic instruments. I used my pitch detector for the flute and saxophone. We used Jam Factory. It was a complex development. We used ultrasound to sense distance, and we used the air drum. Pat Downes developed various things for us, including a detector that I attached to my arm to know whether it was horizontal or vertical. I had an accelerometer on my foot and in my hand. (Chadabe 1997)

Ralf Hutter and Florian Schneider, of the "robotic" electronic pop group Kraftwerk, were also working on human-computer control mechanisms at this time. According to Jim Aikin, "the ultimate, they feel, would be an instrument that 'instantly produces whatever sound you think of' by a direct link with the mind . . . a complete symbiosis of organism and technology" (Rule 1999, 181). Be this as it may, the theme of connections between people and computers was close to much of their work, notably their *Computer World* album. More impressions of their work are given in Toop 1995.

On the global- (rather than local-) interactive scale, Gordon Mumma also considers control by computer-satellite systems by which "the ensemble performances . . . could be achieved by using several satellites at the same time; or collective or ongoing compositions and performances (perhaps even by an anonymous collective) could be achieved over a considerable span of space and time."

One of the most interesting and well documented of the early interactive electronic ensembles was the League of Automatic Music Composers (Bischoff et al. 1985), whose concert on July 3, 1978, in Berkeley, California, is the subject of the quoted article. There were three performers: John Bischoff, Rich Gold and Jim Horton. Each used a KIM-1 microcomputer to generate sound (or, in Horton's case, to generate sound indirectly). Each composer (as they describe themselves in the article) "had programmed his computer with a music program that was by itself able to produce music; however, the programs were also able to input data that would affect the musical content and to output data that would affect another computer's program." A simple circular data flow was used in which Bischoff sent data to Horton, Horton to Gold, and Gold to Bischoff. Sound was diffused over a "high-fidelity music system." The composers used programs that had been written to stand independently and modified them to give and take inputs and outputs. They ranged from that originally planned to be suitable for a "casual" environment and consisting of "long moments of rest interspersed with computer tones" to a timbral generator and a harmonic and melodic function. A similar technique of network text writing is used in Bischoff et al. 1985 to allow the musicians to summarize their views on "network music":

> Independent simultaneous activities viewed as one single activity always bring to mind the idea that groups can work wonderfully together without the anxiety of control structures that supposedly ensure success....
>
> To explore catastrophe hypersurfaces in the relative safety and comfort of involvement with one's friends and neighbors!
>
> At each stage in the development of the network the music changed unpredictably....
>
> When the elements of the network are not connected the music sounds like three completely independent processes, but when they are interconnected the music seems to present a "mindlike" aspect. Why this is so or why we can perceive some but not all activities as the product of an artificial intelligence is not understood. (Bischoff et al. 1985)

The article includes a photograph of a later performance in which Tim Perkis participated; together with John Bischoff, he was instrumental in the establishment of the important successor to the League of Automatic Music Composers, the Hub, which we will discuss later. Other information about the LAMC is presented in Chabade 1997.

George Lewis was also drastically influenced by the LAMC:

Roads: This group was the League of Automatic Music Composers?

Lewis: Yes. Each KIM was connected to a sound generation device, and all of the KIMs were interconnected. Musical data was sent between all the systems. Then, the four composers listened to the output of the machines. Occasionally somebody would halt his program to try a new value in memory or maybe jiggle a wire or something.

Roads: How did it sound to you?

Lewis: It sounded a lot like a band of improvising musicians. You could hear the communication between the machines as they would start, stop, and change musical direction. Each program had its own way of playing. I hadn't heard much computer music at the time, but every piece I had heard was either for tape or for tape and people, and of course none of them sounded anything like this. I felt like playing, too, to see whether I could understand what these machines were saying. I got a KIM as soon as I got back to New York and started trying to learn how to make assembly language programs, cheap digital-to-analog converters, and some other electronic doodads so that I could use the KIM with my synthesizer. But I wanted to play, too, so I had to find out something about getting my sound into the computer. . . .

Roads: So from the beginning of your work with computers you've been involved with interactive programs—programs that interact with a performer.

Lewis: Yes, that's the only thing I've tried to do with a computer.

Roads: How are microcomputers suited to this task?

Lewis: Having your own machine means that you don't have to be tied to a large institution or have a lot of money. And as it turns out, the microcomputer people have explored some areas that are quite different from those studied at the large institutions. That was the interesting thing about David Behrman's programs. You could play beautiful melodies, and they would answer with something that was related to what you were doing. They were interactive. They didn't just respond to input with a predictable transformation. They were very simple, really, but extremely effective. (Roads 1985, 75–76)

SECTION 2

Into the Interface: Instrument ⟷ Computer

THREE

Handling the Hardware

This chapter begins with a brief consideration of the direct interactive possibilities of hardware, instruments and mixers, as distinct from those mediated by computers, my main focus in this book. It then discusses conventional instruments that have been physically modified to permit greater multiplicity of interactive signals being passed to (and sometimes from) computers, known as hyperinstruments. Concomitant with these developments has been the increasing exploitation of amplification, permitting low-level technology to be used as individual and flexible performance vehicles, as in the case of Tom Nunn's constructed percussion boards, the instruments of Max Eastley, and the body of Stelarc (Davies 1992).

■ DIGITAL PERFORMANCE INSTRUMENTS

The archetypal microprocessor MIDI digital instrument was (and is) the Yamaha DX7 keyboard, introduced in 1983. This is a digital synthesizer; it uses wavetables to provide core components that can be used multiply as carrier and/or modulator for FM synthesis. The DX7 permits a wide range of synthesis manipulations to be carried out in real time—that is, during performance. For example, the microtuning of partials of a sound can be dynamically and drastically modified by continuous changing of frequencies of carriers in the synthesis algorithm being used, or more subtly modified by changes to modulators. Feedback levels, panning, and mixing of two different timbres across the keyboards are other examples of controllable parameters.

MIDI capacities on the ultimate DX7, the DX7II, were a full realization of the MIDI specification of the time and allowed a wide range of ancillary gestural controllers to be used to control any synthesis parameters. For example, Yamaha itself sold a breath controller, with a special input on the instrument, while any controller could be attached to its MIDI-in and programmed to control chosen parameter(s). One purpose of this was to permit gestural control that did not involve the hands, thereby leaving both free for playing the keyboard; feet and breath were the two most obvious possibilities. Similarly, for the performer on a MIDI wind controller, there are control possibilities using foot pedals, as well as some specialized keys that can be used to send control signals rather than just to play pitches. However, the MIDI wind controllers (such as the Yamaha WX7s) are themselves really specialized gestural interfaces to synthesizers and samplers.

Unlike the DX7, the Ensonic Mirage, the Kurzweil K2000, and their successors are sample-based instruments. Thus the ROM of the instrument contains a set of sampled sounds, whose magnitude and audio quality has progressively increased. User-generated samples can also be loaded into instrument RAM, so that the range of available sound sources is infinite. Originally, loading was done from floppy disk, necessitating small samples, and was relatively awkward and slow during performance. Currently, zip or jaz (or, less commonly, CD-ROM) drives can be used for larger quantities of loading at a more efficient rate. The range of processes to which the instrument could subject the sampled sounds was initially modest, involving looping, filtering, transposition, reversal, and a few other possibilities. In more recent Kurzweil instruments in particular, a vast array of processing algorithms can be combined to give immense range and can include random components. The interface and learning curve for these instruments is quite daunting. Few players (or even studios) ever use more than a small part of the possibilities, and they use even less of them in real-time performance.

Jeff Pressing has provided a detailed analysis of the ways in which gestural control has expanded the performing possibilities of synthesizers (Pressing 1992), and reader is referred to his book. The ideas concerning synthesizers are equally applicable to samplers, and indeed the distinction between the two types of instrument is progressively breaking down as increasing synthesis powers are built into samplers and vice versa. Probably the factor that now most clearly distinguishes instruments is the range of synthesis and processing algorithms they possess. Few instruments match the processing range of the current Kurzweil series, yet few instruments present more than a selected range of the available synthesis algorithms.

■ MIXERS AND BEYOND: DEDICATED DIGITAL SOUND PROCESSING HARDWARE

The mixing desk has always been central to the production of recorded music and amplified live performance. Since the introduction of digital computer-driven multitrack recording facilities, such as the solid-state logic system, the capacity to use complex digital sound processing (DSP) has gradually moved from the studio into the performance venue and onto the desktop and performers' music stands. Thus companies such as Yamaha have introduced MIDI-controllable mixers, often with significant processing as well as mixing capacity. Because of the advantages of dedicated hardware optimized for DSP, these are still the most common vehicles for realtime DSP. Even so, with many of these mixers it is quite possible to drive the DSP through abrupt extremes that cause audible glitches. These may or may not be a desired part of the performance aesthetic; with software one can choose to build in controls in the form of restrictions, time delays, or ramps, hopefully to avoid such glitches (see the MAX patch MIDIControllerController by Greg White on the CD-ROM that accompanies this book).

In sound amplification for most performance, the public address (PA) sound engineer is not a musically active member of the group, but rather to various degrees seeks to project a sound image that he or she favors and that is acceptable to the group. Generally, however, this is often less than ideal, for many reasons, not least of which is that the performers cannot hear the mix as it is presented to the audience while they themselves are playing, unless there are no acoustic instruments. In contrast, an improvisation ensemble (such as my ensemble, the austraLYSIS Electroband) may well choose to have a coequal member who is also a player but whose role focuses largely on sound projection and the overall DSP of its components. Since digitally generated and modified sound is at the center of computer-interactive sound improvisation, it is only logical to integrate and emancipate the role of sound projection within the music, the process, and the group.

MIDI-controllable mixers such as the Yamaha ProMix series offer considerable scope for algorithmic or gestural control of DSP. Any of the gestural interfaces developed for use with sound-generating instruments can be used with such mixers. An example is the Wacom digital tablet, for which Richard Dudas has written a MAX interface object and the CNMAT group has written valuable software. In addition, the physical layout of the mixer interface allows more rapid transition from one available controller to another than do a computer and mouse. On the other hand, computer control of such mixers may permit a wider range of controls to be readily accessible, and many users have built special control interfaces in software for this purpose, either for specific pieces or kinds of improvising or for more generic use.

Hardware with more elaborate DSP possibilities is the subject of intense development as result of the perceived needs of cinema, surround sound, and the "home cinema." For example, Lake, Roland and Sony are among the companies providing surround-sound and other 3D sound-processing equipment. This work is driven more by commercial factors, such as providing 3D sound through a pair of headphones, than by factors relevant to live computer-interactive sound improvisation.

A long-term collaborator with Lake, Greg Schiemer, has been developing his "improvising machines" for around 20 years (for a detailed review see Schiemer 1999). Schiemer describes an improvising machine as "an instrument which re-interprets input from the real world allowing a performer to influence a musical outcome without entirely controlling it." He has implemented his own on a dedicated microprocessor of his own design, the "MIDI Tool Box," rather than on desktop computers. Two of his most important works use the MIDI Tool Box, in particular its "cyclic code generator" algorithm. This algorithm uses digital feedback to produce repetitive patterns and has been used by many others, such as Salvatore Martirano, and Warren Burt (both in the 1970s). It "uses a single byte of memory called a shift register; each step in sequence is formed by serially shifting a single feed-back bit into the register." Thus a byte 10001000 can become 01000100, 10100010, 01010001, and so on, in a fixed cycle. In his *Spectral Dance,* the cyclic code generator modifies the timbre of a Yamaha FB01 synthesizer (a relative of the DX7). In *Token Objects* it influences a flow of chaotic MIDI traffic that activates a Yamaha TG100 so as "to make interaction between the various independent MIDI message streams less predictable." In the first of these, the performer "swings a mobile sound source—called a UFO—which transverses the field surround a pressure-zone microphone. A sustained audible pitch produced by the UFO is sensed and the signal converted to two pulse trains. These are fed into the MIDI Tool Box" for conversion into the signals that modify the FB01. UFO stands for Ubiquitous Fontana Oscillator, named after the sound artist Bill Fontana. *Spectral Dance* uses three algorithms: "play, which continuously varies the timbre by changing the FM parameter data; map, which translates the mobile audio signal into a stream of MIDI information; and variation, which causes the cyclic code generator to produce aberrations in the patterns generated." *Token Objects* creates a music network of virtual performers that can act independently, though material created by one can be used by another. Four algorithms are critical: "player, which spontaneously creates MIDI sequences; cell, which accesses common musical data assembled from tables; scan, which translates live performer input allowing it to control MIDI traffic; and token, which controls interaction between players." Three piezo-pads allow intervention by the live performer. These set ups have more recently been developed by Schiemer by means of the A4 audio signal processor, developed at the CSIRO Division of Radiophysics, and used in improvised performances. Some of his music using cyclic code generators is available on CD (Schiemer and Leak 1987–1988).

For many sound improvisers, computers offer the ultimate potential and approachability. They may be used either as the site of the DSP itself—especially since the advent of MSP ("MAX Signal Processing," an add-on to the MAX software platform), which has permitted many Power Macintosh users to access these possibilities for the first time—or as providers of control algorithms for digital mixers.

■ HYPERINSTRUMENTS

The interaction between computer musicians and acoustic instruments has driven the development of specialized sensors associated with the essential player-instrument interactions. Specialized instrument "controllers" that detect features of playing instruments, such as finger and mouth sensing, have been developed since the commencement of the MIDI protocol. For example, modified brass instruments have a long history (Dean 1997a). Amongst these are the Perkophone, on which the valves of an ordinary trumpet have been wired and which also uses mouthpiece wind pressure as a source of MIDI information. It has been used by Mark Isham (Pressing 1992, 384) and others.

Tod Machover pioneered an extension of this approach to devise and realize "hyperinstruments." In essence, the concept of a hyperinstrument is that sensors are used to detect aspects of the playing process that can then be converted into quantitative signals and used for aspects of sound production, in addition to, or instead of, the normal acoustic sound of the instrument. In the celletto, a hyperinstrument based on the cello, sensors detect features such as bow pressure and bow speed, which are critical in determining the nature and quality of the acoustic sound but whose detected output can also be used for other sound modification or initiation procedures. The result is that the player can drive an orchestra of sounds or engage in multilayered sound processing with a large degree of control. Players can also learn how to use that control to generate predictable effects, in the same complex way that they can learn how bow speed influences the acoustic timbre of the instrument.

Although Machover's work emanates from a major educational and research institution, the Massachusetts Institute of Technology (MIT), with corresponding resources, and indeed significant teams of collaborators, others successfully use analogous approaches to the design of their own personal performance hyperinstruments. For example, the guitarist and improviser Tom Fryer has developed an effective set-up in which his guitar strings provide analog input into a STEIM Sensorlab interface, which outputs MIDI. In addition, he has an array of foot switches on a relatively compact unit (he contrasts these with his previous performing array of 6 foot pedals, which do not quite match up with his two feet). There are also detectors for pressure, movement, accelerations, and light, together with a joystick. Fryer uses MAX to provide a visual display of the state of his system so that, for example, he can know which effects parameters are operative and get information about the state of his ultimate sound source, currently an ASR10: "The note and controller data from the guitar is sent to the sampler via MAX but no processing occurs. This means that there is no audio output unless I am still playing. My last vestige of traditionalism!!" (Fryer 1999)

The violinist and improviser Jon Rose has also been developing his violin system since 1989, with initial modest institutional support from STEIM:

> I utilize two interface systems which attempt to bring together the physicality and dynamics of improvised music (as played on a violin) with the quick change and virtual possibilities of computer music. The first interface uses ultra sound mounted on the bow or the violinist's bowing arm to measure the actual movements of the bow. The second utilizes a sensor, built into the bow itself, to measure continuously the hair-pressure of the bow on the strings (the driving force or motor for the violin). Naturally factors such as humidity, temperature, how tight the bow was tightened before playing, which end of the bow is being utilized, the pressure used in the previous bow stroke (i.e., after a well dug in bow stroke, the

bow might still be in the process of expanding and doesn't get time to reach its normal rest state before the next stroke), etc. determine a very organic, chaotic and unique character to each concert outing . . . a fundamental necessity for an improviser wanting to take chance or two! (Rose 1996)

He describes the technical aspects:

Within the program are 32 mapping tables. These can be set to work within the standard chromatic scale or choice of notes can be generated by random generator, algorithms, graphic procedures, or interpolation of sequential patterns between fixed points. Superimposition of these structures in real time leads to very complex patterns but these patterns nevertheless always retain a degree of self similarity due to the physical and rhythmic consequence of the bow. This complexity must also operate in an ever changing mode because of the adjacent violin output/performance operating in parallel, against or with it—i.e., those physical actions, movements and techniques of the improvising violinist.

This means that specific areas of interaction can be set up which focus on some found sonic or physical relationship between the two systems. Add to this the voice coming from the violin and there are three pools of information which, through the action of horizontal bow movement or vertical bow pressure combine to form musical structures that appear to be pulled together by some kind of attractor (to use Chaos Theory jargon). (Rose 1996)

Kaffe Mathews is another violinist and improviser who uses a contrasting interactive set-up. In it she focuses on the commercial sampling software LiSa, to which I will return. Mathews's Web site describes it as follows, with particular reference to a CD released from her performances around 1999:

All material is made live, by playing a violin through sampling and treatment system LiSa, in a particular place at a particular time. As well as using sound from the violin, there is also a hidden microphone providing the essential wild card. Grab, select, subvert and game with the consequences as you go. Produces a range of material devoid of any obvious violin sound, yet made largely from violin input. No prerecorded samples are used, and none are taken away afterwards.

In a performance in September 2000 associated with the International Computer Music Conference in Berlin, Mathews instead used a MIDI controller based on multiple sliders to the same ends, though apparently starting with some preformed acoustic samples. Perhaps an essential feature of such a controller is the ease of providing multiple control signals (say, one per finger with a slider controller, or several from the violin) in contrast with that offered by the computer mouse.

Jonathan Impett has made a hyperinstrument of the trumpet (Impett 1994b and 1996) and developed sensors substantially beyond those of the Perkophone. The trumpet is modified to provide information about the

> player's direct contact with the instrument . . . by two pressure sensors fitted where the fingers close around the valve casing, and mercury switches below the bell to read the lateral tilt of the trumpet. The three valves each contain a magnet, the strength of their fields measured by sensors in the valve caps below. Six switches are fitted behind the valves and next to the left thumb, and are generally used to change [software function]. (Impett 1996)

Pitch, bend, and volume are derived by a pitch tracker, and the trumpeter plays in a "$2m^2$ virtual screen" surveyed by ultrasound transmitters so that the position of the trumpet can be detected by receivers. In all, twelve or so streams of information can be sent; Impett originally planned to use breath flow and/or air pressure detectors but found the information so contained was more efficiently represented by distinguishing the volume of the note's attack from that taken later in the note envelope (Impett 2000). Impett refers to his whole system, "an integrated interactive instrument-interface-composition system," in which both computer and player elaborate the composition, as a "meta-trumpet"; but in the terminology of this book, his modified instrument is a hyperinstrument. "My goal was to implement the extension of the musician into the environment without compromising the instrument . . . and without adding extraneous techniques to an already cramped by organic 'technique-space'." Whereas Machover's hyperinstruments are mainly used by other performers, such as the cellist Yo-Yo Ma, Impett is himself a brilliant trumpeter, in both early and contemporary music, and thus he has been able to develop features of the trumpet hyperinstrument which can be particularly useful to the performer-improviser. An important work of his, *Mirror-Rite,* is available on CD (Impett 1994a), and his algorithmic and performance ideas are discussed in chapter 5.

A further glimpse into the motivation for this instrument is given by the composer-instrument maker in the liner notes to the CD on which *Mirror-Rite* is included: "Up until recently, trumpet pieces seemed to be . . . like a circus act in which you see the climax again and again. . . . This is why you have to look for another rhetoric. . . . It's actually a strength to use this megaphone of the soul to express dark, quiet things." Later, of *Mirror-Rite* specifically, he writes:

the music is actually constructed during the performance. I improvise—or rather play at myself—the trumpet part and both my musical and physical actions are processed by a computer.... The instrument is covered with sensors; it looks like a trumpet in intensive care....

To really communicate, music has to somehow pass directly through you and not involving [*sic*] a third party. If the performance situation results in the structure of the music, you're not just giving the composer and the performer the chance to speak directly to the audience, but you're also empowering the listener, because he's part of the situation too. (Impett 1994a)

In a later article on baroque and contemporary performance authenticity in which he argues that "appropriate understanding of the technology of a given culture is necessary for the 'authentic' expression of that culture" (Impett 1998a), Impett quotes Theodor Adorno: "if the musical substance is to develop organically, the intervention of the subject is required, or rather, the subject must become an integral part of the organism, something which the organism itself call for. If appearances do not deceive, it is upon this that the future of music depends."

Hyperinstruments can be used efficiently and knowingly by professional performers. On the other hand, Machover and colleagues' huge *Brain Opera* project (Paradiso 1999) involves some simple musical instrument interfaces, such as tuned percussion keyboards, which were intended to be played by nonprofessionals in an interactive installation context. The Brain Opera was first presented in July 1996 in New York and has been developed since. It is "the largest touring participatory electronic music installation to have been thus far constructed" (Paradiso 1999). One objective was to provide "mappings which allow an untrained audience to intuitively interact with music and graphics at various levels of complexity." There are also instruments for professionals. Amongst the "intuitive" interfaces are the GestureWall and the SensorChair, which use electric field sensors; the smart piezoelectric touch pads of the Rhythm Tree; the instrumented springs in Harmonic Driving; the pressure-sensitive touch screens of Melody Easels; and the multimodal digital baton. There are Speaking Trees and Singing Trees, and a Magic Carpet with an array of up to 64 wires and a pair of microwave motion sensors for upper-body movement.

The Marble Lobby of the first performance, at the Juilliard Theater, was "chaos" from the point of view of the sound fields, as intended: there was no "collective music" there. The casual user, both in the lobby and in interacting with many of the other interfaces, might grasp little more than that there were effects beyond any acoustic sound they made. Nevertheless, Paradiso argues (1999) that there is a need to "bridge the gestural disconnection" and hopes for future interactive environments that perceive and adapt to the skill level of users, which would permit the environment to make the gestural connection more obvious. In the case of casual usage, the distinction between using hyperinstrument controller information and deriving new information from a processing of the acoustic or MIDI input would not be important and certainly would not be apparent to the user. But for the practicing computer improviser, the two possible control mechanisms have radically different implications and possibilities, which I will explore further.

FOUR

Entering the Interface

> I've been working on my stuff for about 8 years now and it seems a natural development from all the deconstructed violin instruments I once made. On the scale thing, I've tried to keep a one to one connection between violin and digital instrument by using only one midi channel in performance. Sort of basic monophonic solidarity! For me, an important aspect of expression comes out of pushing the natural physical limitations of an instrument to the edge of its possibilities, this includes digital ones as well. But the bottom line in all this is . . . that it fulfills a creative need. A sustaining, physically exhausting and sometimes quite humorous experience for performer and audience alike. If it was a repeat show everytime, I for one would soon get fed up with it. In this sense, it's a challenge in the same way that playing with any resourceful improviser can be. The process may be determined by the constituent parts of musician and technology but any definition would be quite reductive in trying to describe the quite beautiful psychological and physical states attained in this kind of music making. We all deal with the man and machine myth, even acoustic guitar players have to twiddle their machine heads. It's simply another (and very actual) possibility for an improviser and does not deny, exclude or compete with the joys of more traditional forms of "free" improvisation.
>
> —J. Rose, *"Improvisation and Interactive Technology"* (1996)

■ INTERFACES FOR SOUND CONTROL

The human-computer interface is a vast area of commercial and scientific endeavor, mainly focused on issues of efficiency, comprehensibility, control, and transparency or detectability (Carroll 1997). For the computer improviser these issues are of interest, but secondary: translating any bodily movement or action into sound-generating mechanisms may be useful. The field has a long history in sound, which springs from early experiments using electrical impulse patterns from the brain (for example, in the work of David Rosenboom mentioned earlier).

To what degree can neural activity be controlled? This is important because it impinges on the question of the extent of improvisatory or compositional control a performer might achieve in a sound work initiated in this manner. Clearly such control can be developed with experience, but it may be that the extent remains modest. These neural-driven performances often used conventional physiologists' electrodes, placed carefully on the head or the skin.

More recently, interfaces between most categories of bodily action and MIDI or other sound manipulation mechanisms have been developed commercially and experimentally. Gloves and other body-covering pressure and movement sensors have been widely used, and software interpreters are available in many forms, including several in MAX. For example, Laetitia Sonami uses her own glove, and her movements are integral to the performance; her *Has/Had* involves improvisatory realization, in which prerecorded sounds and her live speech and voice are subjected to DSP (Marty 1998).

Thunder by Don Buchla, comprises a paired semicircular array of touch-sensitive pads. This is a development of the earlier concept of the percussion controllers, usually built like one or another of the conventional percussion interfaces. Thunder pads use location as well as normal percussive clues. Buchla is also responsible for Lightning, a software/firmware interpreter which is played by movement of an infrared transmitter, often termed the "wand." Bob Ostertag has brought performance with such interfaces to a high art. The radio drum, used by Andrew Schloss and David Jaffe, is a specifically percussive interface of great subtlety and has been used in duo networks with a MIDI violin (see chapter 6). Haken and colleagues have developed a touch-sensitive "keyboard" whose playing surface traces x, y, and z positions for up to 10 simultaneous interactions and uses the information for timbral morphing "between previously analyzed (or previously synthetically generated) sounds in the timbre control space," which is realized through the Capybara/Macintosh sound synthesis system (Haken et al. 1998). The I-cube is a more recent device whose sensors can accept a wide range of physical inputs, including light and other radiations, pressure, and temperature. Several reviews of the range and features of such devices are available (e.g., Chadabe 1997, 213–40; Dodge and Jerse 1997, 404–7).

Such interface devices have the additional ambivalent feature that they utilize a gestural process that is inseparable from the sound work. The gestures may become a visual-theatrical component of the performance, and the interface may itself be designed to provide an aesthetic appearance. For example, speaking or sounding wands have been used by several performers, such as Laurie Anderson, whose "talking stick" (developed with Bob Bielecki and Interval Research) was featured in her work *Songs and Stories from Moby Dick,* as presented in the United States and Europe in 1999–2000.

Clearly the sensor component of such interfaces can be built into natural or man-made environments, including virtual ones. A club dance floor can be criss-crossed with movement or thermal detectors, or a carpet of pressure sensors can be added to a contemporary dance performance. Such larger interfaces make possible both solo and group utilization. Notable interactive environments have been made for many years, such as Rolf Gehlhaar's dance floor, and Wayne Siegel has discussed interactive devices that permit performers to "dance the music" and his own work *Movement Study II* (Siegel 1998), in which he interfaces dancers using David Rokeby's Very Nervous System and STEIM's BigEye. Curtis Bahn has developed a dance piece using simple detectors worn by the dancer and spherical speaker systems surrounding the performance area. These anticipate aspects of the pending fashion (r)evolution of WCs (wearable computers).

Bahn (on his Web page) describes his BubbaBall interface: "The BubbaBall is an alternative controller made to work with 'Bubba' the 23" Sensor Speaker Array (SenSA). The BubbaBall uses 5 force sensitive resistors (FSRs) under squishy foam, a dual axis accelerometer for tilt and shake data, and 5 latching switches. The dodecahedron form for the BubbaBall is from a gutted children's toy."

The possibilities for utilization of such environments of sensors are available to the novice just as to the professional. Indeed, STEIM has put much effort into sensors and instruments that can be used by disabled people. Such sensors are of equal importance in museum and exhibition circumstances; however, in these contexts it is much more common that visual interactions are primary. A delightful children's play area in which their movements played microtonal pitch patterns was used at Singapore's Changi Airport in the late 1990s. Video interfaces, in which video cameras are used to provide data that is then analyzed to provide controls for sound generation, have been widely developed (see Rowe 1993). For example, Warren Burt, an American based mainly in Melbourne, Australia, has developed many pieces on this basis since the early 1980s. He has often used Simon Veitch's 3DIS system, developed in the early 1980s (Chadabe 1997). Other musicians there, such as Steve Adam, have expanded this approach in fascinating ways.

Tactile inputs have been developed further from the initial work of Michael Waisvisz and his Crackle and other "boxes." Waisvisz is best known for his performing interface, the Hands, with which he is a virtuoso (Krefeld 1990). In agreement with Rose, quoted above, he feels that "the physical effort you make is what is perceived by listeners as the cause and manifestation of the musical tension of a work." With his quite theatrical performances, this may well be true for many listeners, even though his body has usually been significantly constrained by dangling cables.

Here is an excerpt from the Web prospectus for Stratifier, used by the Schreck Ensemble in Holland and developed again in the ambit of STEIM:

> The Stratifier is a multi-dimensional controller, which combines a x-y-z pad, five touch sensitive sliders (scanning position and pressure) and four pressure-surfaces, plus two sliders which respond to position placement and serve as default pads. The scanning is done by . . . strips with additional hardware . . . and subsequently sent to STEIM's SensorLab, outputting the necessary MIDI-information to a Power Macintosh running SuperCollider.
>
> The electronics (designed by Schreck's hardware-builder and software-developer Pieter Suurmond) are housed in a white bamboo-casing, measuring 42 cm width, 30 cm deep and 6 cm high. It was designed specifically to the wishes of the creator and built by the sculptor/ instrument builder Hans van Koolwijk. The . . . strips are covered and protected by sheep-skin leather. An important reason for using these organic materials was that it should "feel" and "look" like a "real" instrument—similar to a violin or a clarinet—rather than like an electric appliance like a drill or a chain-saw. . . .
>
> These combinations of materials offer a subtle and tactile control, allowing the user to play with delicate finger movements creating intricate timbral fluctuations, but also large scale changes resulting into huge constellations of sound. Making it a genuine performance instrument for concerts. . . .
>
> The aim was to develop an instrument, that was capable of stratifying patterns in complex signal processing and synthesis techniques in real-time during a performance situation on stage, with the explicit need to control many parameters at the same time. In order to do this, one needs a set of coherent approaches to the mapping of combinations for the full exploration of these possibillities. Some selected approaches were . . . described by Philippe Depalle:
>
> Each independent gestural output is assigned to one musical parameter, usually via a MIDI control message.

One-to-One Mapping: This is the simplest mapping scheme, but usually the least expressive. It takes direct advantage of the MIDI controller architecture.

Divergent Mapping: One gestural output is used to control more than one simultaneous musical parameter. Although it may initially provide a macro-level expressivity control, this approach nevertheless may prove limited when applied alone, as it does not allow access to internal (micro) features of the sound object.

Convergent Mapping: In this case many gestures are coupled to produce one musical parameter. This scheme requires previous experience with the system in order to achieve effective control. Although harder to master, it proves far more expressive than the simpler unity mapping.

A continuum between the untrained, interactive and the more cultivated, improvisatory use is a gratifying consequence of such interfacial facilities.

■ PROPERTIES OF THE INTERFACE

It is important to take account of the nonneutrality of these performing interfaces, just as much as those of conventional musical instruments or the hyperinstruments discussed earlier. Resolution of detection of change may be a significant factor, just as the use of keys on wind instruments affects their capacity for efficient microtuning in comparison with that of string instruments. But more important is that nature of the body movement required to provide a decipherable signal: very complex coordination of multiple movements may be required to give a single signal, or a single movement may be analyzed into multiple component vectors, each of which can be processed sonically. Just as perceptual, motor, and cognitive factors limit real-time improvisation on a conventional instrument, so with a different balance of importance they limit improvisation using a specialized interface.

Modler and Kirk (1999) are undertaking detailed work on the evaluation of architectures for interactive gestural control of sound synthesis. They assess both the physical interface and the computer software with which it is being used, since the overall architecture depends on both. In their analysis, important characteristics of the gestural and synthesis process seem to be "synchronisation with the synthesis algorithms; processing and communication network latency; integration of gestural and synthesis algorithms (multiparametic mapping); distributed processing and scalable run-time performance." These are important criteria, but implicit in the article seems to be a view that to "integrate gestural control algorithms" with sound generation requires transparent event links, whereas, just as improvisation might strive to be nonidiomatic, so might gestural connections in this context. However, the movement toward distributed systems seems powerful, in that it should readily allow expansion of scale of the overall performance operation. Figure 4.1, based on Modler and Kirk, summarizes the processes needed in the streaming of gesture data.

Figure 4.1 Streaming of gesture data.

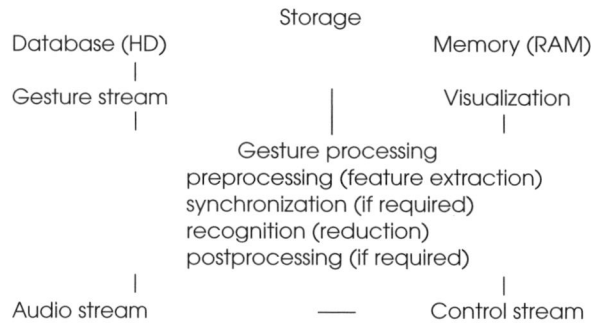

Thus, a key question is, what can be done uniquely with a particular interface? One important factor is that sensors can readily detect and use three-dimensional information about movement and position in space, which cannot be readily achieved directly on most current desktop computers, with their 2D interface. However, more fundamentally, the control may be n-dimensional, where n is limited primarily by the capacity of the user to learn control, rather than by the physical system. Such interfaces have fascinating potential: for example, a solo performer could create and continuously control the streams of an orchestra of sound, though as yet this has been little achieved. The distinction between playing multiple strands of sequenced or algorithmically generated sound on a computer and continuously providing the controlling input to each stream via multidimensional actions is fundamental.

Pressing has argued with respect to gestural interfaces for sound-action mapping:

There is considerable scope for imagination here, and nontraditionally shaped objects may be treated in non-traditional ways. We may have a pulsating blob of jelly or a moving pseudopod that is picked up and stretched, stroked, or scratched to produce sound. It might be made possible to break the object up into pieces, each of which makes its own sound. These pieces might exhibit some attraction for each other and gradually recombine to produce composite sounds. When the pieces coalesce, they might modify the sounds they are making to work in concert, for example by moving to the same scale or key or meter or tempo. (Pressing 1997)

Here are echoes of Bahn's BubbaBall, and Impett's Swarm-ing digital agents (see later chapters).

Pressing also comments of interfaces that "We may . . . set up processes that operate in a rather pathological reality (sometimes termed pseudophysics); the adaptation to this set of novel 'physical' laws (which might change with time) is then part of the learning process for the performer, and it may produce surprising results."

■ AFTER THE INTERFACE: THE SOUND SOURCE(S)

Interaction with a gestural interface is of course directed toward ultimate sound output. For most of the book, that output is either electronic sound from a MIDI instrument or directly from a computer (as we will discuss in the next section of this chapter). However, some improvisers have also developed novel sound sources to complement their interfaces.

A notable early example was the modified acoustic piano used by Alistair Riddell with his PMIS (Performer/Machine Interactive System) software in C running on an Amiga computer to control sound initiation (Riddell 1989). This revealed an unexpected timbral diversity in the system. Riddell writes that "the modified instrument . . . is substantially different from the traditional piano. These differences include the facts that it cannot be played in a conventional manner (since it has no keyboard) and that the strings are struck by wooden hammers with no individual dampers accompanying them." The hammer movements of 24 strings are controlled by solenoids activated from information given at a computer keyboard. When a hammer remains in contact with its string for prolonged periods, it forms an artificial bridge, with concomitant pitch rises, which also depend on the pressure applied. The solenoids are controlled by a cyclic supply of power, so that the string is continually re-excited with the frequency of the cycle while the hammer is in continuous contact.

Riddell comments:

> The sounds produced are at times similar to those of a bowed string instrument, like a cello or double bass. At other times, the harsh, buzzing sound while less immediately appealing is, however, interesting in its dynamic timbral complexity.

and later,

> PMIS enables the performer to control the following fundamental operations:
>
> - Solenoid contact with the 24 consecutive bass strings
> - The energy to the solenoids (the 32 dynamic levels used in the previous systems)
> - Damper mechanism for the lower bass strings
> - System and interface reset
> - Multiple solenoid activations (of limited value)

Among the applications of this system was applied improvisation, and in Riddell's *Black Moon Assails,* recorded and documented in the thesis as the result of "numerous" rehearsals (Riddell 1989):

The four techniques used in the performance to either generate or control the sounds were:

1. Activation of the solenoid, hammer strikes the string (normal operation).
2. Controlled and sustained contact between the solenoid and the string.
3. Use of the damper to control resonance and as a string mute for the percussive mode.
4. Removal of the hammer from the string (the string vibrates freely when the solenoid is deactivated).

■ THE COMPUTER AS SEMIOTIC INTERFACE

Some improvisers have chosen to make the computer and its normal controllers, such as keyboard, mouse, or joystick, their fundamental gestural interaction point. Similarly, visual artists and designers interested in sound have been tempted to design a visual screen interface with which they can interact to generate ongoing image display on separate screens and sound projection perhaps for the dance floor. For example, Toby Grime (a member of Clan Analogue, the dance music collective) has made four interfaces programmed in Director for such use (Grime 2000).

An advantage of the computer as the prime interface is that it can provide a task environment with its own "surprises" (Hamman 1999). Thus we can envisage computers as "generators of semiotic rather than symbolic ordering frameworks." In this context "semiotic" implies a flexible, choosable, variable relation between gesture as seen reflected in the computer interface and music/sound output, while "symbolic" implies a fixed relationship. Thus the computer can be connotative rather than denotative. The former challenges and surprises, while the latter can become a learned convention. As Hamman notes, computers can "problematise" the "historically and culturally bound epistemologies" that constrain action and interpretation; they can provide instruments for "epistemological play." If the episteme is the ground (often hidden) on which a statement counts as knowledge in a particular period, then the computer can permit this to be open and immanent. Interface semiotics have even gone so far as "computers as theatre" (Laurel 1993). As an example, Hamman (1999) discusses Insook Choi's work with a "manifold controller," which generates a 3D graphical display by which "one discovers various integrating and feedback principles through performance and practice" that relate to the ensuing sounds, which are synthesized by a chaotic model.

SECTION 3

Sound Routes and MIDI Maps

FIVE
Algorithmic Processing of Sound and Meta-Sound

Thomas Dolby, in a patent application, has given a synopsis of algorithms he views as useful in generation of music in response to gestures, displayed and physical:

> An improved music generation system that facilitates artistic expression by non-musician and musician performance contexts. Mappings are provided between 1) gestures of a performer as indicated by manipulation of a user input device, 2) displayed motion of a graphic object, and 3) global features of a musical segment. The displayed motions and global features are selected so as to reinforce the appearance of causation between the performer's gestures and the produced musical effects and thereby assist the performer in refining his or her musical expression. The displayed motion is isomorphically coherent with the musical segment in order to achieve the appearance of causation. The global features are segment characteristics perceivable to human listeners. Control at the global feature level in combination with isomorphic visual feedback provides advantages to both non-musicians and musicians in producing artistic effect....
>
> The term "global feature" refers to a segment characteristic exhibiting patterns readily perceivable by a human listener which patterns depend upon the sound of more than one note. Examples of global features include the shape of a pitch contour of the musical segment, an identifiable rhythm pattern, or the shape of a volume contour of the musical segment....
>
> [Methods for] generating a music segment with global features that are isomorphically coherent with the rolling motion of the graphical object. One global feature is the presence of wandering melodic patterns with notes of duration dependent upon rolling speed. The pitch content of these patterns may depend on the axis of rotation. The speed of notes varies with the speed of rotation. After the rolling motion stops, the music stops also (Dolby et al. 1999).

In marked contrast, David Rosenboom elucidates "compositional method" in terms of the following component decisions:

> Choose your universe. . . . How will the universe be ordered? . . . What are the scales of measure for parametric values to be used? . . . What are the levels of significant difference for each parameter? . . . Design the compositional pragmatics needed to make arrangements amongst the distinctions in the universal set. . . . Finally, examine how any particular choice of pragmatics—i.e., a system design—can be extended by viewing the result as part of something much larger than itself. (Rosenboom 2000)

He goes on to classify the "compositional pragmatics" in terms of the "inquiring systems" they might use and gives examples (shown here in brackets): "causal-permutative [combinatorics]; statistical-symbolic [stochastics]; acoustical deterministic [harmony]; gestural-biological [semantics]; and syntactic-teleological [grammar]."

As noted already, Rosenboom is offering the powerful challenge to all creators of music to "invent" their cognitive model for a work or group of works. At another point in the spectrum of approaches to composition and improvisation is the AI- and commerce-driven aim of writing programs that will satisfactorily generate music appropriate for any predetermined or instantly determined function, such as accompanying a film or acting as sound foreground, as in the quotation from Dolby and colleagues' patent application that opens this chapter. Some of these approaches may indeed embody cognitive models, as is true to an extent of the software improvisers of Hodgson, Ramalho, and others.

Ian Cross (1998a, 1998b) has discussed the theories of cognitive parsing of music, notably the ideas of Narmour (Narmour 1977, 1989, 1992), which can be translated into computer code at least for note-centered tonal music. However, Cross has also pointed out elegantly, and in agreement with Rosenboom, that the cognitive process is established anew by every listener to, as well as every creator of, a new piece of music, in a manner significantly influenced by their general and specific cultural context. In this sense, these cognitive processes are outside the realms often claimed by scientific investigation, in which, within the limits of atomic uncertainty, studied physically determinate events are reproducible under a fixed set of (experimental) circumstances. This is because are no such fixed sets of circumstances exist in the cognition of music. Cross concludes that cognitive studies of music

> should proceed by seeking to provide accounts of musical experience that are consonant with the constraints and particularities of embodiment and the concepts of computational logic (see Johnson-Laird, 1983) and with empirically-derived evidence about musical perception, perfor-

mance and creation. At the same time, its practice must be informed by an intimate awareness of the cultural context within which it is conducted, of the meanings that can be borne by its materials, methods and data. (Cross 1998b)

This paradox has not prevented substantial development of computer tools for algorithmic processing of sound and meta-sound. Computer algorithms can effect virtually any compositional or music-structural manipulation of sound material that might spring from the concerns just outlined. Indeed, the algorithms can embody every aspect of a musical entity, and it can be argued reciprocally that all composition is algorithmic (Orton 1996; Hunt et al. 1998). From the point of view of this book, the key concern is how they can process incoming sound or meta-sound (for example, MIDI data) arriving in real time from an improviser. But all the actions can also be put to work on material that is itself generated in the computer, so that they can equally contribute to or fully represent compositions. This chapter tries to illustrate such algorithmic actions at a relatively nontechnical (nonprogramming) level; some of the processes are also represented in functional MAX algorithms provided on the CD-ROM. The key functions are analysis, manipulation, and generation.

We have already distinguished sound from meta-sound. For present purposes, sound is a flow of digital data that encodes a sound directly and can be converted into an audible output simply by a D-to-A converter and a loudspeaker in series. Meta-sound is a flow of instructions, such as those in MIDI, that controls the action of a separate sound-generating machine such as a synthesizer or sampler, which in turn produces the digital output that can be sounded. For the purposes of this chapter it is also useful to distinguish sound "samples" and "streams." A sample is a discrete stretch of sound occupying a finite and conveniently computer-processable length of time (such as a few seconds); a continuous flux of such sound constitutes a stream. Samples are most commonly taken as discontinuous chunks from a stream. Meta-sound, especially MIDI, usually encodes discrete individual events, resulting in sounds that are often very short (milliseconds) but may be longer triggered samples. In the case of meta-sound there is little sense in distinguishing the processing of discrete events from that of streams, since both involve triggering as one or more individual actions; from the computer-processing point of view these are handled identically. Thus I will have occasion in my discussion to distinguish samples and streams of sound from meta-sound.

■ ANALYSIS

Identification In principle, a computer algorithm can be established to analyze input sound or meta-sound for any feature defined as salient by its author. For example, one might wish to identify whenever a particular kind of chord was sounding. With a meta-sound input, the algorithm would check for the existence of a group of pitches with start times less than roughly 50 msec apart; then it would identify the pitches in that group and classify them by comparison with a supplied database. All the required information is supplied in digitally encoded form in a succession of MIDI messages, so that the computer merely has to briefly store and refer to the messages before they can be discarded from memory.

With a sound input, the process is more complicated, but still feasible. In this case, the first step would be the identification of pitch onsets, which requires both discrimination of sound attack features and then determination of the core pitch of the sound (assuming there is one). Neither of these processes is trivial, though, for example, Steinberg's ReCycle software is designed to efficiently segment a sample of recorded sound into constituent individual attacks and works well when the contained sounds are relatively simple drum and bass patterns. Pitch detection can be done by hardware pitch trackers, which provide an estimate of the pitch to the computer, or in software with algorithms such as fiddle~, an MSP object.

In thinking about sound samples or streams one might want to generalize the objective from pitch-centered conceptions of music to timbral and textural ones, such as those of Xenakis (1971) and Wishart (1985 and 1994). To rephrase, our objective might be to identify particular timbres by extracting pitch and energy spectra from the incoming sound and comparing them with a database of such spectra. Such aims become increasingly computer intensive.

Granted powerful enough computers, identification can extend from "events," to larger-scale patterns (be they pitch patterns or rhythmic patterns such as beat recognition), and ultimately to meter identification. Each of these issues is the subject of a substantial research effort, which cannot be detailed here. For example, beat identification has been studied and reviewed intensively by Desain and Honing.

Extraction The same principles of determination of pitch and timbral components of an incoming sound, or meta-sound stream, can be used alternatively for extraction rather than identification. The algorithm might simply record the frequency with which certain events or patterns occur, with relatively little presumption as to their detailed nature. For example, it might identify all pitches sounded in a MIDI stream, record cumulatively the frequency with which they occur (in an array), and make the data available for analysis. Then a motive could be extracted, for example, as consisting of the seven (or any number of the) most commonly sounded pitches.

If the algorithm records all the incoming data of a MIDI stream, then that data can be interrogated from any point of view at any time, though clearly that point of view (e.g., finding the longest 22 notes) may largely determine the pattern that will emerge from the interrogation. If all the data for a certain period is recorded, as in a MIDI sequence, or an audio sample, then all its components may of course be directly reproduced, with or without alteration.

Extraction thus allows a hybridization between identification and extraction of features intrinsic to the sound stream, and superimposition upon it of an external pattern that can be expressed partly through reproducing components of that stream. The degree of hybridization of these two extremes of analysis can be chosen by the user. At one extreme, the hybridization becomes "mapping," in which an extracted feature is automatically mapped to a different feature of the external pattern.

■ MANIPULATION

Of greatest interest to the improviser is the range of processes by which sound or meta-sound stored in or passing through the computer can be manipulated. It is not necessary that there be an analytical phase prior to manipulation, since the performer might choose, for example, to continuously modify everything streaming in, or to use intermittent bursts of the source material for the processing, or to filter that material in some way.

One can conceptualize the general possibilities of sound and meta-sound manipulation in terms of a delay step, however short, in which material is gathered for the subsequent manipulation steps. After the delay any of a range of manipulations can be applied, individually or in any sequence, with or without recursive steps in which the product of one manipulation is fed back into an earlier manipulation step.

One can consider a (non-recursive) chain of such manipulations, ordered from least to most disruptive of the source material. If one considers MIDI data first, then among the main possible functions is REPLAY, in which the material is exactly reproduced after a chosen delay. TRANSPOSER (see CD-ROM and fig. 5.1) might repeat the material with only the pitches changed by a constant amount. REORDER might take a batch of pitches and reverse or repermute them. REORDER with zero change is equivalent to recycling, or looping, the pitches. NEWRHYTHM could alter the durations of some notes, on a logical or random basis. ADD/DELETE would do exactly as it states, but might also be used with a RECOMBINE function (see CD-ROM) in which elements of another batch of data are swapped with elements of the incoming data or added to those remaining after ADD/DELETE has acted. A RESCALE function might use a mathematical or random function to alter the relative pitches, durations, or velocities of the notes. A more complicated version of this would constitute a MAP function, in which any incoming pitch or duration is converted via a mathematical step or a database into a new value before being passed on.

Figure 5.1 An algorithm controlling transposition of MIDI data (written in MAX).

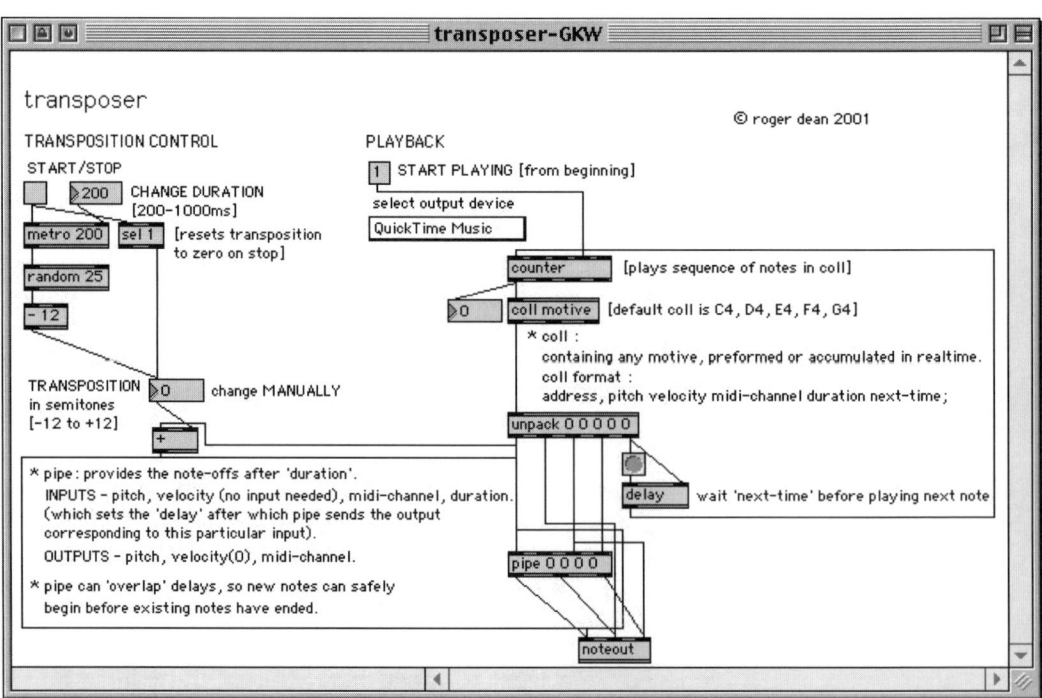

Not only might these manipulations be chained, but also they might be responsive to variables controlled by the user. For example, the user might choose the TRANSPOSE intervals in real time, or provide an algorithmic function with controllable input parameters to do this (see fig. 5.1). The output of one stage might itself carry data that are used as a condition for entry to another (for example, durations might only be changed by NEWRHYTHM for notes shorter than five seconds). Finally, the scale of the input data on which the process operates would certainly be controllable: because of the compactness of MIDI data there is no difficulty with current computers in having stream segments several minutes in length being the subject of the manipulations.

While there can be some logic to a chain layout of such manipulations, an open network configuration is also possible, and an interface might permit the user the opportunity to link any module to any other in real time. The complexity of manipulation is thus almost infinite, and the capacity to sustain the generation of continuously changing structures is readily obtained. The relevance of parallel processing (rather than serial processing) in future computers (Miranda 1998) is intuitively obvious when one uses a network rather than linear arrangement of meta-sound manipulation functions.

Turning from MIDI data to sound samples, some of the processes just described have immediately available parallels. For example, REPLAY and TRANSPOSE are straightforward. REORDERing by reversal is also simple, but a workable concept of permutation requires more thought. One simple approach is to divide the sound into *n* equal segments, which are then playable in permutation. More sophisticated might be to use an approach like that of Steinberg's ReCycle software to segment the sample into individual components with discrete attack points, which could then be REORDERed. These components would also be suitable for the operation of a NEWRHYTHM function, or of ADD/DELETE, RECOMBINE, RESCALE, and MAP. ADD/DELETE might also act by filtering the pitch spectrum or energy spectrum of the unsegmented sample. RESCALE might operate on a segment, on any analyzable component of the sound, or on the sample as a whole. MAP would require the use of segments and chosen characteristics of each (e.g., pitch center, partial content, duration, or maximum volume). The MAP might provide a processing algorithm such as a granulation process, or it might replace a sound segment by another already stored on the computer and referenced by the MAP database. Some of these manipulations, when acting on sound samples, might constitute retexturing or the generation of new timbres, and this could be a defined part of their objective, according to how the function was programmed.

Lastly, let us consider the manipulation of sound streams. Clearly a computer cannot act on an unlimited duration of sound stream; thus, a memory function (buffer) is required that holds the last n seconds of sound, and in which incoming sound data displaces that which is n seconds old. These buffers, often called taps, are commonly used in parallel, with one representing short periods (say, 50–500 msec), one medium (say, 500 msec–10 sec), and one representing the maximum chosen by the user or permitted by the hardware or RAM configuration (for example, on current desktop Macintosh computers, perhaps up to 60 seconds). Although the data in each buffer are continually changing, the manipulation of what is in the buffer at any instant (providing that such manipulation is fast in relation to the time corresponding to the buffer) is essentially similar to the manipulation of a sample. While there are computer hardware and memory timing, routing, priority, and other technical issues, these need not concern us here. They may create practical limitations, but these in theory could be largely overcome.

■ GENERATION

Algorithmic generation of complete musical structures has been one of the goals of computer music since the experiments of Hiller in the 1950s. Even the network of interconnected manipulation modules discussed above, in configurations of moderate complexity, can give rise to diverse and highly structured compositions. The improviser or improvising group may choose to use them for co-improvisation, with real-time control of parameters of the individual modules and their overall routing; but a composer, providing input material as a preformed entity, can use them all generatively. Any specialized algorithm a composer might write to embody the generation of a piece—for example, one commencing with chaotic mathematics, and with preformed sections with different algorithms—could also be configured as an improvising platform, especially with added interface parameter controls for the real-time performers.

■ PRECISION, MULTIPLICITY, AND OVERLAYING FEATURES

One of the most important features of a computer is its reproducibility and precision. For example, the timing of the occurrence of desired future events can be very precise, much more so than that achieved by a group of musicians. The degree of congruence of timed events in different streams of activity (e.g., different polyphonic lines of pitched notes) can also be greater than that achieved by performers (where the most powerful impression of being "together" involves cohesion within only about 20 msec [Sloboda 1988]).

As a consequence, computers are excellent vehicles for establishing and juxtaposing mutiple meters and pulses, which are very difficult to achieve effectively in live performance. This is an area that has been rather neglected in improvisation, even though the concept of polyrhythmic drumming and metrical modulations of various kinds have been central to jazz since the 1960s, particularly in the work of Elvin Jones and Tony Williams (drums) and the groups they powered (of John Coltrane and Miles Davis), and spawned (Chick Corea's Circle). I have analyzed this polyrhythmic development (Dean 1992) and also contributed to it with LYSIS, and more recently austraLYSIS. The latter uses computer-interactive improvisation techniques to permit such overlaying of multiple rhythmic strands (see the austraLYSIS CD *Present Tense*) and also to allow any kind of pulse or metrical transition (Dean 1997b). Figure 5.2 illustrates a simple improviser-controllable "rhythm machine" (software available on the CD-ROM), of which several may be running simultaneously. CNMAT has written a "rhythm engine" for related purposes and also for use in cognitive studies. The saxophonist and improviser Steve Coleman has taken a particular interest in nested looping rhythmic structures, and these are efficiently handled by computer algorithms, where one strand of the algorithm (or one rhythm machine) would be responsible for each pulse or meter and any reproducing pattern it should express. From the late 1980s onward this work was embodied in his Improviser software, and more recently he has worked on his Rameses system, whose name reflects the influence of a wide range of philosophies on his musical thought.

Such multiple rhythm machines also allow inexperienced users to create fascinating rhythmic tensions, and in a related idea I have

Figure 5.2 An austraLYSIS rhythm machine (written in MAX).

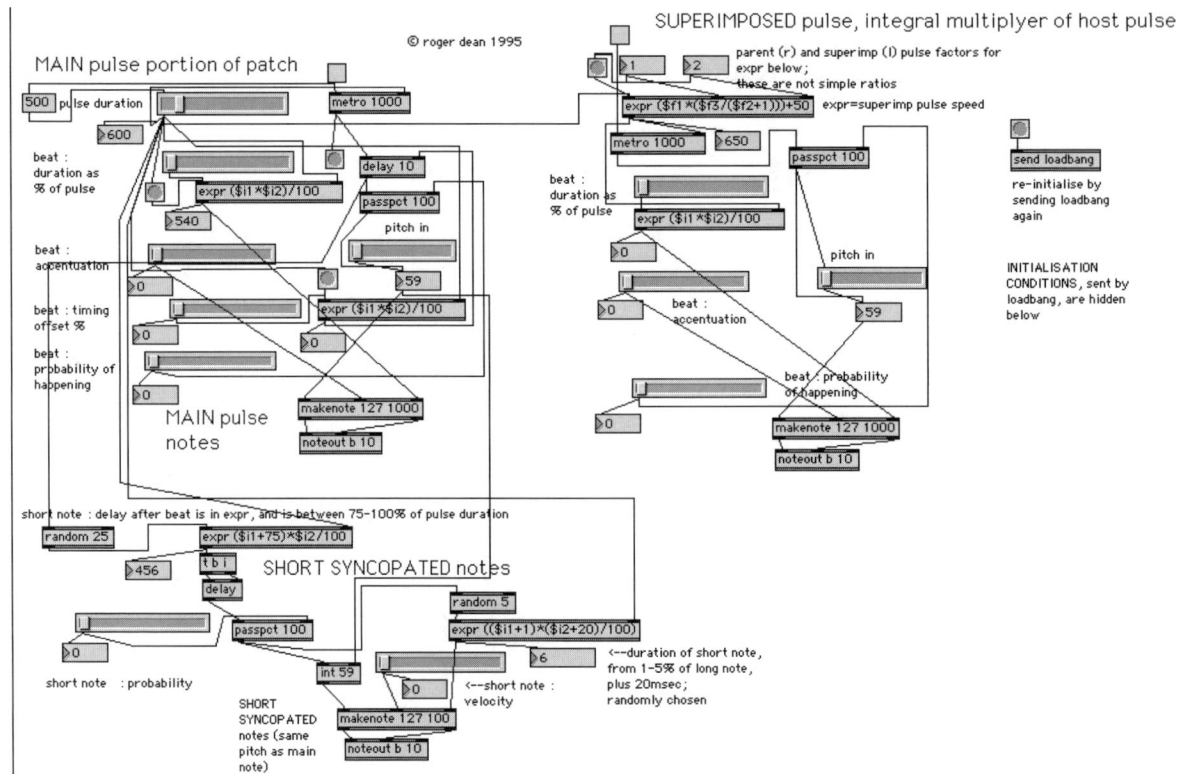

provided a constructive hypersound component (done in MIDI files), within our Web piece *WordStuffs* (included on the CD-ROM). In this, the user can independently drive up to five different MIDI files, which may play from any point, and forward or backward, so that an infinite range of overlays is available. This concept of overlaying fixed rhythmic meta-sound entities is analogous to that of mixing multiple sound samples or streams in real time, which again preserves the possibility of altering their juxtaposition by use of the DELAY function.

SECTION 4

Hyperimprovisation: The Software Shoots

SIX

Software Media for Improvisation

There are myriads of commercial, share-, and freeware programs available for MIDI sequencing and for sound synthesis, manipulation and mixing. Relatively few offer special features to aid the process of composition, of writing a referent for improvisers, or of improvisation. To a large degree this reflects commercial factors, in that software for sequencing and audio functions can be used in every recording studio, and much commercial music, whether popular or for film and media, is still partly built using such software. The development of software for composition was thus primarily the domain of academia, though the earliest algorithmic software emanated from such Bell Labs pioneers as Lejaren Hiller (Appleton and Perera 1975; Chadabe 1997). Subsequently, composers such as Xenakis have used specific algorithms for individual pieces, while IRCAM has developed a suite of software that allows complex modules of musical logic to act as agents successively on input material, in order to derive new output for use by the composer. Some IRCAM programs focus primarily on the generation of notated scores for interpretive performance, though IRCAM has also provided other tools for use by the electronic composer in describing rhythms and notating acousmatic pieces.

If anything, the consideration given to the use of software for improvisation was even less than that to composition. This clearly reflects the sociocultural downgrading of improvisation in the behavior patterns of academia, rather than primarily commercial factors (Smith and Dean 1997).

In this chapter I focus on a representative range of the software that is valuable in real-time performance, notably improvisation. Robert Rowe has contributed an important example of such software (Cypher) and has discussed this area in great detail in an earlier book, though with only limited focus on improvisation (Rowe 1993). Musical software for the Macintosh was brilliantly reviewed in Yavelow 1992, though his book is now inevitably somewhat out of date; a more recent synopsis of such information relevant to the PC platform was written by Warren Burt for posting on the Electronic Music Foundation Web site.

■ HISTORIC CONTRIBUTIONS

Raymond Scott's Electronium (c. 1965) is one of the "earliest developed composing systems that showed interactive intelligence" (Pressing 1992). But Max Mathews and Richard Moore's GROOVE (general real-time operations on voltage controlled equipment, 1968) is probably the earliest program to focus on real-time sound control that has been extensively utilized. Laurie Spiegel, working with GROOVE at Bell Labs, exploited some of its opportunities: "The program I wrote had all Bach's favorite manipulations—retrograde, inversion, augmentation, diminution, transposition—available on switches, knobs, pushbuttons and keys so that I could manipulate the 4 simple melodic and 4 rhythmic patterns with them in the same way that a player of an instrument manipulates individual notes" (Cope 1991, 11).

Later Spiegel herself wrote one of the first pieces of software specifically intended for improvisation and for more general use: the Music Mouse for Macintosh (Spiegel 1986). This was described as an "intelligent" instrument, because it embodied knowledge concerning conventions of scales and chords. The user chooses options in a computer window relating to the preferred mode, and when activated, the program emits a MIDI stream that can play a synthesizer. Originally, the expectation was that most of the sounds would be keyboardlike, or at least sustaining instruments, so that a delightful kind of ambient music, a term contemporaneously coined by Bryan Eno (see article by David Toop in Bell et al. 2000), was produced. The software takes the user parameters and generates a continuous flow of sound; the user can interact as it progresses to change parameters. Recently the program has again been made commercially available by Spiegel herself, and it remains great fun to use.

Components of the "intelligence" of the Music Mouse are stylistic constraints, for example in the mechanisms by which chords are formed in relation to chosen modes. The software is not primarily directed toward the generation of polyphonic music. In contrast, the software produced by Joel Chadabe and David Zicarelli in the 1980s, notably Jam Factory, and its successor M (first version 1986, released January 1987; more recently re-released commercially by Cycling 74'), had motivic input and polyphonic modification at its core. The performer played material into the Macintosh, and the software responded with a MIDI stream related to the material through parameters that were controllable by the user (velocity range, note density, and note order for up to four "voices"). Chadabe has written that the objective in producing M was the "creation of a musical plane that anyone could fly" (Chadabe 1992) and explained its evolutionary origins in Max Mathews's Conductor program (1976) and Sal Martirano's Sal-Mar Construction kit (1969–72). Martirano somewhat similarly stated that "conducting" his own software "consists of telling the orchestra how to improvise" (Chadabe 1992), an impossible task with most symphony orchestras. Historical information about M in particular is available at the Cycling 74' Web site. Amusingly, the program was originally intended to be named Master Composer, then, more tactfully, Rman (Random Manager).

The Ovaltune program not only allowed MIDI output but also graphic image generation in real-time performance. Chadabe's company was called Intelligent Computer Music Systems, again reflecting the emphasis on the intrinsic knowledge state of the software. It focused on ideas such as producing streams within defined meters or keys, which were somewhat less constraining than those in Music Mouse.

Pressing presents another general perspective on the Intelligent Systems software:

> These programs typically allow randomness and permutations of entered note material, often breaking the material into separate cycles of notes and durations. Rhythms can be overlaid at various speeds or stretched in certain ways. Algorithms generating harmony, note density, controller values, duration, . . . may be present. . . . Snapshots of configurations can be stored and recordings of produced pieces ported to sequencers for fine tuning. . . .
>
> The performer interacts with the program, learning it as a novel interactive instrument. . . . A quite different set of performance skills must be developed for each program. (Pressing 1992)

Thus these three pieces of software were not so much examples of artificial intelligence (AI) at work in producing music as "interactive instruments," which will be discussed below. M is again alive, through Zicarelli's more recent company, Cycling 74', and the re-release Ovaltune is planned. I have gained great pleasure from Music Mouse and M, both in their original incarnations, and at the time of writing and still using them for public performances.

As part of the important UK Composers Desktop Project, which sought to bring low-cost computer music tools to composers (initially on Atari computers), a related and stimulating program MIDIGRID was developed (Orton 1992). This uses on-screen boxes, each with a controllable event or process encapsulated and accessible for immediate performance. An ensemble of MIDIGRID performers has been networked on occasion, with apparently powerful results.

A series of academic studies has focused on algorithmic generation of jazz styles. David Levitt's jazz improviser program (Levitt 1984) generated solos from prescribed chord progressions, as did the work subsequently of Paul Hodgson (discussed in Kurzweil 1999; Ramalho et al. 1999). The concept of normalization is central in Levitt's program, indicated in part by the word "constraint" in the title of his article: pitches generated within musical lines were assessed for consonance with the prescribed harmony. Normalization is of debatable and variable utility for the improviser, as I will discuss later.

Christopher Yavelow (Yavelow 1989) reviews several of the programs from the 1980s that offer specific features of use to improvisers, such as M, Jam Factory, Music Mouse, Ovaltune, and also the important and powerful programming platform HMSL, written by Polansky, Burke, and Rosenboom (Polansky 1994). By 1993 large numbers of computer-mediated works had been produced with the involvement of HMSL, and the platform continues to be supported and available. HMSL was written between 1980 and 1985. According to Polansky's highly apt description, it implemented a technology "to do what musicians already know how to do: use a simple improvisational structure and set of predetermined performance relationships to produce strange, sometimes beautiful, sometimes awkward and 'non-musical,' but, I believe, fundamentally new music and sounds." An example of its use in improvisation by Larry Polansky is his *Cocks Crow* (1987–88), "a live improvisation for three performers and computer" that permitted the computer to manipulate the audio rate of a Roland DEP-5 digital signal processor while generating real-time notation and on-screen text commands to performers, which joined with nonelectronic sounds. The piece was performed as a network, and the 1988 version involved Polansky, John Bischoff, and Meloday Sumner (text and reading).

The whole field was transformed by the advent, commercialization, and very wide distribution of the object-oriented software platform MAX, written by Miller Puckette and David Zicarelli (published by Opcode and IRCAM, 1990–2000, with Cycling '74 replacing Opcode in 2000).

■ IMPROVISATORY SOFTWARE FOR MIDI-STREAM GENERATION

Unlike its predecessors, MAX (named in honour of Max Mathews) was intended as a programming platform in which users could write their own software for virtually any purpose expressible as MIDI data streams. For those musicians with limited capacity to program in C (or, currently, Java), MAX offered an assailable learning target, with musically intuitive objects available for common functions and a graphic interface that made the flow of processing more or less readily apparent. It is thus a multipurpose platform, and its potential is almost limitless, taking in MIDI data, storing, analyzing, processing, and outputting it, and also capable of generating data independently. The multiplicity of strands it can handle is limited only by the hardware capacities. The availability of MAX and the dramatic improvements in the price-to-performance ratio of desktop computers have been the major factors behind the development, or at least the widening application, of computer-interactive and computer-improvisatory work in music and sound since 1990. Detailed coverage of MAX programming has been provided not only in the commercial manual accompanying the software, but also in two sophisticated books (Rowe 1993; Winkler 1998), though with primary reference to composition and interaction. Several musicians, such as George Lewis, Richard Teitelbaum, and the members of the Hub, before and after MAX have written and used noncommercial (usually nondistributed) software for their improvisation, and their work is discussed elsewhere in this book. It is interesting, though, that Teitelbaum has had several of his patches (originally written in his PCL [patch control language]) transcribed into MAX, presumably for convenience, and so more recently has the Hub.

MAX has not been without its critics, of course. Peter Desain and Henkjan Honing initiated a series of discussion exchanges in the *Computer Music Journal* on the subject (Forum 1993), arguing that "Max is not a Programming Language" but rather a "data flow language," though noting that C programming can be inserted into MAX. George Lewis contributed to this discussion with particular reference to musical issues rather than programming technicalities and pointed to the desirability of using a complexity and multiplicity of interactive "triggers" in MAX rather than simple switches. It is this possibility that makes MAX particularly appealing musically and permits it to function beyond the norm of a data flow language. For this reason it is normally described in this book as a programming platform.

MAX is essentially a bare programming platform. In contrast, Robert Rowe's Cypher software is more like a sophisticated analysis-control-generate-response mechanism into which the user can interject material and whose mechanisms they can control to certain degrees. Rowe's own description of this mechanism is most pertinent, and figure 6.1 summarizes:

> Cypher is an interactive music system with two major components: a listener and a player. The listener analyzes streams of MIDI data. The player uses various algorithmic techniques to produce new musical output. Both components are made up of many small, interconnected agents operating on several hierarchical levels. The listener classifies features in the input and their behavior over time, sending messages that communicate this analysis to the player. A user of Cypher can configure the player component to react to such messages, where a reaction is the execution of compositional methods producing new music in response. Features characterized include speed, density, dynamic, harmony, and rhythm. Collections of relations can be saved and recalled during performance by a score-orientation section, which tracks human performance and executes state changes at predetermined points in the score. (Rowe 1993)

Figure 6.1 Cypher system overview (from Rowe).

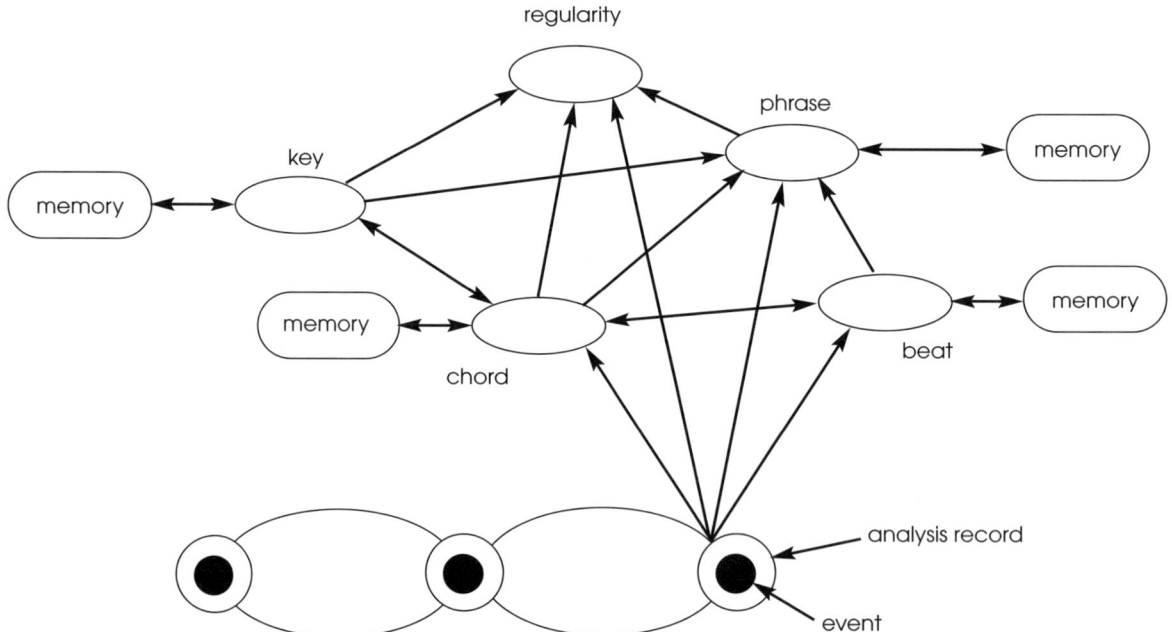

There seem to be some aspects of Cypher the user cannot control in real time, if at all; for example, the nature and details of the analyses performed by the listener and the range of compositional methods. And as its author mentions, Cypher is perhaps hyperenthusiastic about soloing: "it always takes the absence of other input as a signal that it should play more" (Rowe 1993). The compositional methods are many, mostly acting to transform input material. A list of their names gives an impression of this and of their purposes: accelerator, accenter, arpeggiator, backward, basser (which provides a "simple bass line against the music being analyzed"), chorder, decelerator, flattener, glisser, gracer, harmonizer, inverter, looper, louder, obbligato, ornamenter, phraser, quieter, sawer (which "adds four pitches to each input event, in a kind of sawtooth pattern"), solo, stretcher, swinger, thinner, tightenup, transposer, tremolizer, and triller. A range of generation techniques is available. The program includes several "normative" functions, which handle extreme events (e.g., extremely high pitch patterns) by responses that progressively retreat to the middle ground (in this case, midrange pitches). Cypher also embodies concepts of rhythm and pulse that are classically oriented but can be to a certain extent deranged to taste (Dean 1997b). Because of its complexity, Cypher is perhaps best used for compositions and for interactive work, which can be elaborately prearranged: it has great power in this context.

On the other hand, a virtuoso performer, such as its author himself, could use it powerfully in real-time improvisation. Unlike MAX, it is not commercially supported. Accordingly, Rowe 1993 describes some such events. His Concerto Grosso no. 2 [Boston, 1988] was the debut of the software, driven by Rowe, which collaborated with Richard Teitelbaum (piano, and using his own improvisational software, the Digital Piano), George Lewis (trombone), and Robert Dick (flute). Another event, which took place in 1989, at Banff, Canada, was *Universe III,* performed by Steve Coleman (saxophone and synthophone) and Muhal Richard Abrams (MIDI piano) with Coleman's own improvisation program and Cypher. MIDI streams were redirected during performance "so that input to Cypher changed continually between the other human and machine performers and itself." Rowe notes that the "jazz players were able to pick up on the [Cypher] transformations tied to features of their playing and to trigger them at will."

■ IMPROVISATORY SOFTWARE FOR AUDIO GENERATION AND MODIFICATION (DSP)

Several of the audio mixing programs in wide used since the late 1980s, such as ProTools, offer playback features that can be used as improvising tools in live performance. For example, a ProTools window might be arranged as an instrument containing a number of sound files (equivalent to the samples of a dedicated sampler, though usually less limited in terms of sample size and number). The user can then efficiently combine and modify these in some ways that are not feasible or efficient with a sampler instrument. They might choose to play two samples simultaneously, controlling the relative balance and panning. They might actively select chunks of the samples and play them repeatedly (e.g., looped), or collage them together linearly or irregularly, with or without displacements in time relative to each other; reversal is often quite efficient, though sometimes less so than with a sampler. There is also normally a "scrubbing" facility by which one or more tracks can be sounded with varying rates of progression through the samples, giving drastic pitch fluctuation (playing forward or backward). Some of these functions, such as looping, were probably overused in the 1990s by the Ensoniq, Kurzweil, and other samplers. Many performers would now hesitate to repeat them, but some of the possible techniques give access to the innards of sounds in just the way that many improvisers seek those of their instrument, developing unique timbres, extended techniques, and modified instruments.

The influence of the dedicated samplers was such that several authors have written computer-based sample-manipulation programs, of which the most notable is probably LiSa, from STEIM. This makes more efficient the processes I have just described but is also much more oriented toward the intake of new audio during performance (without requiring the cessation of other activity, as was often the case with ProTools versions). LiSa is also useful for control of sample playback from an independent MIDI keyboard, which functions primarily as controller rather than sampler or synthesizer. Such sample playback via MIDI is feasible in ProTools, but with greater limitation and much lesser efficiency. LiSa has thus spawned the endeavors of many live sampling individuals and groups. A common problem with solo performers using LiSa or analogous software is that they are tempted only to use "live" (i.e., fresh) samples. This can often result in a hiatus at the outset of a performance, as in some of Kaffe Mathews's and even of ensembles such as the duo/trio Omnivore (Mitchell Whitelaw, sampling; Phil Slater, trumpet; and, sometimes, Greg White, sound projection, mixing). This feature could be cultivated as an idiomatic component but sometimes seems instead not to receive attention from the performers.

The creation of new loops, beats, and breaks is at the core of techno and of drum and bass, and so Steinberg not only commercialized software that could duplicate the sound of the classic analog instruments of techno, the 303 and 909, but also sample manipulation software. Notably, their ReCycle efficiently identifies component sounds in an audio sample of a potential loop or beat, separating them into individual samples that can then be played back via MIDI and rearranged in time and other respects. ReCycle is used most in studio or home preparation of pieces and is not particularly friendly to real-time use; its functions can be achieved in ProTools, in some ways less efficiently, but ProTools provides a far greater range of possibilities for the process, and these are reasonably achievable in performance.

Grainwave (Berry 1999) is a more recent program, written by Mike Berry. It is focused on real-time sound synthesis and signal processing, unlike LiSa, yet is able to use samples. It again permits MIDI control of sound playback and computer-mediated performance of sound through the 2D interface of the screen, with axes representing pitch and volume. Since Grainwave can serve as a stand-alone sound-generation system, the Hub has used it installed on several remote computers to permit Internet performance in which the Net was used only to transmit meta-sound information (i.e., control streams rather than audio), which was then realised by Grainwave at each location, ensuring that each performer could hear the same results (in the piece *Points of Presence,* 1997; discussed in Berry 1999). Control information (meta-sound) was passed by UDP (user datagram protocol) using MAX objects for the purpose created at CNMAT. Each player had a rendering machine at each location.

Until recently it was unusual or impossible to achieve real-time sound synthesis on most desktop computers. However, Csound, Cmix, and other software can now run in real time on some such platforms, and in particular James McCartney's Supercollider has been exploited by improvisers as a real-time synthesis engine that is open to continuous control input.

An elaborate and flexible platform that combines real-time synthesis with other DSP functions is MSP (1997–), the acronym for

MAX Signal Processing (running on Macintosh). This is an add-on to MAX created by David Zicarelli using ideas from Miller Puckette's Pd. It had its antecedents in work at IRCAM for Next and SGI platforms, which were less widely available. Like MAX, MSP is an almost bare platform that permits most kinds of sound synthesis and almost any kind of digital manipulation of incoming audio signals. Its multiplicity and stability is again a feature of the hardware capacity, but it has already achieved wide acclaim and use. Most of the functions LiSa provides can be readily written in MSP.

■ IMPROVISATORY LOOPING

We will twice in this chapter consider the case of the drum and bass idiom, an aspect of techno. Here we will consider the utility of real-time software-mediated improvisation to loop manipulation, an important feature of the music. The dance and rave context of much drum and bass and related musics such as jungle, big beat, trip hop, and so on is well captured by Philip Tagg:

> [Rave music is] intended for energetic individual dancing in discos or at rave parties. You can dance 'with' someone by just facing them but you do not touch. . . . Rave tracks seem to have an average duration of around five minutes. In formal terms they sometimes divide into two identifiable sections containing slightly different tonal material and variations in instrumentation, at least in the sense of altered presets, muted tracks etc. Just as often, however, techno-rave tracks are horizontally (not vertically) monothematic. Other variation comes from the way in which tracks enter and exit and sound together with (or separate from) other tracks. Rave numbers rarely start with all tracks sounding simultaneously, and often build up several two-bar units of other tracks before the quantised kick drum sets in. All rave numbers feature at least one obligatory break in which the harmonic-rhythmic one or two-bar riff, often heard as sampled piano, plays solo. Sometimes breaks feature other tracks or sounds—a sampled human voice, animals, a siren, etc. (Tagg n.d.)

Tagg then quotes his daughter Maria, a rave enthusiast:

> When the bass drum stops people do different things. If it's an effect or the "tssk-tssk-tssk" noise, some people just stand still; others go round like in slow motion. If it's the piano or another "da-daa-da-dee-da" sort of thing, a lot of people kind of wave their arms about. When the break's on, no one moves their feet or bums much. They do that when the bass

drum starts again. Breaks are dead good: quite dramatic and exciting, because everybody stops and starts again.

This makes clear the importance of breakbeats (breaks) in techno as a complement to the ongoing repetitive (often looping) rhythmic patterns (beats). It is interesting that the differentiation between these aspects of techno is often fiercely argued, yet on very little musical basis. Similarly, Shapiro, in his 1999 book on drum 'n' bass, rather than interpreting breakbeats as gaps in the drumming pattern, even describes them as "the part of the record where the rest of the band 'gives the drummer some'," emphasizing the dropping out of the other players rather than the partial suspension of the driving rhythms of the drum and bass lines. Nevertheless, breakbeats are probably best characterized in musical terms as involving the suspension of significant proportions of the ongoing drum and bass (and sometimes harmony) looped pattern, the beat(s) (R. Brown and Griese 2000). The break seems to have its origin in the street dance and rap discussed in Rose 1994. In the case of street dance the breaks were essentially silent, and hence there was more emphasis on providing contrasted cross-rhythms and sometimes on distorting the length of the break or even introducing a new pulse, which then continued. Components of these more extreme approaches are sometimes used by drum 'n' bass artists, such as the Art of Noise, which several times introduces extra pulses or parts of pulses (beyond those implied by the ongoing meter) into its breaks.

How could a drum 'n' bass performer use real-time improvised loop manipulation? I will discuss this as a suitable case study for the application of software techniques in club performance. (Later in this chapter I will also discuss the totally algorithmic and interactive generation of music related to this idiom.) There are several simple solutions to this objective depending on the degree of "outness" (for example, deviation from the meter and pulse) the musician is willing to accept. The solutions depend on whether the loop is being performed as a MIDI or a sound file. For the purposes of this simple discussion, I will consider the looped beat in isolation.

Most MIDI sequencers now allow real-time manipulation of the MIDI pattern without cessation of playing. Thus notes can be removed, their dynamics changed, MIDI tracks muted, the speed changed, and even the length of the loop (in terms of pulses) altered. For example, with the effective shareware software Easy Beat, all these functions are available, and the software even works well with the general MIDI instrument sets now intrinsic to most computers, such as the Quicktime instrument set. Every conceivable alteration is readily available except for extremely subtle changes in the number of loop pulses: this parameter is limited in many MIDI sequencers, including Easy Beat, to a certain minimum quantization unit. For example, with Easy Beat, the minimum subdivision of a pulse is a triplet 64th note. MAX's Detonate object allows many of these same controls, though it is more time consuming to establish such a convenient interface to the drum kit than with a dedicated MIDI sequencer; on the other hand almost any manipulation of pulse number (e.g., from 8 pulses in a loop to 7.97) is feasible.

The combination of MAX with a MIDI sequencer playing a loop gives infinite possibilities. The inter-application communication driver of the Opcode Midi System can be used to submit MIDI data from the sequencer to MAX before it is sounded. Then MAX can perform any manipulation, random or controlled, including multiple delays, to pervert the loop.

With a loop played as a sound file, ProTools and other sound editors offer some facilities, but often with restrictions consequent on the fact that they are intended for studio rather than real-time use. For example, a loop in ProTools 4.1 could play continuously, and volume (i.e., selective controlling or silencing of individual events) and panning changes could be superimposed in real time, as could track muting. However, subtle alterations to the length of the loop at the beginning of the sound file (cutting out a few milliseconds, for example) required stopping and starting, though those at the end worked in continuous play. MSP provides more flexible ways of manipulating an audio loop, so that the setup is analogous to that with a MIDI sequencer playing into MAX. Just about any conceivable manipulation is possible, including elaborate multiple delay lines. StepTrance and Where/Samples on the CD-ROM are relevant MSP patches.

■ GENERATIVE SOFTWARE FOR SOUND

MAX/MSP is a platform in which complex multilayered algorithms can be written so as to perform continuously or for discrete periods without further intervention. It can output audio and MIDI, and the MIDI can be realized by the inbuilt sounds of the computer, such as Quicktime Musical Instruments. Supercollider can achieve analogous functions for synthesized sound. These platforms are thus excellent for use at any level of audio and MIDI quality, whether internal to the computer or using external sound-generating modules.

When considering sound for the Internet, for most users bandwidth (dictated often by modem connection speed) is still a major limitation. Thus two major specialized paths have been followed toward generative software for Web-specific use: Koan and Beatnik. The former was created by Tim and Peter Cole and has had active input from Bryan Eno, reflecting its tendency to generate "ambient" music. The latter is the work of Thomas Dolby and has mostly been used in similarly New Age and ambient pieces. Both programs provide mechanisms for the use in a MIDI context of very small sound samples provided by the composer, thereby extending the range of the intrinsic sound set of the recipient's computer. They also provide relatively simple programming tools that permit algorithmic composition and some degree of user interaction in exploiting the chosen sounds. The algorithm is usually downloaded to the user's computer together with the small sound files and then runs locally. These tools are primarily useful for creating variability of sound within a site. This is a great advantage over the monotonous simplistic loops that accompany many sites; they also permit some user interaction, though they are not advanced tools for improvisation. For this, MAX/MSP, Supercollider, and their relatives have substantially more potential.

AI and neural net approaches to the generation of music hold tremendous promise for the future of composition and improvisation. However, presently their contributions are restricted mainly to rule-based modeling of particular styles (e.g., Löthe 2000). Valuable steps have been taken toward creating functional artificial performers that can fulfill specialized improvisational functions—for example, the artificial jazz bass player (Johnson-Laird 1991) and the virtual be-bop saxophonist (Hodgson 2000; and Hodgson, personal communication 2000). These will be discussed in chapter 11.

Fundamental to all the generative software is the question of how it can be used productively in improvisation. Clearly a hermetically sealed algorithm that is just started by the user and stops itself or is stopped by the user is not an improvisatory tool. Yet the greater the extent of real-time user-controllable parameters built into the software, the closer the composition becomes to a comprovisation. As I have emphasized, interaction and improvisation with such algorithms form a continuum, and relevant factors include the degree to which the user can learn to exploit the capacities of the algorithm (versus the degree to which algorithmic changes are indifferent to the nature of user input). A generative algorithm might also be conceived as poorly interactive, but providing a sound environment in which other sound is improvised. Unpredictability in the algorithmic output is also a potential positive contributor to its improvisatory utility. In all these respects, MAX/MSP, and to a lesser extent SuperCollider, offer the full ambit of conceivable improvisatory options, while Koan and Beatnik are more concerned with Web projection, musical self-motivation, and simple user interaction.

■ SPECIALIZED FUNCTIONAL OBJECTIVES OF GENERATIVE AND OTHER SOFTWARE: RHYTHM ENGINES AND OTHER MECHANISMS

Most of the software discussed above can be used for a very wide range of improvisatory functions. Conversely, most individual programs (or "patches," as they are usually termed in the context of MAX) are written for specific pieces or events. Many composers and improvisers have been interested in developing hyperinstruments and meta-orchestras for general use. Others have focused on individual functions within music, providing efficient and flexible platforms for controlling these functions specifically.

Perhaps the most widely explored category is that of software relating to meter and pulse. As mentioned already, ProTools and Recycler can be used in real-time performance for the repetitive generation of loops, just as a sampler instrument can. However, like the group at CNMAT, led by David Wessel, I have written patches that facilitate rhythmic control and continuous variation of parameters of rhythm generation usually through a MIDI instrument set-up. For example, a programmed interface should provide an efficient interactive mechanism for defining meter, pulse rate, extent of accentuation, and extent of cross-rhythm generation, and for controlling these continuously in real time. Such a patch (see figure 5.2) can be used for improvised speed changes, subdivision pattern changes (such as 6/8 ↔ 3/4), and more complex metrical modulation (e.g., 4/4, quarter note = 400 msec, to 7/8, eighth note = 266). I have discussed such control previously (Dean 1997b). Matthew Burtner has written a MAX patch for such purposes that he calls his "Polyrhythmicon," aping Henry Cowell, and some of its output is heard on his *Portals of Distortion* (Burtner 1998).

Much research in music cognition has focused on the "beat tracking" problem, which leads to the challenge of providing computer algorithms that can identify beats and meter in an incoming musical stream (Desain and Honing 1999). A whole issue of the *Journal of New Music Research* (vol. 28, no. 1 [1999]) was devoted to the perception and cognition of rhythm. It is worth noting here only that a disparity of opinion exists as to whether rhythm perception involves comparisons with internal bodily "clocks" or bodily physical "resonances" (Van Noorden and Moelants 1999), or rather does not involve perception of time as such but instead the temporal structure of stimulus events. These hypotheses could all provoke distinct computational approaches. Disregarding issues of determination of note attack points in audio streams (which is in any case avoided in incoming MIDI streams), the core of the computational problem is the fitting of the observed timings and accentuations into a coherent pattern, bearing in mind the considerable performance variability in timing regularity in most music. One purpose of such work is to permit computers to accompany live performers through a notated score, making corrections to their timing to accommodate such performance variation. Another is to provide analytical insights that may aid the study of how the brain cognitively processes a given kind of information. Recent evidence suggests that the more complex the rhythmic patterns, the more attentive effort the brain applies (Keller 1999). This reveals a probable psychological constraint upon performance, and hence upon improvisation (Pressing 1998).

While the beat-tracking problem is as yet only partially solved, there is already scope for a parallel development in the programming of rhythm machines to generate unusual rhythmic and articulation features such as swing. Swing is both a subjective experience and a core feature of much jazz, yet many authors evade or admit defeat in any attempt to characterize it. Gunther Schuller (1968) has given a good description with reference to early jazz, which has subsequently been extended (Dean 1992). For the present purposes, it must suffice to say that swing can be generated by a group or an individual playing in any meter, most commonly $\frac{4}{4}$, $\frac{2}{4}$, $\frac{3}{4}$, and $\frac{6}{8}$, by the use of slight displacements of the sounding of accentuated beats in the meter, by frequent and highly accentuated syncopation, and by greater range of accentuation of notes than is common, together with specialized techniques particular to individual instruments. For example, in the case of the piano, it seems to me that components of swing are provided by relative timing of notes in chords and by particular kinds of staccato touch, taken in conjunction with the syncopation and accentuation mentioned already.

Can a computer algorithm generate swing? For at least one software designer, this seemed little problem: he produced an algorithmic rendering of modified melodic derivatives of "My Favorite

Things" in the home style. "The drummer played a traditional ride cymbal figure by attacking on every beat and playing a high percentage of the swing eighth notes between beats" (Fry 1989). More intensive yet still preliminary studies toward this end have commenced. At IRCAM between 1978 and 1986 the project was unsatisfactory (Hodeir 1995), while others continue the effort currently (Dean 1998). It seems that the timing precision of commercial software such as MAX (which can be accurate to roughly 1 msec in its current version) is sufficient, since group performance variability of onset times for a given beat, even when played with a conductor, is around 20 msecs. Subjectively, even relatively simple patches can give the impression of swing, and it seems that gradual changes in note displacement rather than random ones are effective. Certain kinds of instrumental sounds (e.g., drums) may be most readily associated by listeners with swing, and it also seems that algorithms that output multi-instrument ("group") performance are most convincing. These studies need much development, including proper psychological analysis of the outputs and their cognition, before they will be rigorous. The rhythm engine patch shown in figure 5.2 (and on the CD-ROM), especially if used simultaneously in multiple copies, allows control of many of the parameters that so far seem most important to swing.

■ A CASE HISTORY: THE ALGORITHMIC AND INTERACTIVE PRODUCTION OF MUSIC RELATED TO DRUM 'N' BASS

I have discussed the loop and its role in rave music. Other features of most of the genres presented in rave sessions (such as bigbeat, triphop, jungle, etc. [Brown and Griese 2000]) include high basic pulse rates, synthesized rather than conventional instrumental sounds (particularly in the drums), and minor, Aeolian, or Phrygian modality.

A few artists, such as Scanner (Robin Rimbaud), use computer-interactive performance (and some other gestural interfaces) to perform live music with such beats. It is still based on prerecorded materials but in conjunction with a wide range of other sounds, from ambient to noise oriented. On the other hand, even fewer people seem to have addressed the idea of writing software for the real-time generation from scratch of drum and bass. The CD-ROM illustrates an output of my continuously evolving solutions to this challenge, which is used in performances by Dr Metagroove (see mp3.com).

The main mechanism is a model-driven generative approach, written in MAX, with most parameters being real-time controllable by the improvising performer. The model prescribes central features of the idiom, such as the drum patterns, the repeating bass line, and the intermittent harmonies and noises—though it does so in a flexible, avant manner, rather than one close to all the core conventions. Thus, a varying drum pattern is generated instantly from one of several probabilistic mechanisms; pulse rates can change as the piece progresses. A bass line is progressively assembled through stochastic events and then continued unchanged. Keyboard harmonies and melodic and/or noise lines appear intermittently, driven by probabilistic decisions. Melodic lines are partly driven by Markov chains. The time scale of a particular piece is decided at the outset, either stochastically or by player choice.

A subsidiary mechanism is the use of MAX processing of repeating MIDI loop files, as mentioned above. The loop may be precomposed, or it may be generated at the outset of the performance using the mechanisms just described.

Dr Metagroove often has the benefit of live DSP from Greg White, using both direct mixer controls and algorithmic MSP; similarly, I provide an MSP patch that processes some of the computer and sampler/synthesizer outputs. Eric Lyon has taken this approach to other extremes (see, e.g., Penrose and Lyon 2000) in a quite independent development of techno performance. Primarily using preformed recorded loops, Lyon focuses on real-time DSP manipulations, often with a rhythmicity of processing that perturbs the rhythms of the loop. Alternatively, he may use the rhythmic processing to generate the rhythms of the loop, which can be effective with almost any sound source, not necessarily one already looped. Furthermore, the sound source can then be a long sound file, yet emerge technolike. Examples of Lyon's stimulating work are to be found on the Web—for example, at the site of the Bregman Studio of Electro-Acoustic Music at Dartmouth College on its promotional CD-ROM (Bregman Studio 2000)—and there is a relevant example on the CD-ROM attached to this book.

SEVEN

Speaking Locally

> Playing a harpsichord with a shovel or an angel conducting the Crystal Orchestra of the Spheres with the twinkling tip of a fine finger . . .
>
> —*M. Waisvisz (Wanderley and Battier 2000)*

Can the software and hardware just discussed be put to use in improvisation and in improvising ensembles? In this chapter I will first discuss this conceptually, and in the solo work of certain contributors, and then consider in more detail the work of a selection of groups that have been active in the field. The approach is primarily thematic rather than chronological, and so a very brief chronological survey and a discussion of future possibilities are provided as a coda to the chapter.

■ A CONCEPTUAL SYNOPSIS OF POSSIBILITIES IN SOLO AND NETWORKED COMPUTER INTERACTIVE SOUND IMPROVISATION

The idea of hyperinstruments, in which the signaling capabilities of conventional instruments are extended through the detection of specialized features intrinsic to their being played, has already been discussed. Analogous instruments have been devised, for both general and professional use, that are not based on traditional ones, most extensively in the Brain Opera project of Tod Machover and colleagues (Paradiso 1999). There is little distinction between the professional instruments among these and the "meta-instrument" of Laubier and colleagues (Laubier 1998), except that the latter has more complicated interfaces than do most of the Brain Opera instruments, so that the range of possibilities is huge. The meta-instrument can readily be used for large-scale performance works singly or in pairs (by one or two performers). Laubier considers it "more interesting to move a sound around in space if this movement is connected to its spectral evolution." While this is an arbitrary position, the 32 continuous variables (7-bit quantized) of his instrument certainly permit it: the interface comprises foot pedals and a symmetrical array of pressure-sensitive keys and has been used for both sound and parallel image synthesis and for automated light projection.

It is a logical step from a hyperinstrument to a meta-orchestra, and Laubier's instrument can achieve this. By meta-orchestra I mean not only a software-driven simulacrum of a conventional instrumental orchestra, but also, more broadly, a large ensemble of timbrally diverse instruments that can be performed efficiently by one or a small group of players (or silent conductor(s)). The Eminent African-American trombonist and composer George Lewis, with his Voyager software and its antecedents, is one of the earliest practitioners of such an approach. Commonly, his performance set-up has involved one or a small number of desktop (more recently, portable) computers that fulfill two functions: (1) the software processing of incoming musical information as MIDI and the generation of an output event stream, and (2) the playing of orchestral sound samples, usually by means of computer-based samplers, in which sound samples are played usually from an E-mu Proteus 12 or similar internal computer card, allowing up to 12 independent voices to be played by the computer. This method is analogous to one in which a computer performs the first functions, while the second is provided by a sophisticated external hardware sampler such as a Kurzweil, though Lewis's method is physically more compact. Such meta-orchestras can be driven either by a player of an instrument, such as Lewis's trombone, or directly from the computer.

Lewis describes his *Rainbow Family,* an interactive composition for computer with pitch sensor, synthesizer, and an acoustic player. The computer had a listener function, and the piece was done in part at IRCAM and premiered there in 1984 (see IRCAM Web site):

> I'm trying to help my machines understand musical context. Since good improvisors can't listen to everything, they have to keep track of the context in which they place the sounds they're making and hearing. You have to find structure in what you've just played and heard or, if necessary, posit it or another structure as a point of departure. Improvisors often work in terms of rather loosely defined 'shapes', . . . such as volume direction, pitch direction, duration, rhythm regularity, pitch or duration transposition, time between major changes in output or input, pattern-finding, and frequency of silence. You don't need or want an exhaustive transcription, but instead a fast, general analysis of what's happening at any given

moment and what's been happening. This requires massive, but musically important, data reductions. (Chadabe 1997)

Of Voyager, his later program, Lewis added:

> I try to get the computer to do its own thing as well as follow a performer. And as soon as the computer generates something independent, a performer can react to that and go with it. The idea is to get the machine to pay attention to the performer as it composes. So there's an analysis of what's going on, and the analysis informs the composition. (Chadabe 1997)

Having mentioned analyzing pitches, pitch register, mapping into MIDI space, averaging, looking at stability over time, intervals, onset gaps, Lewis continues: "My big thing is averages. . . . Then you can map all of that to the output" (Chadabe 1997). But in fact the generation and performing mechanisms in Voyager "have access to, but may or may not make use of, the . . . output of the listening section" (Rowe 1993). MAX includes an object (Borax) specifically designed to extract several of the derived pieces of information just mentioned, such as onset gaps and note lengths (once the sustain has concluded), and provide them to analytical machineries.

In a conversation with the author in 1999 Lewis elaborated on his aims with Voyager. Like Cypher, Voyager comprises listener and analysis, manipulator, and generator. Since Lewis likes to communicate with the program "only by my own musical behavior" (rather than by directly altering parameters on the computer keyboard), it is not surprising that he views the program as possessing a degree of personality, in fact moving through various "mindsets." A "mind map" of Voyager states exists and if necessary could be organized to provide an overall mind map for a particular piece. However, Voyager aims to be "incarnatic" software rather than "prosthetic," and so Lewis does not favor such an organizational approach, accepting that what is incarnate in the software is in part himself. Lewis mentioned that he has a parameter he tweaks before each performance that dictates the duration of the analysis window on which Voyager operates. For performance with the saxophonist Evan Parker, who can generate multiphonic streams and textures lasting many minutes, Lewis might choose a "glacial" rate of change in Voyager, and hence a very long analysis window; for the more mercurial side of Jon Rose, he might choose a fast change. As a simple example of the influence of analytical information on the mindset of Voyager, Lewis mentioned that if its listener detected increasingly sustained input material, this might well cause Voyager's instrumental voices to switch to sustaining string sounds. He is little interested in using

DSP functions through Voyager (East 1995). Lewis is very clear that what he wishes to do with Voyager is to improvise.

Lewis has written an important and provocative article distinguishing "Afrological and Eurological perspectives" in improvised music after 1950 (Lewis 1996). He says that these "terms refer metaphorically to musical belief systems and behaviour which, in my view, exemplify particular kinds of musical 'logic'." He goes on to theorize them as "historically emergent rather than ethnically essential, thereby accounting for the reality of transcultural and transracial communication among improvisers." From the outset it is clear that Lewis adopts a sympathetic, sophisticated, and flexible approach and is explicitly aware that he is walking on ever-shifting sands. He spends a considerable part of his article characterizing "two major American postwar real-time traditions" centered on Charlie Parker and John Cage, veering respectively to the Afrological and the Eurological. He analyzes the verbal meta-texts surrounding music of the period to reveal how commonly white analysts and composer-authors have neglected or even hidden the influence of improvised music in general, and of African American jazz and related improvisation in particular. Clearly "bebop's combination of spontaneity, structural radicalism and uniqueness, antedating by several years the reappearance of improvisation in Eurological music posed a challenge to that music which needed to be answered in some way. All too often, the space of whiteness provided a convenient platform for a racialized denial of the trenchancy of this challenge, while providing an arena for the articulation of an implicit sensibility which I have termed 'Eurological'." He refers to the white construct of improvisation as "other," and the use of "exnomination." Quoting Fiske (1994) he says that "one practice of exnomination is the avoidance of self-recognition and self-definition," a counterpart to which is to describe the world as if the white view were universal. These points are well taken and should be internalized in the outlook of Eurologicians.

The main difficulty arises in characterizing and distinguishing the two perspectives. Partly because the article is constructed in an episodic manner, the following comments cannot do full justice to the issue, and the reader is encouraged to consult Lewis's article itself. Key is Lewis's awareness of the mutability of both perspectives. However, in characterizing the Eurological he emphasizes the features of being "fixed" or "worked out"—in other words, determinate. He then goes on to distinguish "indeterminacy," promoted by Cage and others, as a very broad process, with unforeseeable outcomes, presenting it as a "subset" of improvisation. Indeterminacy can be viewed in a narrower sense as simply the presentation of composed material whose ordering can be varied in performance, complementing aleatory music in which some events are left for the performers to evolve, and it is fair to see both as subsets of improvisation. At the same time Lewis mentions the "Eurological notion of pure spontaneity in improvisation," but he does not analyze in detail the concept of spontaneity, which, as previously pointed out, is very problematic, possibly unhelpful, in the context of sophisticated (experienced) improvisers (Smith and Dean 1997).

Amongst the key features of the Afrological approach (Lewis 1996) seem to be that "sonic symbolism is often constructed with a view towards social instrumentality as well as form," and the presentation of "personal narrative. . . . Part of telling your own story is developing your own 'sound'. . . . Moreover, for an improviser working in Afrological forms, 'sound,' sensibility, personality, and intelligence cannot be separated from an improviser's phenomenal (as distinct from formal) definition of music." Conversely, "Eurological improvisers have tended to look askance on the admission of personal narrative into improvisative activity," though this could be viewed as the inverse of Derek Bailey's tendency toward "non-idiomatic" improvisation.

Lewis views "improvised music," so called "since 1970" and emerging all over the world, as the result of the influence of Afrological thought, and distinguishes it from "Eurological work 'incorporating' or 'using' improvisation, or featuring 'indeterminacy' or aleatoric practices. . . . A more nuanced view of improvised music might identify as more salient differentiating characteristics its welcoming of agency, social necessity, personality, and difference, as well as its strong relationship to popular and folk cultures." The European improvisers have a "sense of having created a native model of improvisation, however influenced by Afrological forms." The intertwining of the Afrological and the Eurological is therefore extensive, but the perception of their distinct historical emergences is critical. I consider that if improvisation is understood as involving broader freedom of activity than indeterminacy and aleatoriness, then it may be viable to view all improvisation since bebop as heavily Afrological, while Eurological influences are most important for composition. It may be that Lewis also intends to imply this; certainly he wishes to separate improvisation from "real-time composition," for reasons that are otherwise not readily apparent.

In conversation with the author (1999) Lewis commented that software platforms such as MAX already embody the Eurological, and so an important question is the degree to which he feels his

Voyager software does so too. Lewis's response when I directly questioned him on this in an e-mail was subtle and complex, as one might expect. A recent trope he has favoured is that of "multidominance," which seems to refer to the idea of mutual coexistence of multiple separable streams in an artistic work—possibly parallelling Raymond Williams's perception of the antihegemonic countercurrents in larger sociocultural formations.

The idea of meta-composition can embrace a wide range of improvisatory and compositional approaches in which multiple frameworks are prominent and all are simultaneously accessible. There are at least two ways of considering such meta-composition. First, as a system in which a primary composition is subjected to one or more secondary compositional modifications, be they simultaneous or successive. This can happen, for example, in the work of Richard Teitelbaum when a performed improvisatory idea is subjected to a secondary computer manipulation generating a simultaneous stream of output. Or it might be that a transiently stable networked system of interactions between discrete software components, for example in the work of the Hub, gives rise to a subsequent new transient state.

A second way of considering meta-composition is that in which an algorithm permits access to several separate compositional modules, which can be used in any sequence or combination. This goes beyond the idea of Earle Brown and some of his contemporaries, in which the pages of a score might be realized in any chosen sequence, with choice available at the time of performance, for it permits several of the "pages" (compositional modules) to be active simultaneously. It is more like a musical hypertext, in which the performer can jump from any one site to another through a three-dimensional web of choice, sometimes allowing a previous site to continue while a new one also is expressed. To make this process improvisatory, within each compositional module there has to be the possibility of real-time computer interaction, or at least simultaneous sound improvisation as an independent response and counterbalance.

Very relevant here is the work of Curtis Bahn (Dodge and Jerse 1997, 422–25; Bahn 2000), bassist-improviser, and his new and world music improvisation ensemble. Bahn uses the computer to provide sound storage, processing, and presentation. But he also sometimes uses it to provide a graphical performance display to the group members that indicates comprovisational material (for example, three different categories of material at one time), which can be used as the basis for improvisation and which may or may not be sounded by the computer at the same time. This means that the improvisers may use material before it is sounded by the computer, or that is never so sounded. Dodge suggests that this avoids a common impression in computer-interactive performance that the performers are following the computer. This impression occurs in spite of the success of score-following algorithms developed by Dannenberg and Vercoe and the former's use of them even in highly improvising contexts (for example, his piece *Jimmy Durante Boulevard* [Dannenberg 1989]). Bahn's system also exploits computer control, in that there can be a performance display for changing the compositional modules, adjusting MIDI parameters, and changing the sound mix.

```
Main Sound Menu
  /            \
score         sound
selection     scenes
```

As Roads describes it,

> the concept at work is to provide the improvisers with visual clues that will help them to play together. All have had the opportunity to "woodshed" on the material in advance of a performance, so they will be familiar with the particular sounds displayed. The freedom of the musical contribution of the live players themselves is paramount in this system. The visual representations of the three sound files are not coordinated in time. (Roads 1985)

Analogous methods are involved in Karlheinz Essl's *Champ d'Action*, a Web-based music notation system that, to quote the composer from his Web site, "is based on eight characteristic compositional structure types, which are defined as models. By changing the model parameters—by a conductor controlling a computer during the performance—the most diverse variants can be produced, which are turned into sound by the musicians improvisando." The performers read the real-time generated score and use it as a comprovisation. A similar approach has been used by Greg White in his *Scrolls of Time* (1997), in which MAX was used to generate a scrolling score of new material, one line for each player, who was allowed to use the material with defined types of flexibility.

While networked ensemble possibilities are discussed further in the next section of this book, it is important to mention the innovative work of the interactive duo of Andrew Schloss and David Jaffe (Schloss and Jaffe 1993). For example, their *Wildlife* is an "improvisational" duo in five movements for radio drum, zeta violin, and computer-interactive system; it was premiered in 1991 and is available on CD (Schloss and Jaffe 1991–92). Here chains of MIDI processing result in MIDI signals that are realized by Sample Cell, and that may go simultaneously to DSP function; thus, for example, a violin glissando might change the pitch of chords played by the radio drum percussionist. As the creators say, "Independent computer processes are like cattle that are allowed to wander over the open plains and the performer's control is that of the cowboy who reigns them in when it is time to go into the corral." Instead of using a whip, the performer can constrain, for example, by filling a buffer with 100 tremolo reiterations of a single pitch, or by directly interacting with the computer keyboard. Jaffe and Schloss 1994 notes that "in improvisational musical styles, the music is held together by a set of strict stylistic conventions." Presumably the authors meant to imply that this was true of many though not all improvisational styles, for they continued by indicating that the computer could "conquer" this feature.

Certain specific subcategories of meta-compositional possibility are worth delineating in the context of improvisation. Thus one can envisage a powerful application in live improvisation of techno with drum and bass, in which the meta-composition was used as a path through the different breaks and loops the performer (or DJ) chose. As discussed earlier, several composers have written algorithmic drum-and-bass-generating patches (for example, Eric Lyon and the present author), and a drum-and-bass meta-composition might include several such patches. Surprisingly few drum-and-bass artists seem to use the computer as a live performance tool or to contribute improvisation at anything other than the highest level of such a meta-compositional analysis. Most commercially viable, and probably all dance floor-usable, drum and bass comprises very limited disjunctions between the beats of one and the next segment, and countergrooves to the dominant one at any time are rare. On the other hand, a meta-compositional approach can readily permit multiple grooves to co-exist, forming an interesting kind of "hypergroove."

If the hypergroove is considered an example of a meta-composition that permits the exploration of webs of rhythmic fields and the generation of juxtapositions of them into new combined fields, then, similarly, a meta-composition can allow the improviser to experiment efficiently with hybrid pitch or modality webs and hybrid timbral fields. It is worth rejoining the concepts of exploratory and generative hypertexts, as delineated by Michael Joyce. In the former, material exists to be explored and expressed. In the latter, new material is generated as a consequence of the action of the algorithm, as in the case of the networked transient stable states. Both approaches apply in the hypergroove. Specialized generative software exists for a multiplicity of purposes both practical and artistic. This can be useful in an improvising context, especially if the software permits interaction beyond that of merely selecting from among products of a particular generation of outputs before initiating the next.

I wish to conclude this section with a discussion of the higher-level assemblage of meta-compositional components during improvised performance, as powerfully achieved and well analyzed and documented in the case of Jonathan Impett's commercially recorded piece *Mirror-Rite* (Impett 1994a). Some of the objectives of writing this piece, to which the meta-trumpet(er) (Impett 1994b) I discussed earlier is intrinsic, can be gleaned from the following quotation from Impett, from the liner notes of the CD:

> Performing the piece is like speaking a language and getting an answer in some other language that you don't understand at first, but that you know has meaning for you. The performer can't know everything that happens because of his actions. He learns that during the performance and by his learning that his every action becomes part of the performance, the instrument, the piece and the performer become one thing. It's a sequence of chambers of mirrors. You're walking through this chamber and all the mirrors start moving. You don't know how they are moving, and yet they're responding to your own actions.

The composition is "neither notated nor stored, but forms itself as a complex of rule-based structures, transformations and processes around the improvisation of a live performer, its source of both energy and material" (Impett 1994a). One of the most interesting aspects is that early gestures in the piece are used to set the overall time frame and certain other large-scale parameters of the individual performance, while it is recurrent that input analyzed by the software dictates later computer generation processes, time scales, and methods, and not just the material on which these operate. In other words, the large-scale comprovisational mechanism, process, and structure evolve during performance, and not just the sequence of preformed compositional modules. Impett emphasizes that nevertheless the results demonstrate "unity between different performances" (Impett 1994a).

Influenced by dynamic morphogenetic models in biology and elsewhere, Impett discusses the distinction between comprovisational modules that have a fixed relationship and those that have mobile relationships; he also distinguishes between types of communication between modules (that of lineage [parent-offspring] and that of interaction [data transfer between preexisting modules]). This has allowed him to place the developed modules clearly within a functional continuum of "sightedness." A morphogenetic process is "blind" when the " 'parent' or generating module controls the whole structure, independent of the remainder." It is "self-regulating" when "the developing structure organises itself, using communication between existing components." And it is "sighted" when "the structure is aware of its environment." Or, to put it another way:

> "sightedness" [of compositional modules or temporal structures]—the degree to which their future behavior, once computed by the composition from its own rules and material plus information from the performance, is contingent on other events. A musical process may be scheduled irrevocably at the moment of its inception, or it may recalculate itself dynamically in time. The balance of control, autonomy and emergence of musical behaviors in time is at the heart of the matter, both technically and musically. (Impett 1998b)

The composer-improviser has elucidated how several of these different functions occur during the sections of the piece (Impett 1994b).

With these possibilities in mind, I will discuss the work of some interesting group practitioners in a little more detail.

■ THREE CASE STUDIES OF NETWORKED COMPUTER-INTERACTIVE SOUND IMPROVISATION

Three of the groups active in this area offer contrasting approaches. The pioneering group the Hub is perhaps most concerned with the "surprise" of a new state generated as a result of the operation of an initial networked piece of software; their context is normally one of purely electronic sound. The more recent efforts of the austraLYSIS Electroband (abbreviated aLEb hereafter) focus on the use of multiple compositional modules by improvisers, including the idea of real-time high- and low-level interaction with their parameters; our context usually includes acoustic as well as commercial samples and computer-generated sounds. Both groups involve relatively little gestural display in the process of human-computer interaction and challenge conventional ideas that audiences need visual correlates of sonic processes, though aLEb includes the saxophonist Sandy Evans, who also plays wind controller. Sensorband in contrast often presents a dramatic visual aspect, either in the gestural percussive work of Zbigniew Karkowski or in the group's use of a physical web, a strung net, on which players move to create electronic signals sent to their sound-generating computer set-ups.

The Hub, which was active in the San Francisco Bay area from around 1985 until around 1999 (Perkis, personal communication 2001), developed from the earlier League of Automatic Music Composers' work mentioned earlier and incorporated several participants in that work, notably John Bischoff and Tim Perkis. Perkis described its origins:

> The Hub is: John Bischoff, Tim Perkis, Chris Brown, Scot Gresham-Lancaster, Mark Trayle, Phil Stone. The Hub originally came about as a way to clean up a mess. John Bischoff, Jim Horton and myself played for several years in a group called The League of Automatic Music Composers, the first microcomputer network band. Every time we rehearsed, a complicated set of ad-hoc connections between computers had to be made. This made for a system with rich and varied behavior, but it was prone to failure, and bringing in other players was difficult.
>
> Later we sought a way to open the process up, to make it easier for other musicians to play in the network situation. The result was the Hub, a small computer dedicated to passing messages between players. It serves as a common memory, keeping information about each player's activity that is accessible to the other players' computers. I see the aesthetic informing this work perhaps counter to other trends in computer music: instead of attempting to gain more complete control over every aspect of the music, we seek more surprise through the lively and unpredictable response of these systems, and hope to encourage an active response to surprise in the playing. And instead of trying to eliminate the imperfect human performer, we try to use the electronic tools available to enhance the social aspect of music making. (Hub 1989)

John Bischoff's observations about his composition *Perry Mason in East Germany* (recorded 1988, released on the same album) illustrate common and continuing concerns of the band:

> Each of the six players runs a program of his own design which constitutes a self sustaining musical process. Each program is configured so that it can send three changing variables important to its operation out to the Hub and also to receive three variables from other players. Each player reads the variables put out by three different performers, and sends out for use by three different performers as well. This relationship of mutual influence results in a network structure that often yields a special kind of musical coherence; the persistent diversity of the parts is complemented by moments of change that appear to propagate from one part to the next. These linked motions can, in turn, affect global changes

in the music, giving the music structure beyond any individual's planning. (Hub 1989)

The mechanisms might on occasion be more flexible, as Perkis reveals of the group improvisation structure *Hot Pig*, which he co-wrote with Brown and Stone: "As in the *Minister of Pitch,* musical responsibility is apportioned in an unconventional way. John provides a master rhythmic process, which is being computed live and transmitted to other players. The others search for patterns in this input, and play phrases determined by this analysis." As its title implies, *Minister of Pitch* used a somewhat related approach to control of pitch by one player, while others set timing and timbre functions. Exchange of information between the players was not limited to sound components or MIDI-like meta-sound in the precise descriptive sense I have used earlier; in addition, textual "descriptions" of texture and other functions might be passed. Chris Brown wrote of his *Rol' Em:*

> A conductor/computer selects descriptions of musical textures and sends different text messages to each player which are instructions for his part in realizing the current texture. A common clock transmitted through the Hub helps players in coordinating transitions between sections. The sounds made by each player are also being mixed and processed by an electronic system designed by the composer and under the control of the conductor/computer. (Hub 1989)

During a visit to Georgia Tech (April 17, 1997; available on the Web at the time of writing), the Hub performed and gave round tables and presentations. They talked repeatedly of the network as "conversation," emphasizing the importance they attached to needing to be "surprised" by the outcomes. Game elements and rules were part of the process, but "emergent behaviour" was the main focus of interest.

As they summarized in the liner notes to *Wreckin' Ball:*

> The Hub is a computer network band. Six individual composer/performers connect separate computer-controlled music synthesizers into a network. Individual composers design pieces for the network, in most cases just specifying the nature of the data which is to be exchanged between players in the piece, but leaving implementation details to the individual players, and leaving the actual sequence of music to the emergent behavior of the network. Each player writes a computer program which makes musical decisions in keeping with the character of the piece, in response to messages from the other computers in the network and control actions of the player himself.
>
> The result is a kind of enhanced improvisation, wherein players and computers share the responsibility for the music's evolution, with no

one able to determine the exact outcome, but everyone having influence in setting the direction. The Javanese think of their gamelan orchestras as being one musical instrument with many parts; this is probably also a good way to think of The Hub ensemble, with all its many computers and synthesizers interconnected to form one complex musical instrument. In essence, each piece is a reconfiguration of this network into a new instrument.

Originally, we all interconnected through a special computer (also called "the hub") which we designed and built, and which formed a sort of electronic mailbox for players to send messages to each other. (Hear our first CD, The Hub, Artifact 1002.) Since that time, commercial electronic music has exploded, and MIDI, an industry standard for the exchange of musical control information between computer-controlled synthesis equipment, has matured. On this disk, we use a piece of commercial MIDI equipment (the Opcode Studio V) for our hub, and the note-oriented nature of MIDI communication has led to new pieces that somewhat reflect this bias.

But in certain ways MIDI is inappropriate for our uses, and we use it in a way it was never intended to be used. . . . We're interested . . . in music that is situated somewhere: in a real, messy, and admittedly limited social (and technical) situations. We build a quirky complex instrument, which, like any good instrument, has a strong nature of its own; our work is to play it, and bring out its nature. . . .

It used to be common to discuss the computer as an extension of the human nervous system; today, it makes more sense to think of the computer network as an extension of society. These networks have a degree of complexity which prevents us from "controlling" them any longer: we have to participate in a conversation with them. In a conversation, one says things, not knowing what the next person will say, and therefore, not knowing what oneself will say next either. We want to surprise and be surprised by each other, and, in playing together, to also be surprised by our own odd computer network instrument. (Hub 1994)

Perkis has even argued that this feature is in common to a whole experimental music tradition, though in so doing he was focusing primarily on that in the United States:

So the salient feature of this tradition, that all this work shares, and which I think is an important source of inspiration for all the work that I've done, is really a way of thinking about the activity of making music not so much as implementing a vision of the composer, or the will of the composer—something the composer hears in his head—but rather it's about setting up situations that allow the appearance of sonic entities that are more like natural phenomena than traditional music. The practitioners of this type of music build machines, things akin to machines or simulations, that have a behavior of some kind that is unexpected, unanticipated by the composer. (Perkis 1998)

Perkis further defines his focus:

> Self-expression is not what that's about. It's really about listening, and exploring the world. . . . Often when I describe the Hub I like to play one piece designed by one of the members, Phil Stone, because it conveys more clearly than most of the Hub pieces the nature of this process, and people are more often able to hear the interaction clearly on first listening. The piece is called "Is it Borrowing or Stealing?," done in 1987. In this piece there is a very simple specification: the Hub was used as a repository for melodic figures. The only requirement was that whenever a player played a melodic figure, he reported to the central hub what he had played, put a copy of the information specifying the figure up there. Anyone else could take it down, use it, modify it, and play what they want. It's a completely open specification for what each player does: it's just that you have information about what the other players are doing.
>
> Perhaps I should make clear what I mean by "a player"—I mean a person, and the program he has written. Usually the process would be almost completely automatic, the playing of each player is directed by an algorithm running in his computer, no one is playing anything on a musical keyboard, or anything like that—but the players—the people—generally have some knobs and switches they use to fine tune the operation of the algorithm running on their system. It's as if we really are acting more like composers or conductors than performers while in performance, just listening and making fine adjustments from time to time. So the system really includes the people, and the musical reactions of the players would really be incorporated in the social/electronic system. . . .
>
> So here's another piece I did that is based on this idea of simple interacting agents. This is solo piece, the whole process is running on one CPU—there are a set of about 15 simple agents controlling a number of synthesizer voices. The agents are periodic—at some regular rate they wake up, do some one simple thing, and then go back to sleep. Each agent does just one thing—increment or decrement the current pitch of a voice, inc or dec the current loudness of a voice, or actually trigger a voice to sound with these current setting.
>
> There's an additional important side effect to each agent's behavior—according to its own unique table, it increments or decrements the rate at which all the other voices are repeating. Here I'm probably going to embarrass myself by misusing some complexity jargon—but I think it may be forming something like an autocatalytic network, with all the elements bubbling along in a kind of balance, occasionally running away with itself from time to time. (Perkis 1998)

Autocatalysis usually has the possible benefit and excitement of running out of control. Accordingly, Perkis has also described two kinds of music workers:

The Crafters, laboring under the burden of specifying so much, often produce works suffering from a certain lifelessness; The Wild System types are often hard pressed to come up with systems whose behavior provides a close enough match to human perceptual abilities for listeners to perceive any pattern at all. These two ways of working represent two responses to complexity, two approaches to the problem of design. Neither approach is sufficient to work in the increasingly complex world engendered by our computer systems, a network of interacting human artifacts which is approaching biological levels of complexity.

What I see happening now and in the immediate future is the closing of the gap between these two ways of working, brought about by increased understanding of the nature of complex systems, and the increasing sophistication of machine learning and modeling algorithms such as genetic algorithms, neural networks, Lindenmayer systems and other methods based on strong analyses or analogies with biological systems. If the Crafted Object way of working has meant Getting What You Want (and specifying that in great detail); and the experimental way of working has meant Wanting What You Get (being interested in whatever arises from ill-understood systems of interaction), the emergent ways of working based on evolutionary paradigms means Getting What You Didn't Know You Wanted. (Perkis 1998)

Perkis here expresses the same objectives that Jonathan Impett described for his solo systems. Figure 7.1 illustrates one of the physical and networking layouts used by the Hub (based with permission on material from their Web site).

Since the austraLYSIS Electroband is a creative ensemble I myself lead, it is perhaps most useful in the present context if my brief analysis of its efforts and techniques focuses on the musical motivations that led to them, and that I thought could be particularly well accommodated within a networked computer-interactive electroacoustic group. My experience in improvisation before forming the Electroband had been extensive and diverse. I had worked in conventional and unconventional jazz, and in free improvisation contexts that derived from composed music and/or idiomatic improvisation backgrounds.

While improvisation in such environments is extremely stimulating and potential, I had become aware of some potentially limiting factors. One was that compositional material to be used in an improvising context might have either to be given to someone not experienced in interpreting such material with precision, or to someone with such experience but with limited improvisational skill. The combination of both requirements was (and is) not routinely met. Similarly, if an improvised music is to exploit flexibly concepts of swing, groove, and rhythmic subtlety, it may be desirable for the

Figure 7.1 The Hub: set-ups.

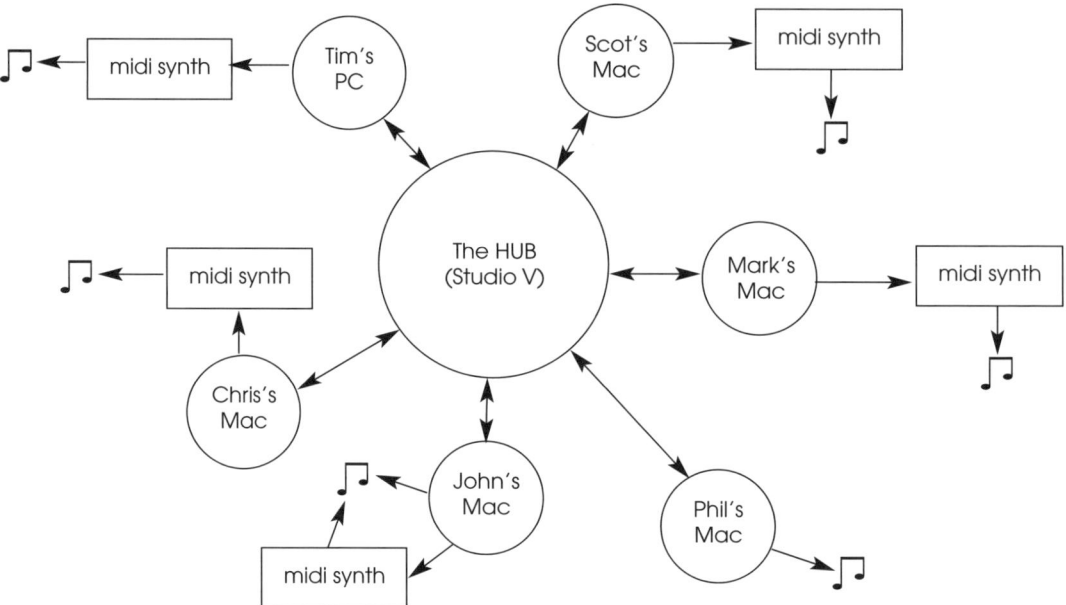

improvisers all to have experience of jazz and other groove-based musics. But such improvisers are not always experienced in precise interpretation of the rhythms of new complexity music, or of metrical modulation, yet such devices can be powerful and desirable in improvisation (Dean 1989, 1992). Lastly, extended instrumental techniques are open to systematic control only in the hands of exceptionally gifted instrumentalists, who may or may not be comparably cultivated improvisers. Computer control of sound generation might avoid this concern.

I felt that all these issues could be overcome more or less efficiently in a computer-interactive improvising group. Furthermore, I saw possibilities in computer networking of MIDI and eventually of all other components of sound, image, and text performance (Smith and Dean 1997). This could allow one to directly and precisely influence the progression of other players during their improvisation, if they were using a computer, or to project their material through one. For example, the parameters of one player's MAX patch could also be accessible and controllable by other members of the group. Such control can be done either hierarchically or in a more egalitarian way; both approaches appeal to me and have been used in some of our pieces. A correlate of this possibility of influencing the progression of others is that of controlling future events. A patch, networked or otherwise, can define events at fixed times in the future. These events might be the introduction of new parameters into the patch, of new musical material derived in advance or in real time, or of controls over another player. A composer uses such time-dependent events to introduce a new but preformed section; an improvising ensemble can use it to introduce a new direction, whose output and precise nature is only developed once the direction commences.

At the highest level, one idea that particularly appeals to me is the possibility of designing complex structural devices that control an overall comprovisation while being able to redesign them during performance. This idea—the control of structure—is perhaps a complement to the interest of the Hub in its emergence from the networked exchange of information itself generated in real time. To view one as a modernist and the other as postmodernist is too simplistic, but it may help to distinguish them. Furthermore, neither the Electroband nor the Hub is (or was) focused on one approach and aesthetic to the exclusion of all others. Equally, this is true of the last group I shall discuss in this section, Sensorband.

Sensorband is perhaps best described in an interview with B. Bongers (Bongers 1998). Although active since December 1993 (the date of its first performance, in Paris), the group has only recently released any recorded material. It is a trio, comprising Edwin van der Heide, Zbigniew Karkowski, and Atau Tanaka. Heide uses a MIDI conductor, in which ultrasound measures his hands' relative distance; Karkowski uses infrared detection to perform "virtual percussion" by movements in a beam-limited "cage"; and Tanaka uses a BioMuse, which tracks neural signals. All may use their SoundNet, "an architectural musical instrument of monumental proportions." It is a giant web, made of 16-millimeter-thick shipping rope, that the performers climb, and that as a result of the imposed tensions and movements sends signals to an I-cube interface that converts them into MIDI. The performers describe Sensorband as "a powerful musical force of intense percussive rhythms, deep pulsing drones and wailing melodic fragments."

The Midi-Conductor was built at STEIM under the supervision of Michel Waisvisz, as a modification of his own Hands (Krefeld 1990). Heide uses distance, pressure, two tilt sensors, movement sensors, and several switches. These go to STEIM's Sensorlab, a programmable microprocessor, and from there to MIDI signals, which are then used for DSP, and in conjunction with Supercollider. Karkowski has

32 IR sensors, 16 transmit, 16 detect, and signals go to MAX and hence to Sample Cell II. The BioMuse was developed at CCRMA and uses signals from the brain, skeletal muscles, and eyeball (electroencephalography, electrooculography, and electromyography). Tanaka uses four electromyograph signals taken into MIDI.

The SoundNet in particular, and other aspects in general, imply that "the notion of control is called completely into question: the instrument is too large for humans to thoroughly master.... Control vs uncontrollability becomes a central conceptual focus of SoundNet" (Bongers 1998). The musicians emphasize the different kinds of interface they have, the triggers—which mainly drive percussive sound—and the continuous controllers, which more often are used for timbral functions. Karkowski commented on the "danger of confusing yourself," despite his remark that "I have hardly changed my sounds in the last 5 years." Sensorband has also undertaken networked performances in which it uses several locations, with ISDN and videoconferencing. Tanaka noted that in these circumstances the audio was "not CD quality," that the video was "like it is coming from the moon," and that the time delays were noticeable. All these features add up to incomplete control, a routine feature of their work in any context. Familiarity with the potential of the group's system is something Sensorband is happy to develop, though this is clearly limited by performance opportunity and frequency: the members comment positively on Waisvisz's great performing ability, as a result of using "the same instrument over [a] long time" (Bongers 1998).

■ A CHRONOLOGICAL SYNOPSIS OF COMPUTER INTERACTIVE SOUND IMPROVISATION

The purpose of this book is primarily conceptual and creative, so only a brief historical and chronological survey is included here. Some of the earliest activity involving computer interaction and its application to improvisation seems to have come from Joel Chadabe and David Zicarelli in their work on Jam Factory and M, and their early patent (see chapter 11 and table 11.1). In a similar period, the League of Automatic Music Composers (LAMC), involving John Bischoff, was developing related ideas, though perhaps with less emphasis on real-time input by the performers and more on the computer-generative processes per se.

The efforts of Chadabe and colleagues spawned a line of software research that led to the Music Mouse and later to MAX, as discussed earlier. MAX, in particular, has become the central platform for such work. LAMC was succeeded by group "jamming," as Perkis describes it, in which several former LAMC members became active, eventually forming the Hub in 1985. Although the Hub commenced by using software written in mainstream languages and a central computer as the "hub" itself, it took more and more advantage of the commercial availability of simpler alternatives. Thus, soon after the advent of MIDI, the group began to use a Studio V MIDI interface as their hub and thereafter mostly programmed their work in MAX rather than a general language. Our aLEb commenced work in 1993 and immediately developed a rather similar system independently with MidiTimePiece and Studio V interfaces, and MAX.

During the 1980s, several performers developed their own idiosyncratic microprocessor or computer-interactive set-ups for improvised performace. Most prolific perhaps, is Jon Rose, the violinist, composer, improviser, and radio-piece creator. His set-up often involves light-detection mechanisms using aspects of the bowing of his violin to trigger a multiplicity of events. Computer algorithmic processing is usually modest, but the range of sound and effect he achieves is remarkable. Rose has developed a whole series of "virtual violins," and other violinists such as Kaffe Mathews have been stimulated by his example.

As mentioned above, George Lewis has since the 1980s written many pieces of software for interactive improvised performance, most notably his large program Voyager, but they are not generally distributed. On the other hand, Richard Teitelbaum, an improvising keyboardist, initially wrote his own Patch Control Language (PCL) in collaboration with Max Bernard and used an assembly of its processing modules, called the digital piano, for solo piano performances with computer processing. In these, Teitelbaum performs on acoustic piano with MIDI interface, which supplied data to the patches. The computer-driven processed accompaniment was often played on another MIDI-driven acoustic piano, such as a Yamaha MIDI grand piano (or, on occasion, on substitute keyboard samples). Later several modules of his work were recoded in MAX, for example by Christopher Dobrian and Eric Singer (see illustration and discussion in Rowe 1993). Teitelbaum shared many of Lewis's concerns—for example, to retain human input, and to drive the program with an acoustic instrument, whose complex (nonelectronic) timbre remained a focus of the piece. Teitelbaum's multiple processing modules can be configured in a chosen chain before performance, resulting in elaborate processing of input material. The names of some of Teitelbaum's modules—transposer and excerpter, for instance—indicate their clear-cut functions (Rowe 1993). The control parameters of the modules are accessible during performance. However, the program did not use a listener function (at least until the late 1990s) and was thus totally controlled by the performer, who remained the sole source of "unpredictability."

Steve Coleman (the saxophonist, composer, and improviser) with his current Rameses project is seeking what he describes as a kind of "cultural transference" through his software composition and interactions with it in performance. He has recently joined the CNMAT group at Berkeley, led by David Wessel since his return to the United States from IRCAM. Wessel and CNMAT as a whole have since the early 1990s been very active in research and creation involving computer interaction and improvisation. He has frequently performed in improvisatory performances (Rowe 1993; Smith and Dean 1997), normally using his own software, written in MAX, controlled with a MIDI device such as Thunder. Commonly he uses both acoustic and MIDI data from a partner improviser, and his software usually comprises listeners, analysts, and generative and/or transformative performers. "Phrase recording" and repetition or transformation is a core technique:

> To be able to transform appropriate phrases, the software must be able to store ongoing musical information and "reach back" to the beginning of phrases when they are called for. For this, Wessel divides the programs memory into short-term and long-term stores. The short-term memory holds MIDI-level information, whereas the long-term memory uses higher level abstractions. With the short-term store, listening assistants perform phrase boundary detection, to notice those structural points that will demarcate the onset of saved phrases. . . . Wessel uses a time-gap detector to indicate phrase boundaries. (Rowe 1993)

The more recent CNMAT rhythm machine project, their plethora of publicly available MAX objects, and their development of networking communication methods for MAX messages are other examples of a whole range of work within their long-term strategy.

Since around 1990, two major new tendencies have been apparent: toward improved and more diverse gestural interfaces, and toward the use of generative programming techniques, including evolutionary algorithms. The futures of these approaches are discussed in the next section of this chapter. Presently, most activity is concerned with the interfaces and is still much influenced by the idea, which I have countermanded, that visual gesture is critical to sonic performance. Probably of more fundamental importance than the interface between instrument or gesture and the computer is the direct human-computer interaction itself. Here, as discussed earlier, there is scope not just for translation of gesture into signal or event into symbol, but for the insertion of new semiotic codes, so that new connotations can be established.

■ SOME FUTURE POSSIBILITIES

I have already touched on the idea that a composition for improvisers, embedded in an algorithmic form, can provide an interface that enables the improviser to modify high-level structures of the composition during performance. This is a quite special opportunity that is difficult to envisage as efficiently available by any other mechanism: it permits a totalizing rather than an associative approach to improvisation, as delineated in the introduction. There is great potential in this. It is as if a sonata form's second subject could at whim be replaced in the development section by processing of a quite separate, previously unheard subject, or as if sonata form itself could be continuously transformed into a song form, a through-composed form, or a totally serial work. And this would be at the choice of the performer-improviser at any time while playing.

The Hub has emphasized the interest and challenge that results when the group's networked interaction, using a single piece of software, leads to a new state. This idea deserves further generalization, in that the capacity of software to integrate or at least share multiple inputs permits multiple improvisers to provide their MIDI or audio streams to a core processing software and generate new output much influenced by the interaction between the inputs. Thomas Dolby, in Dolby et al. 1999 and through the Beatnik software and Web plug-in, is also exploiting this idea: for example, he envisages more than one user interacting with the visual control system for influencing the progression of musical events.

Similarly, while the Hub and the aLEb often have the same software running on the computers of more than one member, the control of the interface parameters of the software on the computer of another group member has probably not yet been exploited maximally. Certainly in the case of aLEb we have experimented with networking software such as Timbuktu either to permit every player to control the parameters of an algorithm on a central processing computer, or to control those of another player. This process can be overt or hidden. When hidden, it takes on some of the character of the unpredictable response of a fellow acoustic improviser in an ensemble, except for the potential availability of the control information on the recipient computer. Numerous combinations of possible use exist for future application.

The futures outlined so far foreground the role of and control by the improviser. On the other hand, the role of the algorithms themselves is rapidly being emancipated. Generative algorithms capable of driving the whole performance and production of substantial pieces and varying drastically from run to run have already been discussed. As emphasized in the idea of an improviser having access to real-time alteration of high-level features of a compositional algorithm, generative software might embody processes for abrupt transformation of the active algorithm. This could either be closed, purely endogenous to the computer, or open, subject to interactive control by the human improviser. With evolutionary algorithms, it is common now for a generation of output to be "assessed," however subjectively, by a human user, before seeding of the next generation with preferred previous-generation products takes place. Again, this process can become important in real-time improvisation, both as endogenous and exogenous to the computer.

The more endogenous these processes, the more it can seem that the computer is taking on features of intelligence. A movement within AI is to go beyond rule-based mechanisms for generation of new artworks that follow a genre to mechanisms that generate new genres. An analogy can be made with current efforts to create new mathematical ideas by combining different rule systems. The potential in music is just as great, though the difficulty in identifying the nature of the innovation may be even greater. A neural net can often "learn" to achieve a particular function, yet will not readily reveal to the user a mechanism by which that function is achieved, though logically the net ultimately does embody the mechanism. Similarly, AI processes may be valuable contributors to novel musical output, but their mechanisms are not translucent. It is not necessary for AI to reach the stage of becoming "creative," since when any individual human conceives his or her artistic or other output as creative, he or she is trying at least to act as the responsive, not the initiating, party. One can equally be responsive to material from other people, or from inanimate computers. The artist may not even know what the source of the material is. These ideas are developed further in the final chapter of the book, where the work of Peter Bentley and others is discussed.

The last layer of future local and networking possibilities I would like to mention is that in which intermedia interactions occur. During a networked group computer-interactive improvisation, huge opportunities for exchange of information or stimulation exist that might use nonsonic streams. For example, individual improvisers could give each other requests or commands expressed in words and transmitted silently, screen to screen, as in Bahn's systems. More subtly, they might provide other stimuli such as images or sounds only heard by the receiver and not made available to the audience. I developed a model of a network of this kind in an earlier book on improvisation (Smith and Dean 1997), and it abuts on the ideas of intermedia work, where multiple types of sensory strands are made available to the audience.

EIGHT

Mixing the Sounds

> Note: All foley and sound effects should be out of sync, never corresponding to their related image.
> —John Zorn, "Treatment for a Film in Fifteen Scenes" (2000)

Two themes recur throughout this chapter. The first concerns how the computer improviser can exploit timbral variation and spatial distribution of sounds. The second addresses how the sounds can merge into or coexist with other media. The discussion will not distinguish between the possibilities for solo and group improvisers, since these are readily discernible on the basis of the previous chapters, particularly chapter 6. A later chapter will consider how sound and other media can be used as the basis of improvisation by users situated remotely from each other and/or from a host computer.

■ THE TIMBRES AND SHAPES OF SOUNDS IN COMPUTER-INTERACTIVE IMPROVISATION

It is easy and common to think of the sound of a violin or trumpet as natural and electronic sound as other than natural. However, we should bear in mind that most musical instruments preceding computers are artificial machines; indeed, the computer is capable, if pressed, of generating sounds are much closer to natural sounds than those of most conventional instruments. For example, a computer can, like most samplers, use prerecorded sounds obtained from natural environments. More fundamentally, sound synthesis by computers (and by some dedicated synthesizers) can be based so closely on physical modeling of natural systems (such as struck surfaces) that the sounds are hardly distinguishable from those observed in nature. Software such as Modalys (IRCAM) has been developed specifically to permit such procedures for making sound, though more commonly the objective is novel rather than natural sounds. Indeed, many composers and improvisors would argue that the most important approaches to computer-derived sound emphasize the role of unique rather than re-creative sounds.

One of the powers of computer-generated sound is to progressively move along axes that distinguish one sound from another by a variety of morphing processes. Thus one can choose to use a sound world aligned to instrumental sound, to natural sounds, or to electronic sound, and to move between such worlds freely, and even gradually. Computers are also particularly powerful in producing continuous sound textures, in which sound is not only uninterrupted, but also almost homogeneous, with slow change and no abrupt disjunctions. The multiplicity of such textures that a single computer can produce in real time is in principle limited only by hardware and software speeds, and thus, increasingly real-time synthesis—for example, using the long-standing Csound system—is available to the performer. Most recently, the advent of MSP, the DSP addition to MAX, has made real-time DSP of incoming sound practical for many improvisers. MSP allows transitions of any kind to be made on sound "bites" of lengths dictated in part by available computer memory. A voice or piece of text can morph into an apparently natural or purely electronic sound. The juxtaposition of sounded word and other sounds can provide a layer of intermedia intertextuality, with all its implications for semiotic exchange. Similarly, purely electronic sounds can also be organized into several strands that possess sufficient referentiality to separate works, sound worlds, or musics to develop a layer of intermusicality and hence another kind of semiotic exchange.

MSP, together with specialized software modules such as IRCAM's Spatialisateur, permit continuous control of spatial distribution of sound, including 3D sound, with systems of two or more speakers. This can readily be used to great effect in live improvised performance.

Evan Parker's Electroacoustic work provides a good example of the improvisatory use of real-time DSP. For example, *Drawn Inward,* his album with the Electroacoustic Ensemble (Parker 1999) involves, besides Parker's saxophones, sound processing by Lawrence Casserley, Walter Prati, Marco Vecchi, and Philipp Wachsmann, and string playing by Barry Guy and Wachsmann. On the liner notes Simon Emmerson comments:

Casserley can take sounds from any or all of the other performers (even sounds already transformed), and process further singly or in combination. But he is a lot more than just a *deus ex machina* coolly manipulating what others create to his own ends; his kit includes drum pads and pedals with which he "plays" the transformations, himself reacting gesturally to the sounds and gestures sent to him. Human presence is sometimes very evident in the electronic transformations. He can transform the spectrums of the four instrumentalists' sounds in real time, for example filtering or transposing, and then control complex patterns of time delay.

Why use electronics at all? All the . . . performers use extended . . . techniques which produce an unimaginable variety of sounds. Especially with amplification some sounds might almost be of electronic origin. Lawrence Casserley remarks that "the electronics may have many different roles from something which is simple accompaniment to being the prime mover in a piece." This can involve processes which differentiate the live performers—making their sounds ever different—to integrating them, usually into a general flux which has great internal variety but which flows as a single stream.

Prati mainly uses brief samples, taken on a Mars workstation; Vecchi performs sound projection and some transformation. As Emmerson agrees, the depth and density of Parker's saxophone playing is not lost but enhanced in this environment, a remarkable and stimulating achievement.

■ THE INTERACTION OF SOUND WITH WORDS AND IMAGES

> Many more examples of digital art (in sound and music particularly . . .) could be mentioned. . . . Interactivity is a new form of visual experience. In fact, it is a new form of experiencing art that extends beyond the visual to the tactile.
>
> —M. Rush, *New Media in Late Twentieth-Century Art (1999)*

The epigraph presents an impoverished but widespread view of sound, in which there is almost absolute foregrounding of the visual in intermedia. It is disturbing in that it comes from a book on new media and a chapter on digital art, and yet the book hardly mentions sound or music (and they do not appear in the index). Interaction itself is taken to be "visual" as well as tactile, but certainly not sonic. There are certainly cultural and possibly ecological forces that sustain the dominance of visual stimuli, and there is some direct psychological evidence to indicate that "when there is direct competition between different modes of ongoing presentation, as in computer-driven displays, in most cases participants' attention is selectively engaged by text, visual display, and user physical actions in preference to acoustic stimuli" (Pressing 1997). The subordination of music is certainly the functional view of commercial filmmakers, though some psychophysiological evidence has been obtained using measurements of skin conductance to suggest that "stressful" music enhances the stress imposed on a viewer who is watching "stressful" film scenes (Thayer and Levenson 1983). However, the available empirical data are limited, and from observing the rapidity of the "click-click" process on the Web, one might still suspect a substantial dominance of visual image over text, and in turn over music and sound, in agreement with Rush's remark. Nevertheless, recent psychophysical evidence has shown that "when a single visual flash is accompanied by multiple auditory beeps, the single flash is incorrectly perceived as multiple flashes" (Shams et al. 2000). Thus visual perception can indeed be altered qualitatively by sounds, at least simple undifferentiated sounds.

I have previously argued concordantly that in spite of conventional views that image dominates over sound, a powerful opportunity for intermedia arts is to exploit a mutual interrogation, as well as sympathy, between the cognitive impacts of the different sensory modalities (Smith and Dean 1997). Neumark makes similar points. In our *Returning the Angles,* a composed and improvised 35-minute technodrama (Smith and Dean 2001), we used a live performed narrative, electronic preformed compositions involving transmuted verbal sounds as well as other electronic sounds, and live computer-interactive improvisation and sound manipulation, together with a meditative 3D-animation written in VRML, mainly of abstract objects but including a few concrete objects and some animated text. We exploited some important structural parallels between sound and image in this piece, for the sounds ranged from synthesized to sampled, and the images from geometrically synthesized to bit-mapped (as in the case of scanned—i.e., sampled—images). In each category, sound and image, the synthesized type contains specific parameters that are logical and effective control points for manipulation, while the sampled type does not, and rather has to be controlled by more generic parameters. The samples in each case are more likely to possess iconic semiotic status, indicating a relationship with a physical object and thus implying a metonymic, associative interpretive stream that may or may not coincide with the large-scale totalizing aspects of the work. The synthesized objects are much less likely to possess such iconicity. Pressing 1997 made a similar point very neatly; Dannenberg 1993 pinpointed the technical issues in software support for such interactive multimedia work.

Let us consider first the interaction between verbal and nonverbal sound. In Trevor Wishart's remarkable *Vox 5* essentially all the sounds are derived by (non-real-time) electronic manipulation of an initial spoken phrase. Other composers, such as Hildegard Westerkamp and Paul Lansky, have also used such juxtapositions extensively. In improvisation, the most common usage is that in which a vocalist enunciates words, often with other vocal sounds, and these are then used as performance triggers and source material for live electronic manipulation. An important example of the former is the piece *Hub Renga,* performed by radio and Internet hook-up by the Hub. In this work, parts of written texts provided by multiple online participants in the WELL were read by the poet Ramon Sender, and also used as musical triggers in response to which the Hub musicians played certain preformed segments (organized in advance as responses to chosen "power words") or made less specific responses (Povall 1997). The vocal sound per se might be used via a pitch to a MIDI controller to trigger a MAX patch to perform some transition, and a verbal performance might contribute to the ongoing sound melee while undergoing electronic manipulation, as in several of our own pieces. In a related way, Warren Burt has described one of his own performances in 2000:

> I did an improv with Tom Fryer at the Planet [a venue in Melbourne, Australia] on Tuesday night. I had 6 patches prepared of various stuff with samples and audio mulch [commercially available PC real-time audio processing software by Ross Bencina]. At the start, totally spontaneously, I started a harangue into the mic about the frigidity of Melbourne sex life, then had the mic trigger off Ruth Westheimer samples, so the electronics were talking dirty back to me, then aimed the mic at the speakers, so Ruth auto-erotically triggered off herself, then played the samples of Ruth saying things like "necrophilia," "sodomy," [and] "pre-marital sex" with a keyboard, then played some percussion samples, then fragmented a loop of Debussy with audio mulch, then played the intro to "A Man and A Woman" again and again and again, etc., all the while while Tom was improvising with his electronics as well. I used maybe 5 of the patches I'd prepared, plus a couple of unexpected patches on the fly. (Burt, personal communication 2000)

Rowe 1993 discusses several examples of real-time interactions between image and sound processing and presentation, including the work of the video artist Don Ritter and his program Orpheus, an interactive animation system. This software uses MIDI input to drive the display of stored video frames and the transitions between them (70 different transition types are available).

> Correspondences stem from a user-defined control file which indicates relations between various musical parameters, and the visual effects that will appear in response. For example, a control file may define that an increasing musical interval in the third octave will cause the display of a bouncing ball in a forward motion; a decreasing interval however will display the ball in a backward motion. . . . Because it is capable of characterizing some salient feature of an ongoing musical performance, Orpheus can change its behavior in ways that are not known in advance but that nonetheless demonstrate correspondences which are immediately apparent to an audience. (Rowe 1993)

Interestingly, such features are amongst the much later commercial claims of Thomas Dolby for his interactive system patent (Dolby et al. 1999).

In the mid-1960s Laurie Spiegel developed her VAMPIRE "visual music system" as an outgrowth of her work with GROOVE. One (physically very large) computer generated both image and sound on the basis of real-time performed inputs: "I had begun to conceive of music not specifically as a sonic art, but as the art of composing abstract patterns of change within time. Such composed functions of time could be modulated variously onto either sonic or visual parameters as their carrier media" (Spiegel 1998).

Most commonly in contemporary sound and image performances, a video camera system detects and displays some movement action and at the same time sends digital information to the music-performing or controlling software, which then constitutes or affects the ongoing processing of the MIDI and/or audio streams. More recently, a range of new software has become available that facilitates such interactions, notably image inputting and processing systems such as Big Eye (STEIM), NATO (a MAX/MSP adjunct), and image generation systems such as Bliss and Bomb, which permit limited influences of MIDI events on the ongoing algorithmic generation of a progression of images, often with a fairly psychedelic orientation. Bomb allows the user to choose input images for manipulation, which may allow a different visual style. Recently UIO software's Videodelic offers processing and interaction opportunities, though again with a primarily pscyhodelic or VJ orientation, as implied by its name. Miller Puckette's Pd, in which the capacity for visual image generation has been developed by Mark Danks, permits coordination of sound and image at more fundamental levels, operating as a programming platform in a manner rather like MAX/MSP/NATO. Puckette described a piece of his own in which short temporal-span analysis of musical input from a player was used to provide input to Pd, then transformed into both image and sound, in part using advanced spectral analysis (Puckette 1999). Puckette described the piece, in relation to all its output, as "borderline cubist."

Elegant composed "computer music animations" have been produced by Joran Rudi since 1987, and he has described his "cross-disciplinary mapping of data from the musical domain into the visual domain," used in what he calls "concert videos" (Rudi 1998). In the mapping, sonograms of the sound of the piece are converted into 3D images and then "filmed" by a moving camera. He is concerned "to never have the *camera* [i.e., the resultant projected image] work against the music," and the display at any moment normally represents ("maps") many seconds of current and imminent music. This is a very specialized, relatively literal mapping system, and as yet is too computer intensive for real-time use. On the other hand, Hunt and colleagues describe models for real-time algorithmic composition of music and image using their developing Tabula Vigilans Audio Interactive (TVAI) (Hunt et al 1998). As described earlier for the Hub's use of Grainwave, these authors advocate supplying meta-information for remote rendering to permit Web delivery and even real-time performance.

Sidney Fels and colleagues have developed a "graphical musical instrument," MusiKalscope, for live performance. They describe it in a synopsis as

> a new multimedia system for musical and graphical expression called MusiKalscope contains subsystems that support computer-assisted jazz improvisation (RhyMe) and kaleidoscopic imagery (the lamascope). The Graphical Musical Instrument Interface (GMII) connects these subsytems and lets performers create images and music as they play virtual drums. A functional map matches the images' mood to the music played. (Fels et al. 1998)

The system sounds highly engaging, though the stylistic ranges of the images (kaleidoscopic) and the jazz (tonal/modal, conservative rule-based pitch choices) are quite modest and probably intended more for nonprofessional users than for professional improvisers. The researchers explicitly envisage developments more directed toward enhanced "expressive" power for "experts."

Perhaps the most fundamental real-time improvising opportunity would exploit algorithmic exchange between the ongoing sound and image generation. This requires either exceedingly expert programming using the APIs of the two categories of software, one controlling image and the other sound, so that data resulting from the live improvised processes interacting with one could be sent to influence the process of the other; or the use of software that contains both functions. MAX, for example, contains modest image-generating functions that can receive data from anywhere within the patches, but these are too limited for satisfactory exploitation; the addition of MSP/NATO overcomes this, allowing complete algorithmic continuity between image, sound, and MDI. Miller Puckette's current platform, Pd, uses similar approaches to MAX but focused on real-time image generation, though it is as yet only available on a limited range of computer systems. This might facilitate formatting data outputs from one program in a convenient way to usefully and logically influence the other. Much remains to be done to fully exploit this possibility of intermedia algorithmic, as well as semiotic, exchange.

■ CHRISTOPHER YAVELOW'S "MUSIC IS THE MESSAGE"

Some taste of the possibilities to come is given by the remarkable interactive installation and software *Music Is the Message* by Yavelow and his team (Yavelow 1997–98, 1999). The core of the CD-ROM of this work is a short film clip, an apparently unexpected interaction between an actress who is removing her make-up and a man; the narrative is intentionally ambiguous in its import and, as it progresses, in its direction. Mart van den Busken, the filmmaker, refers to it as a "polyvalent" film. The purpose of the software is to "generate film and video soundtracks. The program continually adapts its internal compositional models according to feedback from its user or users. . . . [It] models the actual compositional process." Yavelow terms this "adaptive music," and while he recognizes its relation to AI, he is careful to distinguish the two. "The program [generates] new music in three moods: Romance, Comedy and Thriller. Certain musical characteristics are assigned to each mood, for example, those relating to form, tempo[,] rhythmic patterns, and key" (Yavelow 1997–8). The user configures the "rhythmic world, melody, allowable textures, and volume curve, the orchestration," and up to 28 coordination points with the movie. Alternatively, the user may leave most of these fresh choices to the computer, which, summing the nature of the inputs, may decide that the degree of "serendipity" chosen permits it to "inject a completely random configuration" (Yavelow 1997–8).

The software then generates a soundtrack. Soundtracks can be tonal or atonal, simple or complex, and even on a laptop computer running Quicktime they are generally impressive. Soundtracks are highly variable from run to run, so that while the movie stays constant, its impact changes drastically, as Yavelow intends. He goes so far as to state that "its interpretation rests solely upon the soundtrack." After the showing, the user is asked to rate its "effectiveness"; an archive of showings can be maintained, and other users can review previous renderings and add their scores. "The software then uses these ratings to determine which soundtracks should be considered the next time it adapts its compositional model." In the installation setting in which the work was first seen, at the Metropolis Science and Technology Center in Amsterdam (1997), *Music Is the Message* was "configured to adapt ('learn') at a specified time each day."

When the CD-ROM was released, Yavelow and his team had planned 400 compositional algorithms and implemented 40. There are ten fixed constraints, influenced by the overall choice between the three "moods." For example, in orchestration,

> Romance uses the chamber trio as its default, Comedy defaults to the jazz band, and Thriller chooses between chamber ensemble and string ensemble.... Besides these ten fixed constraints (regarding which the user has little or no control), the other factors of making the music lean toward their personal view of "romance," "comedy," and "thriller" are left to their experimentation with the controls provided for them. That's why it becomes important to give the software time to "learn" and continually adapt to the (collective) user's taste (Yavelow 1997–8).

There is no intermedia algorithmic exchange in *Music Is the Message,* as its title might imply. Even so, the power of the semiotic undercutting between sound and image is remarkably strong. Such impacts may be enhanced in future work permitting such data and compositional exchange between sound and image.

NINE

Notes and Annotations: Into the Ear and Eye

Many individual works have been discussed already in this book. The purpose of this brief chapter is to solidify some of the ideas and approaches we have considered, with reference to a limited selection of complete recorded performances, albums, and/or comprovisations in the form of MAX patches or specifications. The works discussed are chosen for this purpose rather than for their musical value or standing. The chapter concludes with brief annotations concerning a limited selection of other fascinating recordings. Other material is listed in the bibliography, and some is provided on the CD-ROM published with this book.

■ THE HUB: TWO ALBUMS ON ARTIFACT

Let us first consider two Artifact albums by the Hub (Hub 1989, 1994), the successors to the League of Automatic Music Composers and very early practitioners of networked (and computer-interactive) sound improvisation, to whom I have made repeated reference already. These albums reveal clearly the emphasis on detailed specifications for compositions that will be realized in performance, and that on emergence, whereby through networking information, usually in a ring-token passage mechanism, sonic processes emerge that were not obviously intrinsic to the specifications. The first album presents recordings made in 1987 and 1988 and uses the prototype computer hub discussed already. There are works credited to individual musicians as "composers" (John Bischoff, Chris Brown, Phil Stone, Scot Gresham-Lancaster, Tim Perkis, and Mark Trayle) and two credited each to three "composer-performers." Rather than seeking improvisatory control or freedom, the pieces embody quite rigorous processes, followed through diligently. Quite commonly, information from one player's computer is passed to the next in the ring, or alternatively, is made accessible to all others by means of the Hub. It is the use of such information that is often quite rigorous. For example, in *Perry Mason in East Germany,* each of the six players "runs a program of his own design which constitutes a self-sustaining musical process," but "each program also must use three variables it reads from three different performers in making its own music decisions." Presumably as a consequence, the sound worlds quite often appear almost monodic, though quite heavily textured. Most of the pieces have recurrent rhythmic patterns, where samples or musical structures repeat with gradual change but occasional disjunction. The repetition is as if a set of musical data were successively realized in sound by each node of (or player on) the network; in some cases this is probably literally what is happening.

As Perkis writes in the liner notes: "I see the aesthetic informing this work as perhaps counter to other trends in computer music; instead of attempting to gain more complete control over every aspect of the music, we seek more surprise through the lively and unpredictable response of these systems, and hope to encourage an active response to surprise in the playing." In other words, and simplifying, process leads, diverse improvisatory response follows.

By the time of *Wreckin' Ball,* the Opcode Studio 5 MIDI interface had taken over as the Hub, and the general musical perspective on the album is somewhat different. Rather than sonic textures, which seem to evolve in one stream, the music here is sometimes more note or event oriented, and indeed there are many acoustic sounds, or sampled sounds with instrumental connotations. There are also instrumental collaborations on one piece from the Rova Saxophone quartet, and on another from Alvin Curran. Tim Perkis again emphasizes the value of the unexpected in this work: "We want to surprise and be surprised by each other, and, in playing together, to also be surprised by our own odd computer network instrument" (Hub 1994). A marked exception to the event-oriented focus is the first track, "Crybaby," by Mark Trayle, in which one player provides samples of heavy metal guitar and "the unholy racket of 'monster truck' engines," and these are sonically processed by cascading through each group member's sound processing gear. Sonic artifact is cultivated.

"Waxlips," by Tim Perkis, appears in two versions, the second involving changing pitch sets as section succeeds section. The first version aimed to minimize the amount of musical structure planned in advance, in order to allow any emergent structure arising out of the group interaction to be revealed clearly. The rule is simple: each player sends and receives requests to play one note. Upon receiving the request each should play the note requested, and then transform the note message in some fixed way to a different message, and send it out to someone else. The transformation can follow any rule the player wants, with the one limitation that within any one section of the piece, the same rule must be followed (Hub 1994).

"The Glass Hand" (by John Bischoff) requires each player to composer a number of sonic textures, and these are also generally used as if they were individual events, triggered and modified, but separable rather than continuous. Triggers are sent from player to player (a → b in the ring), as well as texture transition speed information (a → c in the ring). "Therefore, each player receives control information concerning how often and how fast to move between texture from two independent sources (Hub 1994)."

The Hub work is diverse, imaginative, and emergent in a highly stimulating way. It is also the result of sophisticated thought and immense application.

■ PER ANDERS NILSSON: *RANDOM RHAPSODY*

This album was released in 1993 and juxtaposes pieces involving MAX programming by Nilsson with acoustic pieces. It includes one piece ("Acoustic Attractor") in which "the bass line was originally created in the computer, then interpreted and played acoustically" (liner notes). Nilsson is both composer and saxophonist, playing soprano and baritone saxophones. The performers are all eminent idiomatic jazz musicians (Anders Jormin, bass, on the single track mentioned; Karin Krog, voice; and Peeter Uuskyla, drums), and a variety of instrumental combinations are used to create a wide-ranging album that is nevertheless clearly rooted in jazz.

"Fractal Fantasy" is the first piece on the album using Nilsson's Virtual Chaos Band, in which the "rhythm section" has been programmed and created using fractals. The core of the relatively simple patch (figure 9.1) is a Gaussian function, and this provides numerical values for note parameters that are realized on electronic instruments; there is no input of data from the other performers. The patch itself has a preset panel, which allows choice of starting conditions or conditions at any time during its operation. However, once established these parameters are usually subject to continuous time-dependent modification through the "gauss 2" subpatch. The three basic instruments of the rhythm section—keyboard, bass, and drums—are driven independently, with no mutual exchange of parameters. Thus the rhythm section can at times be totally multirhythmic, so much so that the listener does not hear a coherent core pulse; or it can be apparently polyrhythmic or even monorhythmic, by chance, such that core pulses are sensed. On the album these possibilities are all exploited with versatility and sensitivity in additional appropriately named pieces: "Diverse Directions" and "Random Rhapsody."

Nilsson continues to develop this work and has presented further pieces at the International Computer Music Conference, while also extending his interest in computer algorithms for use in sound installations.

Figure 9.1 MAX patch for Per Nilsson's Virtual Chaos Band.

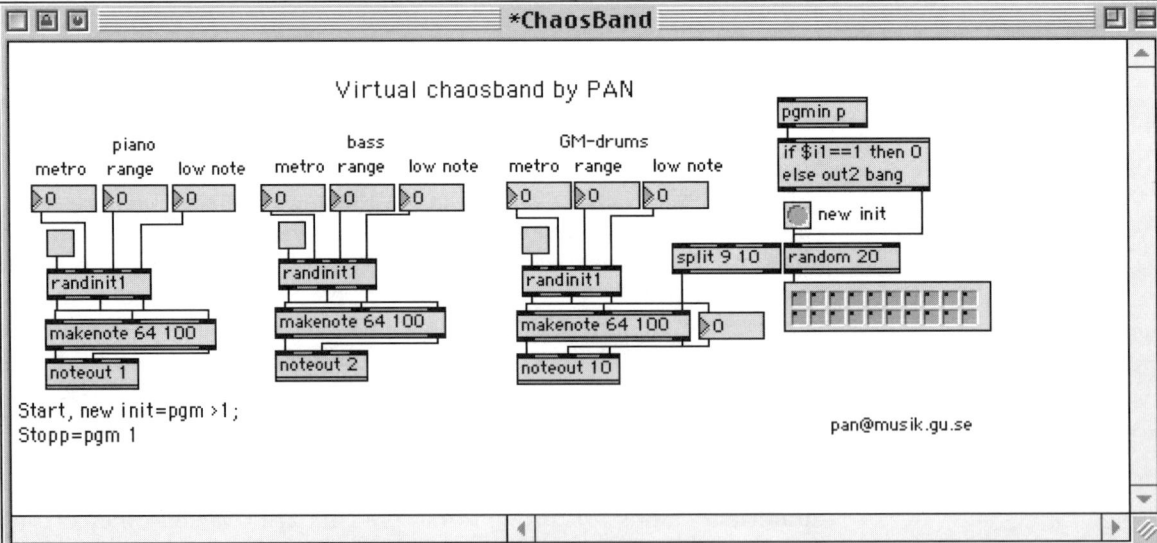

■ THE austraLYSIS ELECTROBAND: TWO ALBUMS ON TALL POPPIES AND FUTURE MUSIC RECORDS

My group, the austraLYSIS Electroband, started in networked interactive improvisation shortly after the time of the second Hub album and similarly used a MIDI interface as its hub, though for very different, complementary purposes. As I have indicated earlier, in essence our objectives were to maximize improvisatory scope, in the sense of range of sound sources accessible simultaneously, and to amplify precision of real-time control of large scale improvisatory structures and instrumental "performance." The large-scale contrasts between our two major albums (austraLYSIS Electroband 1997, 2000) are almost the mirror of those of the two Hub albums discussed above. Our first album featured much note- and event-oriented music, some strongly rhythmic, some groove based; it also featured extensive microtonal components and sound manipulation. However, our second album used extensive sound synthesis and sound modification in performance with MSP. It was also more texturally and noise oriented. Rather than focusing on data exchange between computers, we commonly used a core computer that controlled most of the electroacoustic sound sources and was operated by one player directly, whose patch state was sometimes subject to modification by other players across the network.

Figure 9.2 shows the MAX patch and interface for "Ostinato" (austraLYSIS Electroband 1997). In the recording the performance starts with a slow 8/8 groove, played by the patch. This repeats in a four-bar pattern with the bass-line pitches on a sampled piano and accompanying drums. Acoustic playing, on saxophone and acoustic piano, begins virtually in the groove; the music is almost idiomatically true to jazz. The acoustic improvisation evolves somewhat more meta-idiomatically, and some audio processing is apparent. Then both pulse speed and the pitches on the sampled piano are progressively altered via the MAX patch. The groove speeds up drastically, and pitches first spread over a huge range and then largely migrate to very high ranges. Eventually a completely anti-idiomatic state takes over, in which first the apparent position of the beats changes.

Figure 9.2 The MAX patch for "Ostinato."

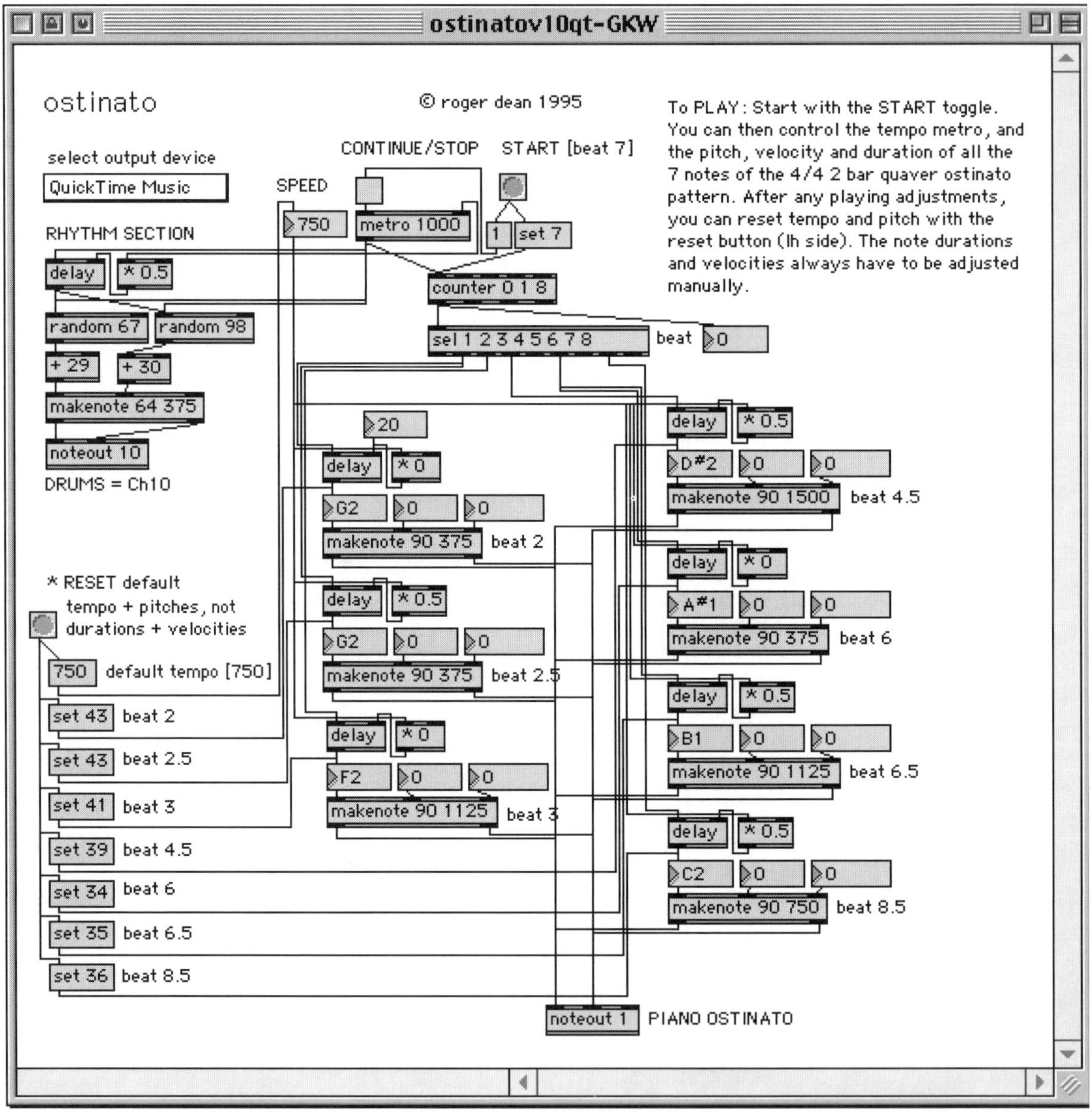

Later the groove is no longer recognizable, partly because it is realized on untuned percussion and accompanied by an additional percussion part driven by a separate patch, akin to the austraLYSIS rhythm engine discussed earlier. The piece concludes in this free state. Some other performances have used the patch further—for example, returning the speed gradually to the outset tempo, with or without returning the instrumental voicings, or abruptly restarting the groove in exactly its original form, from within the anti-idiomatic section. Although this is only a simple example, it illustrates how the comprovisational structure can be made a flexible one, both at the micro level (pitches, for example), and at the macro level (for example, whether or not a groove is apparent). In this case, the groove can be vanquished either by high pulse rate, by silencing enough of the pitched events, or by using instruments capable of sustaining long tones; the patch could readily be extended so that the pattern could be made of variable length segments, or other groove disruption mechanisms could be made available.

The unreal levels of virtuosity mentioned earlier in the book are exploited in "Sloping," particularly in the case of the computer-driven bass line. Rhythmic precision is also achieved in "Fibonacci" to a degree that would at least be very difficult in human group performance. Finally, "The Present Room" presents an intertextual reference to the preceding austraLYSIS album, *The Next Room*.

The second Electroband recordings (part of a double CD that also contains earlier work by LYSIS) focus more on sonic textures and MSP processing, both of samples and of real-time acoustic or synthesized sound. "The Engine" flirts with generating a groove, together with complex chordal patterns on an electronic keyboard, by a process of assembly, almost the converse of that in "Ostinato." Some examples of MSP and MAX patches relevant to the work of the Electroband are included on the CD-ROM.

■ ANNOTATIONS ON A SELECTION OF ELECTROACOUSTIC IMPROVISATION, SOME ANTECEDENTS TO COMPUTER INTERACTIVE WORK

MEV: "Spacecraft," 1967 (Musica Elettronica Viva, 1967; CD: Various, 2000)

This is a newly accessible example of the work of a pioneering electronic improvising ensemble. The material is a six-minute excerpt from a long performance, taken from the tape archive of Richard Teitelbaum, one of the founding members. Teitelbaum notes in the CD insert:

> Our first group piece, Spacecraft (1967) combined internal meditative processes with electro-acoustic techniques to create a kind of "space" designed to dissolve barriers between individual egos and merge them into a collective consciousness. By mixing and highly amplifying each musician's signals through a common (and cheap) sound system, the inter-modulation, distortion, inherent unpredictability of analog devices, and the physical displacement and movement of sounds between distantly placed loudspeakers created out-of-body sensations and loss of individuality in the dense noise textures produced. The performances, which lasted as long as six hours, tended to oscillate between peaks of intense collective violence and valleys of meditative peace. (Teitelbaum 2000a)

As he goes on to say, the piece does reveal those extremes. It includes much vocalized indecipherable verbal or pseudoverbal sound. It also foreshadows very strongly some of the ideas of individual submergence into an emergent whole that characterize the work of the Hub, as Tim Perkis has noted elsewhere.

Richard Teitelbaum: Concerto Grosso, 1985 (recording released 1988)

Based on a baroque concerto form, this important large-scale work features as "concertino" Anthony Braxton (winds, etc.), George Lewis (trombone, etc.), and the composer (piano and synthesizer). The "ripieni" are provided by "two digitally controlled acoustic grand pianos, one Yamaha TX 816 and two DX7s, with one Kurzweil 250 Digital Sampling keyboard." Figure 9.3 shows the layout of the performance, based on a diagram in the CD insert. The piece uses the three-piano system Teitelbaum had developed earlier in conjunction with his Patch Control Language, discussed earlier in the book. Here, one grand piano part is read into computer memory as it is played, then it is processed and played out by two Marantz Pianocorder Vorsetzer units attached to two additional grand pianos. Besides this original system, there is also a four channel MIDI interface, such that the Marantz could be controlled also from a synthesizer, and by acoustic instruments via pitch-to-MIDI converters. As the composer says, this created "the amusing and unique situation in which a wind player could simultaneously 'accompany' himself on one or even two acoustic grand pianos which would follow and interact with him. Through the use of the Kurzweil 250 . . . the acoustic soloists can also control and interact with sampled sounds they make themselves." The use of this instrument creates a generic continuity of some aspects of the sound world with that of the first austraLYSIS Electroband album mentioned above, in which the K2000 is used. Besides Teitelbaum's own software for musical interaction and pattern modification, FORTH programs by Lewis were also used. Teitelbaum states that

> the programs are designed to "listen" to the acoustic instrumentalists and respond to aspects of the musical gestures they hear by modifying their outputs accordingly. In the PCL programs, there are no pre-stored musical sequences. . . . These interactive programs can for instance change the pitch, tempo, rhythm, direction and instrumentation of the musical output in response to changes of articulation and phrasing in the music simultaneously (or previously) played into them by the musicians. (Teitelbaum 1985)

The "human concertino" is contrasted with the "robotic ripieno," to use Teitelbaum's suggestive terminology.

It is interesting, and consistent with aspects of the concerto grosso concept, that much of the orchestral range of instruments played by the synthesizer emerge at any one time as if forming a monodic stream, often because the note durations and rhythmic patterns are relatively uniform over time and across the different

Figure 9.3 Richard Teitelbaum: performance layout for Concerto Grosso.

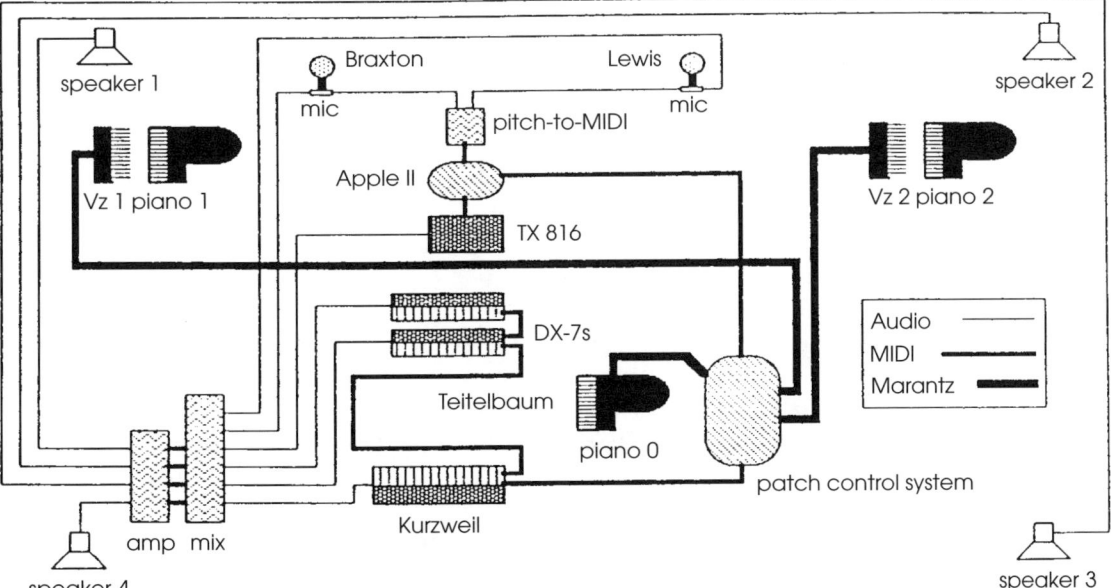

voices. Polyphony is produced mainly between the concertino and the ripieno, and within the concertino. The work is a major achievement in terms both of the application of the technology and of the development of a highly controlled large-scale musical form that harnesses mainly micro-improvised musical elements.

Teitelbaum's 1995 work *Golem* (an interactive multimedia opera) is equally fascinating, though the use of live improvisation is less dominant. Lewis and Teitelbaum again perform using computer-interactive systems, and they are joined by vocalists such as Shelley Hirsch and David Moss and the electronic violinist Carlos Zingaro.

Bob Ostertag

Ostertag is a wizard in interactive sample performance, and an excellent and relatively transparent example of his work is *Attention Span* (1989; released 1990 by RecDec). On tracks 1–26, Ostertag plays samples of John Zorn playing alto saxophone; and on tracks 27–32, he plays samples of Fred Frith playing guitar. In both cases he manages to produce music at times idiomatic to the original materials, and at others nonidiomatic. Some of the samples are computer manipulated before use. In "Slam Dunk," the first set, they are then performed on an Ensoniq EPS sampler in real time. In "Sleepless," the Frith set, both musicians perform live. Ostertag is heard playing in an ensemble of four on *Say No More in Person* (1993), but again with the influence of the "mirror" of recorded samples. As Ostertag says in the CD booklet, in this case "each musician was asked to learn parts derived directly from his own improvisations. In effect I was sitting each player down in front of a mirror image of his own music. But the mirror was curved into prisms and lenses which were the results of the transformations I had made in the process of creating the 'band' from the original solos."

Chris Brown

Brown, a member of the Hub (as discussed in this book), is involved in improvisation in a variety of contexts, including some jazz-oriented work as pianist with Glenn Spearman and others. He has released several albums that involve computer-interactive work. On *Snakecharmer* (an album of solos recorded between 1987 and 1989), his likable penchant for rhythmic grooves, deformed or straight, is repeatedly evident. As Brown mentions in the sleeve notes, on each piece "a different acoustic . . . instrument is played through an electronic system that responds automatically to the sounds and actions of the performer" (Brown 1989). The system uses information from the sampled performance to influence the nature of the signal processing it effects. The works use composed scores, and the degree of improvisation involved is not clear. "I want electronic sound that is alive to the nuances of human gesture and spontaneous musical thought. And I want it to enhance our experience of acoustics and of playing instruments, extending what we already do instead of trying to imitate, improve upon, or replace it." The sound world of this album is relatively homogeneous, reflecting the substantial impact of the sound-processing components, though in places the system drives other sound modules, rather than deriving sound directly from the input by modification. The former method is central to the piece from which the album takes its title. Here a "computer monitors the input from a microphone, transposing pitches and quantizing rhythms according to a program, then playing them back through an FM synthesizer and a harmonizer. Since the computer's pitch follower also hears the electronics the systems chases it's [sic] own tail (c.f. Ouroboros, the Snake), feeding back in modes than can be influenced by an acoustic performer (the Charmer)."

Brown's *Duets* (recorded 1992–96) includes "Sync or Swing," a duet with Ikue Mori in which rhythmic processes are again dominant. According to the sleeve notes, it is "an improvisation between two drum machines, one trying to synchronize with the other. Ikue Mori's machine lays down the steady beat, and Chris Brown tunes his rhythm software to a tempo that nearly, but not perfectly, matches it. As the two systems drift apart, Brown's machine interprets the discrepancy as 'swing,' and tries to match it by imparting the same feel to its performance" (Brown 1996).

George Lewis Lewis's improvisation and his software are well represented on his album *Voyager* (recorded 1993). Figure 9.4 from the CD sleeve lists some of the modules contained within the software and gives an introductory impression of its organization, as discussed earlier (Lewis 1993). The album consists of duo improvisation, mostly between either Lewis or Roscoe Mitchell (saxophones) and the computer-driven system, though an acoustic duo concludes the album. The eight "computer duos" use a modest sound palette (45 instruments) driven by a Macintosh Powerbook on an Emu Proteus/2 sample player and synthesizer. As David Wessel notes on the sleeve, the software produces quite different music in response to the two different improvisers. A microphone input to an IVL 4000 Pitchrider (audio-to-MIDI converter) supplied the data to the computer. It analyzed more than 30 parameters to create a "state" model of the input, which was then used to drive the output. As Lewis says, "the program exhibits generative behavior independent of the human performer. The system is not an instrument, and therefore cannot be controlled by a performer." One aspect of its independence is the recurrent use of random numbers generated by the system to influence some of its parameters; these allow the system to perform continuously without performer intervention when so desired. "What the work is about is what improvisation is about: interaction and behavior as carriers for meaning." This is a key album of computer-interactive improvisation, embodying very different notions about the possibilities for the computer role from those either of the networked emergent Hub or of the interactive control mechanisms of austraLYSIS.

Figure 9.4 Layout of George Lewis's software used on the album *Voyager* (by permission of the author; taken from published articles and the CD-sleeve of Voyager).

Voyager's top-level phrase behavior word, written as a FORMULA active process

```
:ap setphrasebehavior (--)
   ::ap" general phrasing"    (task recurs at intervals of 5000-7000 ms)
   5000 time-advance 11 irnd 200*5000+to cycle

     begin
        ::ev
       bodymusic 0=           \in this version this red light is always zero
          if calcork          \set up new group of players, including number and
position in space
          else allplayersoff     \turn off all groups and start over with a new
group.
          then
\set up how system will follow input; set MIDI timbres
       setfollowbehavior      setreplies         setvoxbehavior

\set melody algorithms, pitchsets, reverb and chorus type
       setwavebehavior        setscalebehavior        setreverbbehavior
       setchorusbehavior

       computer-solo?              \if no one is playing, I have a solo

\set volume and velocity, microtonal tonic transposition
          if setvelbehavior    setvolbehavior    settonicbehavior
```

Figure 9.4 continued.

```
\set octave, interval range, duration range
            setoctbehavior       setintbehavior       setwidbehavior
            setlegatobehavior

\set length of notes
            bodymusic 0=\in this version this red light is always zero
                if setrestbehavior \set up average degree of silence
                then

\set portamento, whether or not to follow tempo, and tempo ranges
            setportabehavior      settempofollow       setspdbehavior
            then

      ;;ev
   cycle time-advance
   again
   ;;ap
;ap
```

Voyager's input response word, written in Forth, sets parameters based on analysis of MIDI input

```
:setresponse (--)
 setinputbasedur                    \set tempo ranges based on input note durations
 bodymusic 0=                       \in this version this red light is always zero
      if setinputplayprob    \probability of note or rest, based on input
      then

\set duration range and length of notes, interval range
 setinputlegato      setinputwid      setinputint

\use pitchset based on last few input notes; set octave and microtonal tonic transposition
 setinputscale setinputoct     setinputtonic

\set MIDI volume and velocity
 setinputvol    setinputvel
```

Pitchset construction, Voyager, written as a Forth table representing the well-known 43-tone scale of Harry Partch, with approximate values given in cents. The word "s" translates values in cents to MIDI note numbers with 8-bit microtonal pitchbend offsets, and then compiles the 16-bit result into the next available byte pair in the table. The word "i" creates a transposition factor that allows the program's melody generators to perform a rough mapping of the microtonal data in a given pitchset to 12-space data received via MIDI. This permits the program to use these scales with effective interval widths analogous to those in 12-space, if desired.

Figure 9.4 continued.

```
create partch43 43 i,
0 s,      21 s,    53 s,    84 s,    112 s,    151 s,    165 s,    182 s,
204 s,    231 s,   267 s,   294 s,   316 s,    347 s,    386 s,    417 s,
435 s,    471 s,   498 s,   519 s,   551 s,    582 s,    617 s,    649 s,
680 s,    702 s,   729 s,   765 s,   782 s,    814 s,    853 s,    884 s,
906 s,    933 s,   969 s,   996 s,   1018 s,             1035 s,             1049 s,   1088 s,
115 s,             1147 s,           1178 s,
```

Lawrence Casserley

Casserley is a longtime proponent of many aspects of computer music. In 1997 he released *Solar Wind,* improvised duos with Evan Parker (saxophones) (Parker and Casserley 1997). The core of this music is the use of a long digital delay line, which provides a buffer of sound whose processing can be interactively adjusted some time after it was played. In current set-ups Casserley uses MSP with sample buffers corresponding to around two minutes of sound (Casserley, personal communication, 2000). The result is a spacious, sustained, textural music into which Parker's continuous multiphonic polyphony, or dense rapid action, is merged. Parker responds to the improvising environment by a significant moderation of his flux of sound; the result is powerful and unusual. In another collaboration by these artists, in the Electroacoustic Ensemble album *Drawn Inward,* recorded in 1998, the same processes are at work, but "live electronics, sound processing" is provided not only by Casserley, but also by Walter Prati and Marco Vecchi (Parker 1999). There is a much greater density of electronic sound; and there are also three other instrumentalists (two of whom provide some additional live electronics) providing sound to the processing pool. Again the usually prolix free improvisers (such as the virtuoso bassist Barry Guy) find effective ways of using a less dense input than they might usually apply.

Other Artists and Works

The use of real-time audio processing by computer is by now quite common in improvised performance of most kinds. An example in a genre quite removed from the albums listed so far is Chris Cutler's work *p53,* recorded 1994; (Cutler 1995). Parodic and sometimes almost reverential musical quotations are treated with imperturbable unity by the real-time processing of Lutz Glandien, while

Cutler complements the grand piano performance of Marie Goyette and Zygmunt Krauze with objects, low-grade electronics, and drums, to which Otomo Yoshihide adds turntables and home-built guitar (Cutler 1995).

A complementary approach, akin to using applied improvisation to build up a composition, is rather to use it to build up an instrument for improvisation, as exemplified in the piece *Traverse* (Eckel and Royer 2000). Gerhard Eckel has collaborated with the violist Vincent Royer, elaborating over a period of time and rehearsal a computerized database of viola-derived sounds that he performs from a Macintosh G3 Powerbook, using a MAX/MSP patch, in duo with the violist. "The computer player controls his or her part more on a structural level than by creating individual events" (Eckel and Royer 2000). The musicians emphasize "playing together," an aspect of which is to merge the sound worlds of viola and computer, while also providing some disparate vocalized elements. Whereas the processing of string instruments, or of saxophone, in the work of Lawrence Casserley and others brings a trail, an aurora of sound, following an initial acoustic impact, this work focuses on discrete events progressing rapidly, and with elements of indeterminacy in the control of the computer. Instrumental performance also inevitably involves imprecisions, and these musicians can respond efficiently with precise or imprecise sounds, as they see fit.

SECTION 5

Into the Ether

TEN

Into the Memory and across the Ether

> Musical experiments with distributed processing and global communication links among geographically distributed performers have been taking place for some time. These may be producing new kinds of organization and conception that could not have been predicted just by knowing the connections.... Such experiments have been a major focus at the Centre for Experiments in Art, Information and Technology at the California Institute of the Arts.
>
> —D. Rosenboom, "Propositional Music" (2000)

Sound improvisation can now proceed locally or remotely. A group may perform with its members working from several parts of the world; or a comprovisation may be distributed to any part of the world for use by others in an improvisation performance, domestic or public. The burgeoning possibilities in collaborations of such kinds are the subject of this chapter.

■ CD-ROMS, DVD-ROMS, AND DISTRIBUTION OF MATERIALS FOR COMPUTER-INTERACTIVE SOUND IMPROVISATION

There is a long-standing tradition among both composers and improvisers of chain or reciprocal exchange of sound files by cassette tape (originally analog, now digital). This allowed one musician to create the basis of a piece, which was then modified or added to by another and built upon further into a "final" piece. The building often went by repeated successive contributions of two people, sometimes by a chain of people, often not known to each other. One of the possibilities intrinsic in this was that any musician might provide an improvising substrate for another, or for a nonexpert user.

Such possibilities are now vastly enhanced by the exchange of both sound and meta-sound data by means of CD-ROM (or DVD, with its much enlarged data capacity). A CD-ROM of 650 megabytes allows, for example, 50 minutes of uncompressed CD-quality audio and large quantities of algorithmic software. More sound (in terms of duration) can be included by modest compression mechanisms, which, with little loss of sound quality, allow three- to fourfold compression (e.g., the IMA mechanisms). Sound files 10 or so times longer can be included by the less than desirable compression mechanisms such as Quicktime, mp3, and RealAudio, and yet in some cases achieve most of the intended sound effects. Many powerful programming platforms allow algorithms to be saved as freestanding applications, which do not require the original software (perhaps expensive and inaccessible to many users), as is the case with MAX. Thus such CD-ROMS can be the vehicle for transfer of sound files and software from one improviser to other people, so that the recipients can improvise with the supplied comprovisation.

The recipients would normally copy most of the CD-ROM contents onto their own computer so that they can use the faster speed of the hard disc to play and manipulate audio data; however, sometimes playing from the CD-ROM itself suffices. Once a sound work is in progress on a computer, then there is the possibility of "patch-memory" (Walker et al. 1992), in which the closing state of a piece of software in one user's hands becomes the starting condition for the next user. Such a state may be passed to another user of the same computer or transmitted across the Internet or on removable disc.

Mara Helmuth's *SoundColors* (Dodge and Jerse 1997, 418–420) is such a piece. It can run in real time on a computer, though it was originally written for the now-defunct NeXT computer. The listener/user first selects which of seven sound files to play, and then, using an interface program ("Collage!") provided with the piece, activates the computer to mix "the specified sound files stochastically within the guidelines set by the listener." The user has "for each sound file, control by means of sliders over the general amplitude level and its variability; the general range of durations and its variability; and the silence between plays and the variability of that attribute of the mix." Helmuth is quoted as writing (in 1996) that "*SoundColors* creates a sound environment of shifting colors." The piece is intended not for concert performance but for "a relaxed environment in which to contemplate the sound. . . . It may be placed in front of large windows, where people may look out while manipulating the sounds (Dodge and Jerse 1997, 418–420)." Other examples of such works distributed on CD-ROM are those released by the International Computer Music Association on its first CD-ROM (1999), which includes several multimedia works. Amongst these, our *Returning the Faultlines* is for nonexpert users, who can juxtapose up to three simultaneous sound files and activate a changing visual display of moving texts. Real-time DSP written in Director (originally in MAX) is effected on the multiple sound files, and in a way that varies from interaction to interaction. The users' control is restricted to start-stop controls of the independent multiple sound and text flows, providing modest improvisatory possibilities in the sense that the interactions are constructive and not simply exploratory. Other works on the CD-ROM are interactive, but primarily exploratory. The possibilities for inclusion of more extensively interactive software on CD-ROMs have been mentioned in the supplements to books such as that of Robert Rowe, and in didactic CD-ROMs on composers (such as Robert Winter's series released by Voyager), but so far not widely beyond.

The future for "digital cinema," in which much production is done by purely digital means, is bright (see Manovich, pp. 173–192, in Lunenfeld 1999). Digital cinema is not only a mechanism by which Hollywood production values can be subverted, and in which the required financial input is decreased exponentially, but also one that can permit interactive narratives in which the audience is as active as the producers in determining the final output. As with Web hypermedia, the interaction may be constructive and/or exploratory, and sound is (or should be) unrestrained by bandwidth. However, the relatively submissive position of sound in the production budget needs to be undermined before this will be fully revealed. In asynchronous cinema (Kahn 1999; cf. Youngblood 1970), sound might proceed image; certainly it should be able to question, countermand, unlike that in most film, even abstract film, as analyzed in Kershaw 1992.

■ IMPROVISATION ACROSS THE ETHER: IMMERSION

Openfield (1994) is an interactive work for the internet, produced during my residency at Xerox PARC. Openfield continuously broadcasts a live audio space world-wide to users of the internet. Using web browsers and VAT, an audio conferencing tool, users shaped the behavior of virtual "agents" who make sounds in this common space and interact with the agents defined by other users currently working with the system.

> Consider the analogy with a natural environment: it's amazing to me how the various birds and insects "multiplex" the channel of the outdoor acoustic space, each species differentiating its signal from the others in the space. I'm interested in seeing what kind of ecology may emerge as multiple simultaneous users try to create agents which can be heard. As in an open field, there is a harmony that arises out of each agent just trying to make itself heard among the multiple voices in this acoustic community.
>
> —*Tim Perkis, on his Web page found at the time of writing at* http://www.artifact.com/perkis/p_openfield.html *(as of 2001)*

MUD and MOO interaction across the Web now has a long history, mostly dominated by image and visual avatars. However, several systems have begun to develop audio exchange. For example, NTT's InterSpace (see discussion by William J. Mitchell in Lunenfeld 1999, p. 120) allowed audio communication in a virtual space.

> In InterSpace, users speak into microphones at their computers, and the voices are mixed according to the angles and distances among their avatars in perspective-rendered three-dimensional spaces. Avatars are controlled by joysticks, and take the form of robots with video monitors for heads . . . [which] display live video images of the faces of their owners. . . . It's as if the phone handset becomes a remotely controlled, speaking-and-listening video popsicle.

The medium for transmission of audio or meta-sound contributing to tele-improvisation (in which participants are physically remote from each other) is only relevant insofar as, at present, it confers limitations on speed of information transfer. Most people still access the Web by modem dial-up at speeds up to 56K, which means that streaming audio has to be drastically compressed, and little else can happen simultaneously on the communication line. Although these limitations are diminishing, currently the only generally applicable solution to such issues is to transfer only meta-sound, such as MIDI and DSP control information, to distant "rendering" computers, whose responsibility is simply the generation and reproduction of the entrained sound. This then entails the use of other computers at each participating site for manipulation of algorithmic information originating both locally and distantly. Such a mechanism has been used by the Hub and by Richard Teitelbaum performing remotely with MEV, as well as others. In contrast, sounding audio, across audio receivers such as radio, is useful as a component of ongoing improvised sound and can be subjected to DSP or other use at the receiver's end, just as it could locally if received live.

It is not appropriate to give a detailed discussion of the continuing conquering of these bandwidth limitations. It can be safely assumed that, at least with reference to current demands, the victory will be complete within a short time. Toward this end, streaming audio mechanisms, such as those provided by Quicktime and RealAudio, have been valuable, even though they are based on compromise through compression. Similarly, the contributions of both Beatnik and Koan (Garrigus 1999) in providing widely available mechanisms for use of very small (file size) sounds determined by the user rather than by the computer manufacturer have already been important stimuli. They provide unique sound opportunities, even though sample brevity, if not necessarily compression, is still intrinsic. The discussion that follows presumes that such bandwidth issues are not relevant or have been overcome.

The commercial versions of Koan in particular provide mechanisms for programming interactivity for the Web. Koan is primarily an algorithmic generator and has been widely used by Brian Eno and others; however, its intrinsic flexibility is limited compared with that of MAX. Beatnik is more concerned with the merging of MIDI and audio data into single files, in a unique format (.rmf). The most interesting aspect of both is perhaps their capacity to receive input from JavaScript (or VBScript). In principle, this could permit not only an interactive interface, but also one with enough variety on the control-stochastic axis for real improvisation. (Quicktime, even in version 4, was still somewhat resistant to such interactions.) Beatnik provides a library of JavaScript methods. Elaborate use of it is made in William Duckworth's *Cathedral* (on the Web). The stimulating possibilities had been little used at the time of writing the bulk of this book (mid-2000), judging by extensive Web searches. Furthermore, the progressively enhanced sound capacities within the more widely available visual and animation plug-ins and software, notably Flash 4, probably indicate that interactive and improvisatory sound might be most usefully and accessibly developed for that software (which is also JavaScript controllable), though the most recent releases of Quicktime also permit some JavaScript controls.

Several sound-only or sound-focused Web works have been produced. Playable Web "drum machines" have been developed by Eric Lyon and his Japanese students and colleagues and are genuine improvisation vehicles, though little different in possibility from commercial ones. On the other hand, *Netfield* (1996), by Philip Perkins, Bill Thibault, and Tim Perkis, provides the remote user with a 2D visual space representing a sound field that is controllable by the computer's arrow keys. In this work, one axis represents a gradient of "wetness" while the other refers to an "urban-rural" aspect, and it uses 25 "continuous environmental recordings" made by Perkins. Transitions between positions in the sound field are done by 3D spatialization and mixing, whereas in a related audio/computer installation piece (1995–), *InterZone Transfer,* morphing and other more computer-intensive transformations are used, and the original source recordings have been computer processed to generate additional overtly nonenvironmental sounds. Perkis comments: "It's interesting, to my ears at least, that after being prepared by the experience of the frankly fake and noisy interzone, the rain forest recording is almost completely non-functional as a representation of anything: it too is revealed clearly as the hissing and jangling of a cheap loudspeaker, and has been stripped of its mythological content (again, from the Artifact web site)." Natasha Barrett and Oyvind Hammer, conversely, developed a physical modeling-based sound installation, *Mimetic Dynamics,* and displayed it in Oslo (1999) while simultaneously making some simulations of it available on the Web for remote participation. The modeling was in part based on the fluid dynamics of oil droplets and their interaction with surfaces. David Rokeby has also developed some fascinating Web objects. The works just mentioned offer substantial levels of interaction across the Web, though they do not provide much improvisatory scope. On the other hand, Karlheinz Essl's Web site describes several of his interesting sound and text projects, such as *Amazing Maze* (1996). His *Playing Strategies* (1998) was developed as a user stimulus in the form of a JavaScript that generates random displayed verbal "text 4-liners (quoted from Essl's web site)." In several of these works, notably *fLOW* (1998–99) and the massive *Lexikon Sonate,* real improvisational possibilities exist, though the Web is used primarily to make the software available for download rather than for real-time sound improvisation across the Web.

Two very exciting possibilities are that all the approaches to computer-mediated improvisation will be accessible to a team of users remote to each other, and that intermedia work will be just as efficient as the purely sonic. The use of algorithms available to each player from a single server remote to most is a trend that is already developing in the use of commercial software and is unlikely to be a retarding factor in this evolution. Noncommercial MUDs and MOOs exist for mutual music making—for example, some ever-changing sites specialized in the techno areas, others more generalist. Some developers have focused on providing software that trawls the Web for sound files and then collages them, or that uses remote data of other kinds as source for automated translation into sound. For example, the Java application Earshot (www.deepdisc.com/earshot) is an effective tool for such purposes.

The ether may be traversed locally (as in a computer-interactive installation) or remotely, and as I have emphasized, the significant bandwidth limitations of the latter will not be present for much longer. But at present the construction of maximally immersive environments is still focused on local usage. Pressing 1997 describes an interesting example done in 1993 for presentation in Melbourne, Australia—"Total Immersion." In this collaborative work, two improvisers used a precomposed structure. One wore a head-mounted display and a cyberglove to drive both sound and image generation through a series of scenes; the other performed at a synthesizer. The piece had an ambient field based on water sounds, "with faint incursions of pitch-shifted incongruous mechanical sounds" that were precomposed. The work used MAX patches to generate sound control from the gestural performer and was presented in a museum/conference environment.

Many other efforts toward immersive environments featuring sound are ongoing, some large scale, such as the CAVE (at the University of Illinois), some smaller scale, at least financially, such as the efforts of Garth Paine (see his Web site). These VR environments offer unique sensory experiences in which sound may take a prime, if not dominant, place. However, at present the improvisatory opportunities they offer are more restricted than those mainly discussed in this book, almost as are those offered across the Web by Koan, Beatnik, and others. However, this need not remain the case.

Some of the interactive sound developments are driven by objectives primarily related to the film industry, as with digital cinema itself. For example, Thomas Dolby's patent concerning user-controlled generation of music to accompany visual images (Dolby et al. 1999) specifically envisages the interaction between at least two users and the possibility that their intentions might conflict. Major companies such as Microsoft have also entered this patenting arena, to the consternation of many computer composers and academics. However, in some cases the patents contain little that is not already in the public domain, and their level of "reduction to practice" is often slighter than that of the composers, so such patents may not be defensible or valuable (see Table 11.1 and related discussion).

Remote interactive performance will also undermine the present prejudice regarding the relationship of visible gesture to event, as discussed already. A contributor's gestures will be observable to few if any besides that person. Similarly, the distinction between expert and nonexpert participants can be removed, and even that between computer performers and human performers. These are some of the subjects of my final chapter, on the future of computer-interactive sound improvisation.

SECTION 6

Some Futures of Computer-Interactive Sound

ELEVEN

Evolving Futures

> Despite commercialization, working with computers in music is still both an end in itself and a means of creating music and expanding human understanding.
> —L. Spiegel, "That Was Then—This Is Now" (1996)

> "A computer network is an extension of society. These networks have a degree of complexity which prevents us from 'controlling' them any longer."
> —T. Perkis, quoted in review by J. Mazolli (1996)

■ IMPROVISING SOUND: EMERGENCE

Throughout this book references to the limitations of hardware, memory, access speed, and bandwidth appear. The power of computers and the speed of access to the Internet will continue to improve—no doubt drastically in the first case and modestly in the second. Undoubtedly, within a few years the limitations as presently perceived will be overcome. For example, it will be routine for a user at a remote computer, perhaps at home, to be able to exchange several CD-quality audio streams and a video stream or two, and to undertake algorithmic processing of a range of software modules, some held locally, some distantly, while inputting and outputting the resultant data. These improvements will lead us to make exciting new demands and expose new limitations. However, from the point of view of quality of sound used and generated, current problems seem eminently solvable, and the future is open.

More interesting to consider now in relation to future computer-interactive sound improvisation is the impact and development of evolutionary programming and related AI endeavors. Several classes of AI programs are currently claimed to exhibit "emergent" behaviors. For example, cellular automata (digital replicating entities within a computer) may possess certain activities as individuals, yet when placed in a community of modest complexity, reveal unexpected "higher"-level functions. Analogies are often made with cooperation between multiple individuals in certain animal communities. If an AI program is directed solely toward exploring a space of possibilities dictated by input rules and data (for example, the Virtual Bird or artificial Mozart minuet programs discussed earlier), then it is likely that the products will be unexpected only to a modest degree; as Paul Hodgson emphasizes, the space is directly determined by the rules and data, whether or not its extent is obvious to the human user at the outset (Hodgson 2000; also, hear the excerpt of Virtual Bird on the CD-ROM). Robert Rowe makes a similar point in discussing both the Experiments in Musical Intelligence software of David Cope and the work of Todd (Rowe 1993).

On the other hand, if members of a community of replicating functional digital entities are interacting, can an evolutionary process take place? Can a superstructure evolve with the capacities and achievements of human intelligence? Note that we can if we wish separate this question from that of whether a computer can become intelligent: intelligence can be considered a biological property, and what we are concerned with here is the capacity of machines to generate products that humans would normally generate by processes we call intelligent. More subtly, it may be argued that emergence is simply any distinction between an observed system and an observer's model of it, as several authors have argued. This view implies that there are grounds for questioning the view that what emerges was not already intrinsic. It might indeed have been present but not known, nor expressed. However, biological evolution (which does use a physical system) seems to have given rise to properties neither originally present, known, or expressed, such as self-replication of complex structures (organisms), their capacity for homeostatic control of limited parts of their environment, and eventually analytical symbolizable intelligence.

As a professional biologist as well as a musician, I would respond to the idealistic optimism about evolutionary computation by pointing out that not only has biological evolution been active over a very long period, but also the complexity of the constraints (environmental pressures) under which it has operated have been far greater than anything a computer seems likely to be exposed to. Even looking crudely at this issue, one can note that no biological entity is really part of a definable closed system. Every part of the worldwide system influences to some degree the activities of every organism, whereas a computer, or even the network of all computers in the world, is a system with a finite number of components separated almost completely from the majority of the world and its living contents except the few humans who operate on it. The evolutionary pressures thus seem slighter, however confident we are of our human intelligence. Perhaps a cautious position would be that evolutionary programming might well evolve higher functions, but the speed and ultimate extent of that evolution is as yet unclear.

So what are the possibilities for music and improvisation? Jonathan Impett has put forward thoughtful and provocative views on this. He is impressed by Lyotard's concept of a

> "tele-graphic" culture—a culture that can work at a distance in both space and time—in terms of three Freudian categories of memory. First . . . the memory of habit, . . . then that of search and recall, which includes the transposed resynthesis of phenomena ("scanning"). [Lyotard's] vision for the new technologies lies in the third, "anamnesis." . . . The new technology will be turned not on itself, as in scanning, but against itself; "to pass beyond synthesis in general. Or if you like to pass beyond the reminder of what has been forgotten, the point would be to recall what could not have been forgotten because it was not inscribed." (Impett 1998)

He is also enthusiastic about Adorno's *musique informelle,* " 'a type of music which has discarded all forms which are eternal or abstract or which confront it in an inflexible way'." He sees the possibility of flexibility (as discussed earlier in relation to his software for *Mirror-Rite*) and also of emergence: "A complex adaptive systems population of musical behaviours inhabits a landscape which in turn is shaped by a process of description and redescription of the events which constitute its environment" (Impett 1998). Emergence is no longer just that of a physical system reaching a new order; rather, "we pass to a situation of *emergent* knowledge; what we *didn't know* we knew; new cultural knowledge as the result of forces we *don't* have direct assess to. *Anamnesis* . . ." (Impett, in press). Currently, Impett is building his dynamically hierarchical describing and redescribing system in the computational simulation environment SWARM.

Perhaps it is also worth rehearsing the various algorithms already existent by which efforts have been made to generate preexisting styles of composition or improvisation; for when and if the algorithms run in real time, then they could be used equally in either context. Most cases published so far have involved a person extracting salient examples of a style, and even in some cases extracting data therefrom. The data is then formatted in a computer-friendly way as an accessible database. The computer algorithm then reads a specification of the context in which it is to operate, if any, and searches the database for the most appropriate musical fragment(s). Modest modification procedures are applied to the fragments, which are then sounded or scored according to rules of various degrees of elaboration that reflect other aspects of the style as understood by the programmer.

It is clear that there are several major stages at which computer-identification and evolutionary strategies could in principle take over from the human intervention, thereby reducing the extent to which stylistic boundaries are set by the programmer. Firstly, just as AI has developed commercially viable approaches to visual pattern recognition that allow individual body parts to be identified, so an algorithm can be established that simply observes the features of the formatted input data (still chosen by the programmer-musician). The extraction of features would then be limited largely by the data-formatting mechanisms, rather than by human preconceptions. For example, rather than analyze data with the concept of bars or meter embedded, the program can analyze it "neutrally," perhaps as do "free" improvisers in many contexts in which pulse and meter may yet sometimes emerge. Peter Bentley, from University College, London at the time of writing (personal communication, 2000; see also his Web page) claims that such an approach can generate excellent computer drumming, and efficiently recreate rhythmic patterns from cultures foreign to the programmer-musicians.

If the extraction of features (which could correspond to the "signatures" of which David Cope talks) can be relatively style neutral, then so can their exploitation. The extent of modification of the computer-generated database could then be controlled, from random to consistent, permitting production of music with any degree of relationship to the initial styles supplied. While musicians would immediately think of specifying the degree of variation along conventional musical parameters (pitch structures, rhythm, harmony, etc.), the program might well extract features couched in other terms. Yet it could be constrained, if desired, to focus on such conventional musical elements. This would allow the control of modification of material to act globally, or in quite different ways from those of musicians, on the formatted data of the computer; and to generate internal features and rules that were again not those used previously. Because the data at several stages is in a format not specific to music, it is also easy to envisage data exchange between visual and sound-generating components of the algorithm. An analogy exists between the "black box"-style independence and flexibility of such an approach and the capacity of neural nets to learn certain functions for which human intelligence as yet cannot provide analytical solutions; this implies that a solution is intrinsic to the successful net, but still not revealed, and certainly not expressed in the analytical language of our intelligence. The feature extraction component of the envisaged evolutionary algorithms is related in concept to the "listener" of Cypher or George Lewis. It is the nature of the analysis (degree of style independence) and exploitation that differs, with the potential for diversity rather than "normative" direction being considerable. There is also an analogy between the large-scale interacting community of the evolutionary program and the network approaches of computer bands discussed earlier. The visual and sonic experience of Rod Berry and colleagues' "Listening Sky," sampled on the CD-ROM, is indicative of such possibilities.

Evaluation is a recurrent stage of an evolutionary algorithm. Here again it is conventional to superimpose human choices or criteria defined by them. But it is also possible to envisage computer generation of evaluation algorithms that, like the feature extraction algorithms, do not involve a preconception of stylistic ideas. At the low level of data representation such evaluation can still be used to guide "focused" evolution or to choose diversity.

In sum, evolutionary computation, in part by the generation of complexity, may soon permit both style consistency and style flexibility in automatic music generation. Such an emergent achievement would be analogous to the supposed emergence in music itself, as viewed from the "immanentist" position outlined in Cross 1998b. Once this is achieved, multiple opportunities for real-time interaction between musicians and algorithms would exist, permitting new kinds of improvisation. For example, a global variation controller would certainly be a more diverse controller than any built into current MAX patches or other improvising patches. Conversely, controllers based on particular formalizations of the data manipulation might be made available that could not be described in terms of known musical features but yet drastically influence the ongoing performance of the algorithm. Finally, because ultimately the data generated by the computer has to be reformatted into sound or meta-sound, at some point in the chain data would become accessible in all the forms in which we currently use it. As always, a group of musicians could perform the software, and perform with it, and transform its output.

■ COMPUTERS IN THE ANALYSIS AND MODELING OF SOUND IMPROVISATION

I commented earlier in the book on several efforts toward software production of genre-specific music. Here I discuss work that is specific to modeling and generating improvisatory styles, and the continuous feedback cycle between analysis and modeling, where any generative mechanism involves the analysis of a model and the extraction of usable features, whose utility is then further analyzed in terms of effectiveness so that they can be further modified.

Modeling approaches may be an adjunct to, or based on, any analytical approach. But because of the convergence between computers, artificial intelligence, and cognitive science, the last is perhaps the most relevant for further discussion here. Narmour has proposed some relatively simple rules that might underlie the cognitive processing of melodic information. These depend on the comparison of successive pairs of intervals formed between a series of pitches $a, b, c. \ldots$ If $a \rightarrow b$ is a rising interval, then $b \rightarrow$ may constitute a continuation (if it is also a rising interval), or a reversal (if not), and the relative magnitude of the intervals is also assessed. Refinements are overlaid so that essentially there are five major rules in Narmour's "implication-realization" model (Narmour 1977, 1989, 1992). Experimental studies by Schellenberg tested the preferences of nonprofessional listeners who heard part of a melodic phrase for a succeeding pitch that was to "continue" rather than "complete" the phrase (Schellenberg 1996). This showed that the preferences were remarkably consistent with the predictions of Narmour's model, whether with tonal folksongs or atonal Webern song fragments; and with subjects born and living in the United States, or born in China and living in the United States. Indeed, Schellenberg was able to achieve just as precise a concordance between theory and experiment on the basis of only three of the rules, pointing out that the intercorrelations between several of the original five and their logical description implied that they were in part merely expressions of the same feature(s). He pointed out that in view of the success with only three rules, the likelihood that Narmour's claim of universality might be upheld was perhaps increased, though he took care to indicate that the universal might be learned, rather than necessarily innate. Rapid virtually universal learning seems to take place in relation to pitch recognition and tuning (Sloboda 1988), so the possibility of such learning in relation to melody is plausible. Narmour and Schellenberg might therefore support the idea that universal implication-realization is supplemented moderately by style-specific features and thus give strong support to the idea that computer modeling of musical styles could be successful. They arrive at a complement to the style-specific "signatures" of David Cope discussed earlier. A hybrid of the "physicalist" and "cognitive" positions on the nature of music, outlined by Cross, would emerge, as he clearly recognizes (Cross 1998b).

Many efforts have pursued such cognitive-based paths to the computer generation of music, and just as Margaret Boden has emphasized the relevance of breaking constraints to creativity (Boden 1991), so improvisers can use such computer algorithms as targets for rupture as well as cooperation. The experimental psychologist Philip Johnson-Laird early on produced relatively simple algorithms that model the jazz bass player, though, as he himself said, the results were only acceptable rather than impressive (Johnson-Laird 1991). The composer Klarenz Barlow has written his complex Autobusk software. Paul Hodgson has developed his Improviser program since about 1985: it is intended to generate jazz solos in boppish idioms to provide examples to those learning to play in the style by an imitative approach. Subsequently, he has extended this in his Virtual Bird, which, given a performed chord sequence as a MIDI file, analyzes the harmonies, determines the chordal progressions (e.g., I → II → V → I) and their scalar implications, and then very rapidly generates a solo ready for playback. The process involves using a repertoire of Charlie Parker phrases chosen by Hodgson and stored in the computer. These are indexed in terms of rhythmic pattern, pitch pattern, and home key. Suitability of a phrase is gauged by comparing it with the progression at hand (regardless of key). Several phrases may be ligated to form a longer phrase for use in the progression space. Chosen completed phrases, transposed to the appropriate key, are then if necessary cycled to fill the rhythmic space available. Modifications of the phrase may include omission, chromatic notes, and transposition of certain notes. The results are impressive (see CD-ROM), even though the database of material is modest, and the modifications to the materials that are inflicted by the software are also limited (Hodgson 2000a, 2000b). Random pattern components can be included.

In an unpublished conference article, Hodgson emphasizes the psychologically intensive nature of improvisation, in terms of its high flux of both perceptual and creative cognition (Hodgson 1994). This issue was also discussed in Pressing 1998. Hodgson views Improviser as a "pedagogical method for boot strapping people into creative improvisation." He emphasizes the relationship between the selection and remodeling processes his Virtual Bird applies to the database of Bird materials and the cognitive processes he envisages as intrinsic to human musical improvisation. But, as he says, "It doesn't actually tell you how the patterns were created in the first place" (Poole 1998). Nevertheless, the first comment of the well-known British saxophonist Courtney Pine after first trading phrases with Virtual Bird was that it was "bloody brilliant."

Neural network (trained learning) approaches have also been used in the context of modeling improvisatory styles. For example, Toivainen has modeled the related jazz style of the hard bop trumpeter Clifford Brown, with some success (Toivainen 1995a). He has also demonstrated that the tonal hierarchies and pitch usage of bop and hard bop are similar to those of European art music (Toivainen 1995a).

Other work in the direction of cognitive modeling that takes careful note of Hodgson's has been done by Ganascia and Ramalho (Ramalho et al. 1999). Their IMPACT program generates jazz bass lines against the backdrop of a previously decided "scenario" (for example, the chord sequence of a standard jazz tune, together with a soloist). As with Hodgson's work, IMPACT has been given 354 extracts of patterns from recordings of the eminent jazz bass player Ron Carter and uses a feature-based extraction protocol. The fragments are represented in memory and indexed for ready access on the basis of quite elaborate features. The authors view the process as one of problem solving, where accommodating the progression between two successive chords is the core. The program is provided with the chord progression and for any particular chord interface generates Potential Actions (PACTS) on the basis of their harmonic properties. From the PACTS a particular case is chosen and then subjected to modest modification before being performed. As observed in other contexts, the activation rules involve several normalizing concepts. For example, if the soloist is playing many notes per unit of time, the system will "play with low density"; if the overall scenario "temperature" at a particular point is "hot" (which means many notes, loud, highly syncopated, and higher tessitura), the bass will also play hot (Ramalho et al 1999). A series of modifications of the PACTS can operate involving deletion, combination, propagation. Peter Gannon has patented and commercialized some similar ideas (see Table 9.1), and Ramalho compares the performance of IMPACT with this and NewSwing, another commercial package. Even the author of NewSwing prefers IMPACT, but though successful, it is clear that it is an artificial accompanist rather than an improvising partner. As the authors note, self-evaluation, such as is found in Cypher, is needed for the enhancement of IMPACT.

Al Biles' GenJam (short for Genetic Jammer) is an "interactive genetic algorithm that learns to play jazz solos. It may well be the only evolutionary algorithm that is a 'working musician'" (from his Web page, http://www.it.rit.edu/~jab/GenJam.html). In the version current at the time of this writing, a GI-10 Roland pitch-to-MIDI converter is used to allow the program also to listen to Biles's acoustic trumpet playing and then to use the material when alternating four- or eight-bar soloist's phrases within mainstream jazz idioms. There are preprogrammed tunes (of which there were around 150) and harmonic knowledge, and styles for the virtual rhythm section (which, unlike the soloist, performs in a largely fixed manner). When producing four-bar breaks, the computer listens to the majority of a human-generated acoustic four-bar break, then maps the input to "four measure chromosomes and one phrase chromosome," where a chromosome is a string representation of data. It "stops listening to the human, applies a random selection of its mutation operators to the phrase and measure chromosomes, and then performs the result as its next phrase." There is also a mechanism for ensuring the consistency of the chosen notes with the harmonies of the pre-programmed tune or style, which does permit some chromatic passing notes. This constrains the computer solo to be "competent," but it cannot be "creative." Elsewhere Biles has indicated that, consistent with the algorithmic possibilities already summarized in this book:

> The available mutations on measure chromosomes include (1) reverse—play the loci in reverse order, similar to retrograde, (2) rotate—rotate the loci a random amount from 1 to 7 positions to the right, (3) invert—subtract the locus value from 15 and rescale the result to the pitch range of the original measure, and (4) transpose—raise or lower the new note events by a random amount. The available mutations on phrases include (1) reverse—play the measures in reverse order, (2) rotate— rotate the measures a random amount from 1 to 3 positions to the right, (3) repeat—select a random measure and repeat it, replacing the measure that would have been played with the repetition, and (4) sequence phrase—build a special phrase beginning with the last measure of the human's four, repeating that measure one or two more times and filling out the remainder of the phrase with other measures from the human's four. (Biles' web page, as at the time of writing)

Alternatively, the software "evolves populations of melodic ideas under the guidance of a human mentor(s), whose feedback provides the environment under which individual ideas either survive to breed or die off. GenJam also uses its genetic algorithm machinery as a real-time melodic development paradigm to evolve phrases played by a human into its improvised responses in chase choruses" (Biles' web page again). Feedback can be given by an individual mentor, collectively by an audience, or in real time by performers, this being a partial solution to the difficulty of otherwise deriving an evaluation routine. Tim Perkis's TouchTyping software/ hardware instrument permits related evaluation to be done on real-time evolved entities based on a genetic programming approach, and he has used this in real-time performance in many contexts. Other related endeavors are Rod Berry's "musical breeder" *Feeping Creatures,* an interactive display with associated sound (see also CD-ROM), and Sony's Firefly evolutionary rhythm. It is interesting that Berry has associated "genetic" properties with sounds per se and rhythmic material with "energy flow through the system"; he also describes a distinctive biological pressure, that of food supply. To quote from his Web site (as of 2002: http://www.cofa.unsw.edu.au/research/rodney/FC_table.html)

> Description of Feeping Creatures 2.0 as installed in Perspecta '97 . . .
>
> You walk into a darkened room. In it you find a large projected video screen taking up one wall. On the screen is an image of a 3D environment populated by a number of moving shapes. The shapes on screen are clearly seen to be interacting in some way and, after more observation, some appear to be mating causing new shapes to appear and begin wandering the landscape. Some shapes remain static and represent a kind of plant material as various mobile shapes seek out and eat them. In the middle of the room, you find a positioning device such as a joystick which allows you to alter your point of view and to navigate your way around the 3D environment. There are also some basic instructions and suggestions about how to begin interacting with the work. All the time you are aware of sound coming from loudspeakers located either side of the screen and behind you. When you move the positioning device, you notice that the sound changes as well as the image on the screen. You find that various sound events (melodies, rhythms, timbres) are associated with different creatures in your field of view, becoming louder or softer depending on their proximity to your imaginary position in the environment. Each creature produces a series of musical notes which remain unchanged throughout its life but its rhythmic material (the lengths and loudnesses of the notes in the series) keeps gaining elements as a result of the creature eating plants (or other creatures) or losing them through starvation, and ageing. When two creatures mate, their offspring inherits a combination of each parent's note series. The new creature sounds a bit like each of its parents. It then has to go and find food to build up its body and its rhythmic structure and eventually

mature enough to reproduce itself. Pitch material is genetic in nature whereas rhythmic material represents energy flow through the ecosystem (via the food chain)....

While journeying around this space, you find that different groups of creatures have distinct kinds of harmonies, melodies and rhythms. These 'cultures' emerge from each creature's ability to evaluate certain aspects of a neighbouring creature's music (such as how they fit together harmonically) and its own inherited preference for particular kinds of harmonic relationships. For example, creatures who prefer consonant harmonies with a neighbour tend to group together and have consonant offspring with an even more profound consonant preference. After a while, they might tend to get inbred and sound a bit 'new agey' with the occasional mutant child exiled to seek out a more dissonant crowd. Eventually, you leave wondering what musics will have evolved in a week's time. Will there be any recognisable descendants of the ones you've been in amongst today, or will it be a whole different world? (2000: http://www.cofa.unsw.edu.au/research/rodney/FC_table.html)

The evolving artificial-life (A-life) visual arts community is more extensive than that concerned with sound, but some of its participants also pursue sonic outputs, as for instance does David Rokeby (see his "Giver of Names"). A useful recent review of genetic techniques for music generation with discussion of the issues of evaluation is available (Burton and Vladimirova 1999).

■ THE COMPUTER AS IMPROVISER

If the evolutionary computing agenda outlined is successful, then it will generate entities that can learn to behave in various human(oid) ways. Many projects are addressing this already, such as the Talking Heads project of Sony Computer Science Lab, Paris, and a group of academic collaborators, which has been exhibited and is available on the Web (Wellcome Trust 2000; Talking Heads Experiment 2000). This project addresses how language and meaning originate in digital "agents" and how they can be developed and transmitted between generations. The agents can be exhibited as robots, exposed to real-world stimuli via camera, or remain hidden and purely digital but still stimulated; the information they progressively share is exchanged over long distances by the net, the process of "teleportation." To do this, agents create words and try to establish mutual agreement on their association with objects.

Each agent possesses "a mechanism to 'grow' new distinctions by expanding discrimination trees. Each tree discretizes one sensory dimension. . . . Trees can go as deep as necessary to carve out smaller and smaller subregions of a continuous space" (Luc Steels, catalog to Wellcome Trust 2000). The agents negotiate with each other in a gamelike manner, which permits them to evaluate whether a given object is associated by several agents with the same new lexical entity. "The distinctions which are not successful in the game are pruned. This way the conceptual repertoire of an agent can continue to adapt to the needs of the agent."

While there are certainly crude analogies in this process to those in real-time improvisation, perhaps more important is the idea of gradual emergence of lexical power. If the project achieves higher levels of complexity of the language the agent community shares, then at least in terms of object discrimination, an impressive step will have occurred. It will remain to be seen how generalizable the process is, for example to nonobjective concepts and logical argument.

Robert Rowe and colleagues have superimposed interactive and improvisatory capacities on the character animation system IMPROV, which was developed by Ken Perlin and colleagues at the New York University Media Research Laboratory and creates animated characters with individual personalities. Rowe's Interactive Virtual Musicians (IVM) allows external inputs, such as movement and video, to control the behavior of the characters, and endows them with sound-generating mechanisms based on MIDI and real-time synthesis. It also can generate improvisation in the form of constrained random lines, patterns based on chord changes and Markov-based lines. Other methods from Cypher are incorporated, and some of the analytical aspects of Cypher, particularly those to do with chord recognition and rhythmic patterns, are extended.

■ UTILITY AND EXPLOITATION

Computer-interactive sound improvisation will lead to several practical applications, some of which I have touched on briefly. Educational utility is one of the most obvious. I have alluded to the use of CD-ROM and computer and Web interfaces for teaching jazz improvisation in the bebop style or understanding of the works of Beethoven or Stravinsky. Tod Machover, Morton Subotnick, and others also have great hopes that computer-interactive improvisation may facilitate children's development of musical skills. Subotnick produced a CD-ROM for this purpose and subsequently offered related materials freely on the Web (Subotnick 1995). The segment of this software entitled "Mix and Match" was amusingly retitled "Max and Match" in a review in the *Computer Music Journal* (Ames 1996).

Computer-interactive improvisation will also continue the current trend for the production of much music for worldwide consumption by musicians who neither want nor need conventional musical training. These musicians, who often create music on home computer systems, do not necessarily require notation or an understanding of metrical approaches to rhythm: these can be substituted by appreciation of a proportional space-time notation, as has been used in some avant-garde music for more than 50 years (e.g., the works of John Cage and Morton Feldman). An example of a system for both educating users about computer music and allowing them to create novel soundtracks for media work without sophisticated musical knowledge as prerequisite, is WorldBeat, on permanent display at the Ars Electronica Centre in Linz, Austria (Borchers and Mühlhäuser 1998). This uses "Musical Design Patterns . . . an approach to developing interactive, music-oriented systems for use as novel media content." In the exhibit, computer sound generation is controlled by a user armed with a pair of Buchla infrared batons. These can drive menu choices and also generative parameters. To allow the system to be used by nonprofessionals, there are many "corrector" functions, and the supplied materials database is canonical. Users can play instruments with joy sticks, conduct prerecorded pieces with virtual batons, query the database for material by humming, customize design patterns, and perform with others over the Internet (this function is undergoing further development at the time of writing).

Commercial issues also need to be considered. Patenting methods for computer generation or computer-interactive manipulation of music for use in film, advertising, multimedia, environmental ambience creation, videorecording, and so on has expanded considerably in the last three years, as mentioned earlier. Table 11.1 is a selective listing of interesting, or at least challenging, patents in this area. The surprising degree of predictability of pitch-centered melodic lines on the basis even of simplified Narmour rules (above) suggests that related computer-generative techniques should be quite successful in producing functional music for these contexts.

Table 11.1 Selected US patents relating to computer-interactive sound improvisation

US4341140 07/1982	Ishida. Casio Computer Co. Ltd. Automatic performing apparatus
US4399731 08/1983	Aoki. Nippon Gakki Seizo Kabushiki Kaisha. Apparatus for automatically composing music piece
US4468998 09/1984	Baggi. Harmony machine
US4526078 07/02/1985	Joel Chadabe. Interactive music composition and performance system
US4704682 11/1987	Manfred Clynes. Computerized system for imparting an expressive microstructure to succession of notes in a musical score
US4716804 01/05/1988	Joel Chadabe. Interactive music performance system
US4745836 05/1988	Roger Dannenberg. Method and apparatus for providing coordinated accompaniment for a performance
US4926737 05/1990	Minamitaka. Casio Computer Co. Ltd., Automatic composer using input motif information
US5085116 02/1992	Nakata et al. Yamaha Corporation. Automatic performance apparatus
US53150557 05/1994	Land et al. LucasArts Entertainment Company. Method and apparatus for dynamically composing music and sound effects using a computer entertainment system
US5355762 10/1994	Tabata et al. Kabushiki Kaisha Koei. Extemporaneous playing system by pointing device
US5393926 02/1995	Johnson. Ahead, Inc. Virtual music system
US5451709 09/1995	Minamitaka. Casio Computer Co. Ltd., Automatic composer for composing a melody in real time
US5455378 10/1995	Paulson et al. Coda Music Technologies, Inc. Intelligent accompaniment apparatus and method
US5496962 03/1996	Meier et al. System for real-time music composition and synthesis
US5513129 04/1996	Bolas et al. Fakespace, Inc. Method and system for controlling computer-generated virtual environment in response to audio signals

Table 11.1 continued

US5627335 05/1997		Rigopulos et al. Harmonix Music Systems, Inc. Real-time music creation system
US5648627 07/1997		Usa. Yamaha Corporation. Musical performance control apparatus for processing a user's swing motion with fuzzy inference or a neural network
US5663517 09/1997		Oppenheim. International Business Machines Corporation. Interactive system for compositional morphing of music in real-time
US5670729 09/1997		Miller, et al. Virtual Music Entertainment, Inc. Virtual music instrument with a novel input device
US5736666 04/1998		Goodman et al. California Institute of Technology. Music composition
US5773742 06/1998		Eventoff et al. Note assisted musical instrument system and method of operation
US5753843 05/1998		Fay. Microsoft Corporation. System and process for composing musical sections
US5952599 09/1999		Thomas Dolby et al. Interval Research Corp. Interactive music generation system making use of global feature control by non-musicians
US5990407 11/1999		Peter Gannon. Automatic improvisation system and method
US6051770 04/2000		Andy Milburn et al. Postmusic. Method and apparatus for composing original musical works

The table arbitrarily focuses on US patents, simply to provide examples of the range of claims. The data shown here are: patent number; issued date (mm/yy); key protagonist(s); title. There are several public domain sites making patent information available, normally reference details and patent abstract. See for example: http://www.patents.ibm.com.

Another commercial trend is toward generation of sounds on the basis of verbal specification so that a composer or soundsmith who did not require formal training might be able to generate and then string together sounds for film on the basis of such descriptions. Eduardo Miranda is developing his ARTIST program to this end, currently at Sony Computer Labs. He has also emphasized how the development of parallel computing architectures, in which multiple tasks are processed simultaneously by different functional modules within a single computer, will be beneficial for such approaches in particular, though of general applicability (Miranda 1998). Together with AI and evolutionary computation, these approaches should ensure an important practical future for computer sound generation.

The improviser (or composer) will always be able to overlay special controls, features, and structures in real-time (or meditated) work and thus take advantage of these software and hardware futures.

■ EVOLUTION

The possibilities for future computer-interactive sound improvisation and its cooperation in intermedia improvisation are thus exciting and immense. They are certainly undergoing replicative divergence. To continue the biological analogy, I would conclude that for substantial evolution and emergence to be achieved, it will be necessary to invoke comparably diverse selective pressures. A single alogorithm on a single computer may not produce surprising output; but multiple algorithms on multiple interacting computers, given plenty of time and large numbers of selective input forces, may do so. Happily, many of the intermediate products, if used as musical processes, will be fascinating. Unlike the case of evolving a railway network for a city, the case of music is more forgiving, more implicitly understandable, and less subject to practical criteria. I look forward to the emerging future.

APPENDIX 1

The Questionnaire and Selected Responses

During the period March–September 2000, I e-mailed a questionnaire to 89 relevant musicians and researchers. It resulted in 21 written responses, and one of the respondents was also interviewed in person. In addition, I interviewed or conversed less formally with 25 others amongst the 89 people on some or all of the topics of the questionnaire. These 46 people are listed below and in many cases have been mentioned in the body of the book and in the references. Here, after reproducing the questionnaire I wrote and used, I provide a brief synopsis of the comments that were made specifically in response to the questionnaire, whether given in writing or in person. This is ethnographic information, and I make no claim for its representativeness of the field as a whole.

■ QUESTIONNAIRE IN RELATION TO FORTHCOMING BOOK ON COMPUTER-INTERACTIVE SOUND IMPROVISATION

From Roger Dean, austraLYSIS, Sydney
(last revised 2000/04/04)

Dear Colleague,
I am writing to you as someone interested in computer-mediated sound generation, and/or with knowledge adjacent to, overlapping, or focused on improvisation. I would be very grateful for your responses, brief or extended, to the following questions. I am undertaking the necessary research to write a book in this area, contracted to A-R Editions, perhaps the leading publisher in this area besides MIT Press. I would therefore like your permission to

quote (directly or indirectly) from your comments when appropriate, and I will assume this to be given unless you indicate otherwise.

I will present the perspective of an improviser, and emphasize process, real-time interaction, and computer/body interface issues. I will also discuss the use of sound in intermedia contexts, again in relation to interactive and real-time issues; for example, algorithmic transfer between visual- and sound-generative processes will be a relevant topic.

In three previous books, two with Open University Press (*Creative Improvisation,* published 1989; and *New Structures in Jazz and Improvised Music since 1960,* published 1992), and the third written more recently with Hazel Smith (*Improvisation, Hypermedia and the Arts Since 1945,* Harwood Academic, 1997), I have developed some theoretical frameworks for the discussion of improvisation, which will be used in the new work. I indicated there that it is fair to view composition and improvisation as forming a continuum, along several axes, with no clear demarcation point on any of the axes. Thus, I am sending this questionnaire to some people whose main public output seems to be more compositional than improvisatory, because I will appreciate their comments and insights as much as those of colleagues closer to the cores of improvisation. I will be addressing techno and its offshoots, as much as free, avant-garde, and classical- and jazz-related computer improvisation; distinctions between popular and elitist musics will not be barriers in the book.

I would emphasize that questionnaire responses have proved extremely valuable in my previous work, especially in the book with Hazel; many comments were documented therein, and added importantly to the thrust, continuity and diversity of the book. The names of the many responders were listed in the book. So I do hope you will be able to find the time to respond to this request; and I give you my thanks in advance. You may find it convenient to fill in your responses on the e-mail below, and return it; or you can paste it into your word processor and proceed from there. For ease of access, if possible please return your resultant document by email. Naturally, the form of your responses is up to you; I would appreciate even yes/no responses, but be interested in some elaboration of all the points that strike you as worthy of any more comment.

You can respond to me by e-mail at my long-term address, dr.metagroove@mindless.com, or by snail mail at the address below.

QUESTIONNAIRE from Roger Dean related to Computer-Interactive Sound Improvisation

(1) Do you make computer-interactive sound works?
    (1a) Do you make them as compositions?
    (1b) Do you make them for use within improvisation or to include improvisation?

(2) Who can interact with the computer to influence sound output (in these works)?
    (2a) Yourself only?
    (2b) Performers?
    (2c) Recipients (i.e., audience; "screeners" or "sounders," in the case of Web or CD-ROM work)?

(3) How many people can interact with computers during the process of the(se) work(s)?
    (3a) Do they do so on a one person-one computer or a networked basis?

(4) How can people interact with your computer-interactive works? Where necessary, please indicate distinctions between the possibilities available to yourself, to performers, and to screeners, respectively.
    (4a) What are the physical means?
    (4b) Are the interactions offered in live performance?
    (4c) Are they offered over the Web or on CD-ROM?
    (4d) Can the computer user drive the process (which would otherwise rest), or just modify its progression?

(5) Do you intend that the computer users be able to identify the results of their interaction?
    (5a) Can they simply stop/start defined processes, and will this be detectable to them?
    (5b) Can they influence processes in a more subtle way, and will this be detectable?
    (5c) Is the relationship between the user input and the subsequent computer response fixed or variable, and if so, how?
    (5d) Is input information aggregated in any way, so that only the resultant cumulation is responsible for output? How does this work?

Where necessary, please indicate distinctions between the possibilities available to yourself, to performers, and to screeners, respectively.

(6) Do you view the computer, or the computer network, as itself being in some degree an improviser? Please elaborate.

(7) Is your use of the computer "embodied" in algorithms you write? If not, please elaborate on your usage. If you do write your own algorithms, then do you see them as
(7a) Compositions?
(7b) Material for comprovisation?
(7c) An improvising entity?
(7d) A hyperinstrument?
(7e) A compositional superstructure that is explored?
(7f) Exploratory or generative algorithms (in the sense developed by Michael Joyce for discussion of [the] hypertext literature, in which a generative hypertext creates new entities in response to input, whereas an exploratory one reveals entities which were already completely formed but not displayed)?
(7g) Something(s) else??
Please elaborate in each case relevant to you.

(8) Why do you make computer-interactive work?

(9) Can computer interaction provide unique opportunities/outputs? If so, could you elaborate?

(10) Are there any aspects of computer interaction you would like to point out as important to sound improvisation? Please elaborate.

(11) If convenient, please send me a list (or give me a Web address) of your relevant work, and indicate which of it I could obtain from you at cost if necessary. Naturally I have an extensive collection of relevant material, but new sources and details are always important. If you have reprints of any relevant articles you have published with any relevance to the topic, I should also be most grateful for these by mail to the address above; again, I have and continue to acquire many critical reprints, but access is not always efficient, or even possible.

(12) Please indicate whether you have software that might be suitable and available for inclusion in a CD-ROM accompanying the book. I have in mind algorithmic patches in MAX, MSP, or other platforms, including audiovisual work. There will be scope for some relevant sound examples also. I am also interested in any material you might suggest beyond these confines.

(13) Please list a few of your musical peers relevant to the field of computer-interactive sound improvisation whom you think of interest yet unlikely to be known already to a British Australian musician living in Sydney.

Again, thanks for your contribution. I will let you know the likely release date of the book once completed, and I may follow up your responses with some further questions if appropriate.

Yours,
Roger Dean
Artistic Director, austraLYSIS
PO Box 2039, Woolooware, NSW 2230, Australia
www.australysis.com

The respondents and interviewees/conversants:

Curtis Bahn	Philip Johnson-Laird
Peter Bentley	Douglas Kahn
John Bischoff	Eric Lyon
Chris Brown	Bruno Nettl
Tony Buck	Per Anders Nilsson
Phil Burk	Tom Nunn
Warren Burt	Garth Paine
Lawrence Casserley	Joe Paradiso
Joel Chadabe	Tim Perkis
Chris Cutler	Larry Polansky
Roger Dannenberg	Jeff Pressing
William Duckworth	Scanner (Robin Rimbaud)
Gerhard Eckhel	Greg Schiemer
Magnus Eldenius	Eric Singer
Simon Emmerson	Hazel Smith
Karlheinz Essl	Laurie Spiegel
Sidney Fels	Lindsay Vickery
Jim Franklin	Martin Wesley-Smith
Tom Fryer	Greg White
Greyworld	Mitchell Whitelaw
Mara Helmuth	Christopher Zavelow
Paul Hodgson	David Zicarelli
Jonathan Impett	Carlo Zingaro

■ A SELECTION OF THE RESPONSES

The responses from Greyworld were given by Andrew Shoben, apparently representing shared views. Some of the responses from George Lewis included delineated sections quoted from previous writings; these delineations are retained as quotation marks below.

(1) Do you make computer-interactive sound works?
 (1a) Do you make them as compositions?

Greyworld: We make them as generative environments. They are not complete, or even fully authored until experienced.

George Lewis: I wrote this in response to a query from the Leonardo Music Journal people: "*Voyager*'s unusual amalgamation of improvisation, indeterminacy, empathy, and the logical, utterly systematic structure of the computer program, is described throughout this paper not only as an environment, but as a 'program,' a 'system,' and a 'composition,' in the musical sense of that term. In fact, the work can take on aspects of all of these terms simultaneously—considering the conceptual level, the process of creating the software, and the real-time, real-world encounter with the work as performer or listener. Flowing across these seemingly rigid conceptual boundaries encourages both improvisers and listeners to recognize the inherent instability of such taxonomies."

Carlos Zingaro: Rarely, as I rather prefer to take advantage of the real time risks of interactive performance . . .
 (1b) Do you make them for use within improvisation or to include improvisation?

Greyworld: If you mean improvisation in a musical sense, i.e., to accompany some other fixed sound elements, then no. Ultimately though, our work allows the creation of complex sound environments through some sort of physical, friction-based interaction. No knowledge of musical structures or theories is necessary; it is public art for public spaces.

George Lewis: Voyager is all about improvisation. Everything is improvised: "*Voyager* is a nonhierarchical, interactive musical environment that privileges improvisation. In *Voyager,* improvisers are engaged in dialogue with a computer-driven, interactive 'virtual improvising orchestra.' A computer program analyzes aspects of a human improviser's performance in real time, using that analysis to guide an automatic composing (or, if you will, improvising) program that generates both complex responses to the musician's playing, and independent behavior that arises from its own internal processes."

(2) Who can interact with the computer to influence sound output (in these works)?
(2a) Yourself only?
(2b) Performers?
(2c) Recipients (i.e., audience; "screeners" or "sounders," in the case of Web or CD-ROM work)?

Sidney Fels: All of my work can be used by anyone. MusiKalscope, Sound Sculpting and Glove-Talk II are more focused on performers since expression improves with practice. The Iamascope is intended for recipients; however, it has been used in performance.

Greyworld: People passing through an urban space. A supermarket, a foot tunnel, an underpass.

George Lewis: Voyager is a piece for up to two experienced improvisers—Roscoe Mitchell, Douglas Ewart, J. D. Parran, Evan Parker, and myself are among the artists who have performed the piece.

Mitchell Whitelaw: Much of my work has used live sampling, so that while I can interact in detailed ways with the computer to influence sound output, the material I work with is entirely supplied by other player/s or sources. So partly myself, partly other performers.

Carlos Zingaro: Just used the audience some five years ago in a very basic set-up, again for a dance performance. The audience was being recorded with shotgun mics when coming into the venue and while waiting for the performance to start, and this was being looped, manipulated, and triggered by the dancers' movements during the performance. Of course the audience was not active (triggering) during the performance, unless we consider occasional sounds of surprise or laughter when some voices or snippets of conversation were recognized. . . .

(3) How many people can interact with computers during the process of the(se) work(s)?

Greyworld: Depends on the installation. It is not limited by the system, although for meaningful interaction, where each person is aware of [his or her] individual contribution, numbers are reduced. Having said that, [I find that] often people understand the process even in busy commuter areas.

(3a) Do they do so on a one person-one computer or a networked basis?

Greg White: My aim is always a networked environment. In the simplest (most complex?) sense the network is between the ears of the performers and interacts with the acoustic space. The computer as instrument (hyperinstrument, as you would say).

(4) How can people interact with your computer-interactive works? Where necessary, please indicate distinctions between the possibilities available to yourself, to performers, and to screeners, respectively.

Roger Dannenberg: Usually, I write programs that "listen" to the performer, analyzing various features of the performance and sometimes classifying features into a performance style. Music and graphics are generated according to this analysis. Usually, the whole piece is also guided by some sort of overall plan that is not necessarily strict, but which helps with the musical development, taking some of the burden of large-scale structure off of the performer.

Greyworld: They walk on a sensitive floor, they eat from a sensitive table, etc.

George Lewis: Except for the commands "start playing" and "stop playing," which are executed from the computer's keyboard and essentially define the duration of the piece, there exist no means by which the soloist can non-maskably "trigger" the occurrence of a certain kind of musical behavior. The soloist and orchestra must therefore communicate by means of sounds alone. If the soloist wishes to explore a particular musical area, this must be done by improvising in such a way as to influence the direction of the orchestra. If the orchestra "understands," or rather seems to respond to the directions proposed by the soloist, this will immediately become apparent to the soloist, and perhaps to the listeners as well. For a number of reasons, the soloist may at times find inappropriate the orchestra's response to the current musical situation. Since there can be no recourse to a "magic button" that would automatically bring in the desired behavior set [see answer to 5a], the soloist's only recourse must be to attempt to influence the orchestra by playing in the desired manner. Moreover, the orchestra may at times fail to respond (or appear not to respond) to the direction that the soloist is proposing. In such cases, a prudent course of action in terms of the performance might well be for the soloist to go along with the direction proposed by the orchestra until such time as the orchestra seems more amenable to outside influence. On the other hand, the soloist could regard a particular direction proposed by the orchestra as musically or structurally desirable. In this case, the soloist might improvise along the lines suggested by the orchestra, being influenced by it.

Finally, one approach might be for the soloist to simply take a break, that is, to stop playing for a while and let the orchestra play on by itself.

>(4a) What are the physical means?

Roger Dannenberg: Usually microphones or pickups. I've used 3D sensors with a dancer, optically sensed paddles for an audience, and seat-mounted buttons for an audience. Additional input sometimes comes from MIDI keyboards and computer keyboards.

Greyworld: We have developed our own system for the articulation of public spaces called the Layer.

>(4b) Are the interactions offered in live performance?
>(4c) Are they offered over the Web or on CD-ROM?
>(4d) Can the computer user drive the process (which would otherwise rest), or just modify its progression?

Curtis Bahn: My "rig" is a "composed instrument." It is necessarily personal and idiosyncratic, demanding a great number of hours to program and tailor (via sensor mapping and scaling) to my playing and my body. My bass and sensor interface allow approximately 20 streams of continuous gestural control over the computer algorithmic aspect of my performance at any time. Additional buttons and sliders allow the context and mapping of the sensor interface to be adjusted during performance. The meanings of the mappings can change constantly during performance and thus create not a generalized performance interface, but a greatly personalized one. The components of the interface are designed as much as possible to allow them to be configured in any way at any time, feeding into each other, etc.

Roger Dannenberg: Usually, the performer drives the progress of the piece, but some of the "steering" is under computer control even if the performer has the "gas pedal."

Joseph Hyde: Mostly the latter—find this more interesting as a less linear cause-effect relationship.

George Lewis: In a performance of *Voyager,* it is more appropriate to speak of the flow of performance *influence.* According to the musical and philosophical model at the heart of the composition, this flow must be bidirectional. Basically, I look at my pieces as embodying dialogue; the progression won't be known to anyone in advance, though certain behaviors tend to recur, as they might in any system. In both theory and practice, this means that both human musicians and computer programs play central organizing and structuring roles in any performance of these works; neither party should "drive" the process in a dominating way.

Larry Polansky: All my pieces, as far as I can remember, are software platforms for live interaction where the computer is at least reasonably intelligent.

(5) Do you intend that the computer users be able to identify the results of their interaction?

Phil Burk: Once in a museum installation, I was showing someone the abstract shape editor in HMSL, which was directly driving a single melodic line. They used it intently, exploring the various transformations possible. Suddenly, after five minutes, they stood up and said, "Oh my god! The music from the speakers is changing when I use this program." So sometimes even the obvious is not so obvious to anyone but the programmer.

George Lewis: I don't look at the performers as "users." In *Voyager,* the computer system is not an instrument, and therefore cannot be controlled by a performer. Rather, the system is a multi-instrumental player with its own instrument—a battery of synthesizers.

Eric Singer: Yes! This is of utmost importance in new media works. If users cannot identify the results of their interaction, they will be more confused than engaged.

Martin Wesley-Smith: Yes; users need to know what effect their actions are having. The audience, too, needs to see and hear the interactivity working as a performance gesture.

(5a) Can they simply stop/start defined processes, and will this be detectable to them?

Curtis Bahn: The gestural control of my sound processes is an important aspect of my performance, and the musical result. It seems that people can identify, parse, and understand the music better when they can identify its source (in terms of both means of production and location). However, since my sensor mappings change often, it can become confusing, and I don't think anyone would be able to identify exactly what I am doing or controlling in performance, just that my gesture most often relates to an identifiable result in the music.

George Lewis: Generally, I avoid instrumental paradigms wherever possible. One of my personal quibbles with using "magic buttons" to introduce precomposed material, or to force the program to work with a particular set of materials, is that using them interferes with the sharing of the decision-making process as it normally occurs in my pieces and substitutes the button pusher as the final arbiter of what will occur in the performance. The use of magic buttons tends to make difficult or impossible any occurrence of the kinds of events I want to hear in the performance—most especially those kinds of events that relate to the behavior of the composition. In extreme cases, they can even make it difficult to hear whether or not the input analyzers actually work. I would say that using these kinds of structures constitutes a certain gap in the formal structure of the music, which is in turn reflective of a gap in my approach to composing with behavior—in short, not a magic button, but a panic button.

(5b) Can they influence processes in a more subtle way, and will this be detectable?

Phil Burk: In "Nuke" the players control the absorption of "note-rons" in a simulated nuclear reactor. Note-rons are generated by simulated fission events and passed around a MIDI ring. The level of activity is controlled by raising and lowering virtual "control rods." I initially had trouble stabilizing the reactor. It would blow up from positive feedback cycles. I called a friend who worked on a nuclear sub. He explained that as reactor activity levels increase, the reactor heats up and expands, which lets more neutrons escape, thus slowing the reaction. By incorporating this effect into the piece, I was able to make the reactor model stable at any level of activity and thus playable.

Sidney Fels: The influence that I strive for is continuous control. Thus, users/performers typically have analog control over various parameterization of the sound space. The control is usually detectable (at least in the more successful work).

George Lewis: Especially in an open-ended piece like *Voyager*, it's hard to say whether and under what conditions something is detectable. If people detect things they tend to look for other things to detect, and sometimes they construct their own belief systems regarding what has been detected. This construction of belief is more interesting to me than worrying about a one-size-fits-all notion of detectability.

Mitchell Whitelaw: Yes . . . sample- [and] channel-specific parameters include volume, pitch, pan, loop start, loop end, resonance/distortion, [and] playback "pattern" selection. Meta-controls include low-frequency oscillators, which can drive any of these parameters, and sequencers, which can record and play back changes in these parameters.

Carlos Zingaro: That would be ideal, though the problem might be, with most unaware audiences, for them to think that's just prerecorded sounds/music and to not understand the process involved. . . . But then again, is it necessary to "show off" the tech aspect just for them to understand? . . .

> (5c) Is the relationship between the user input and the subsequent computer response fixed or variable, and if so, how?

Phil Burk: The effect is consistent, but sometimes they are controlling a stochastic process, which can have a variable response. But a given gesture will always have the same effect on the probabilities.

Sidney Fels: In Glove-Talk II and Sound Sculpting, the relationship between user action and sound is fixed. This stems from the main focus of the works being for performers and the deterministic behavior is more suitable for learning. In MusiKalscope and Iamascope, this is not the case. In MusiKalscope the relationship changes in accordance with Berkeley jazz theory plus the play from the performers. In the Iamascope, the key structure is modified by the computer so the sounds that are played are not the same for the same body motion. However, the relative note offset is fixed. The fixed relationship, though, is not usually exploited, in my experience.

George Lewis: I guess [my] foregoing [comments] mean that this relationship is designed to be variable. If the computer is not treated as a musical instrument, but as an independent improviser, difference is partly grounded in the form of program responses that are not necessarily predictable on the basis of outside input. *Voyager*'s response to input has several modes, from complete communion to utter indifference. It is a fact that the *Voyager* system is designed to avoid the kind of uniformity in which the same kind of input routinely leads to the same result. This aesthetic of variation and difference is at variance with the information retrieval and control paradigm that late capitalism has found useful in framing its preferred approach to the encounter with computer technology.

In *Voyager,* an aperiodic, asynchronously recurring, global "behavior specification" subroutine called *setphrasebehavior* runs at intervals of between five and seven seconds, continually recombining a set of 64 monophonic MIDI "players" into new ensemble combinations with defined behaviors. This subroutine (or "word," in FORTH parlance) first makes determinations as to how many players will be part of the next ensemble. Additional options include turning off all players in all ensembles and starting afresh with this new group, turning off just the most recently instantiated ensemble, or allowing the new ensemble to enter the fray with the groups that are already playing. The top-level phrase word specifies for the new ensemble choices of timbre, the choice of 1 of 15 melody algorithms, the choice of approximately 150 microtonally specified pitch sets, and choices of volume range, microtonal transposition, tactus, tempo, probability of playing a note, spacing between notes, and interval width range, as well as MIDI-related ornamentation, such as chorusing, reverb, and portamento, and how such parameters as tessitura and tempo can change over time. Moreover, each new ensemble chooses not only a distinct group sonority, but a unique response to input, deciding which improvisers—one, both, or none—will influence its output behavior. Further options include imitating, directly opposing, or ignoring the information coming from the improvisers.

Figure app.1 *Voyager*'s top-level phrase behavior word, written as a FORMULA active process.

```
:ap setphrasebehavior (–)
   ::ap "general phrasing" (task recurs at intervals of 5,000–7,000 ms)
   5,000 time-advance 11 irnd 200*5,000 + to cycle

   begin
   ::ev
   bodymusic 0 =    \ in this version this red light is always zero
      if calcork  \ set up new group of players, including number and position in space
      else allplayersoff  \ turn off all groups and start over with a new group.
      then
\ set up how system will follow input; set MIDI timbres
         setfollowbehavior    setreplies      setvoxbehavior

\ set melody algorithms, pitch sets, reverb, and chorus type
         setwavebehavior       setscalebehavior      setreverbbehavior       setchorusbehavior
              computer solo?                \ if no one is playing, I have a solo

\ set volume, velocity, and microtonal tonic transposition
         if setvelbehavior     setvolbehavior     settonicbehavior
```

Figure app.1 continued.

```
\ set octave, interval range, and duration range
setoctbehavior        setintbehavior        setwidbehavior        setlegatobehavior

\ set length of notes
    bodymusic 0 =        \ in this version this red light is always zero
        if setrestbehavior \ set up average degree of silence
        then

\ set portamento, whether or not to follow tempo, and tempo ranges
        setportabehavior      settempofollow       setspdbehavior
                    then
        ;;ev
        cycle time-advance
        again
        ;;ap
        ;ap
```

The response task word, *setresponse,* which runs asynchronously to the phrase behavior task, processes data from both the low-level MIDI parser, which collects and manages the raw data, and a mid-level smoothing routine, which uses this raw data to construct averages of pitch, velocity, probability of note activity, and spacing between notes. This information is used by *setresponse* to decide in greater detail how each ensemble will respond to elements of the input, such as tempo (speed), probability of playing a note, the spacing between notes, melodic interval width, choice of primary pitch material (including a pitch set based on the last several notes received), octave range, microtonal transposition, and volume.

Figure app.2 *Voyager*'s input response word, written in FORTH, sets parameters based on analysis of MIDI input.

```
: setresponse (--)
    setinputbasedur          \ set tempo ranges based on input note durations
    bodymusic 0 =            \ in this version this red light is always zero
    if setinputplayprob      \ probability of note or rest, based on input
    then

\ set duration, range and length of notes, and interval range
    setinputlegato        setinputwid          setinputint

\ use pitch set based on last few input notes; set octave and microtonal tonic transposition
    setinputscale         setinputoct          setinputtonic

\ set MIDI volume and velocity
    setinputvol           setinputvel
;
```

(5d) Is input information aggregated in any way, so that only the resultant cumulation is responsible for output? How does this work?

Where necessary, please indicate distinctions between the possibilities available to yourself, to performers, and to screeners, respectively.

Roger Dannenberg: I usually collect some history, e.g., with histograms, to try to statistically characterize what the player is doing. This avoids a simple direct connection between input and output, which gets boring, and allows more high-level judgments by the computer as to what the performer is doing.

Joseph Hyde: It is in the case of my latest installation, which "learns" over the course of its six-week showing period.

George Lewis: In *Voyager,* the only elements that are really aggregated are the last five notes played. There are averagers and smoothers (low-pass filters) for pitch, volume, duration, and silence that, by introducing a limited hysteresis, tend to have a similar aggregative intent, though not quite the same function.

In any event, these are all short term. Why is this so? Well, I never saw the need or mandate for the arbitrary reintroduction of prestored material into the improvisative space, simply because the computer made it possible to do so. In fact, I regarded this supposed amelioration (suggested to me by many, many people) as essentially Eurocentric in nature. From an improvisative standpoint, the big formal danger is that reintroducing the material often conflicts with where the piece is actually going. Instead, I proposed an environmental, state-based model in which the global aggregation of sonic information, considered in a temporal sense, is privileged over moments of linear development. Of course, one could create an algorithm that analyzes prestored material (however and whenever gathered) and looks for moments in the prestored stuff that seem compatible with what is currently going on. I suppose I prefer to have the system use that analysis to create new music that is similarly compatible.

Eric Lyon: I generally do not require intelligence from the computer.

Larry Polansky: I've done lots of pieces that collect and analyze information over time. I think this is an important thing to do, much like you would if you were simply improvising together.

(6) Do you view the computer, or the computer network, as itself being in some degree an improviser? Please elaborate.

Curtis Bahn: No.

Phil Burk: No, they are generally just using some algorithm described by the composer to spew out sound under the performer's control. So the computer is acting somewhere along the line between composition and instrument. I believe only the human performer can "improvise" by listening to other musicians or themselves, making musical decisions, and then expressing them on the computer.

Roger Dannenberg: Absolutely. The computer in my pieces generates music, so it becomes a sort of partner to the performer. My goal is to encode some of my compositional ideas into the computer so that they can be realized in performance. This is an alternative to traditional notation. It imposes something on the performer without dictating note-by-note what the performer should do. Ideally, this gives the freedom to improvise and inject new ideas into the piece, but I want there to be a well-defined piece at some level, and that's where the computer's generation is important. I want it to be essential that the performer work with the computer and be guided by it. At the same time, the computer is influenced by the performer.

Jim Franklin: Yes. I choose to "forget" the rules I have programmed, and treat the machine as a partner—sort of an alter ego, since I write the rules. That is, it's my own choice to view the machine in this way.

Greyworld: Yes, we see three authors in our work. Clearly Greyworld are always identified as the authors. We create the installation. But the computer mediates the interaction and creates new sonic elements based on its algorithmic mind, the world we have constructed for it, and its external input. And lastly, the public, when they participate within the work, author their own sound structures, based on their speed, weight, direction, etc.

George Lewis: "A performance of *Voyager* is conceptualized interactionally as multiple parallel streams of music generation, emanating from both the computers and the humans—a nonhierarchical, improvisative, subject-subject model of discourse, rather than a stimulus/response setup. In both theory and practice, this means that both human musicians and computer programs play central organizing and structuring roles in any performance of the work."

Eric Lyon: Not really. More as an environment for growing sounds.

Larry Polansky: Of course.

Eric Singer: Yes. By use of controlled random elements, I have implemented algorithmic computer-generated improvisation.

Greg White: Absolutely. Algorithmic processes can be responsive to other entities on the network.

Carlos Zingaro: That would be the ideal step for me. Of course I'm not intending to replace live musicians by the computer possibilities, as I'm fortunate enough to play with some of the best. On the other hand, I can always give "orders" to the computer—when to play or shut up. . . . That's something that would never cross my mind with other fellow musicians.

(7) Is your use of the computer "embodied" in algorithms you write? If not, please elaborate on your usage. If you do write your own algorithms, then do you see them as
    (7a) Compositions?
    (7b) Material for comprovisation?
    (7c) An improvising entity?

George Lewis: I suppose that this comes closest—*Voyager* as technology-mediated animism.

    (7d) A hyperinstrument?

Phil Burk: That's pretty close. Every instrument affects the type of music played on it. On a computer the effect is more variable.

    (7e) A compositional superstructure that is explored?

Greyworld: No, large elements do not exist before the installation is used.

Larry Polansky: I don't write algorithms, I write software that uses algorithms, which are just ways of doing things. If there's any embodiment, it's the embodiment of ideas, hopefully musically deep and philosophically rich.

    (7f) Exploratory or generative (?) algorithms (in the sense developed by Michael Joyce for discussion of [the] hypertext literature, in which a generative hypertext creates new entities in response to input, whereas an exploratory one reveals entities which were already completely formed but not displayed)?

Greyworld: More like this. . . .

    (7g) Something(s) else??

    Please elaborate in each case relevant to you.

George Lewis: First, please see my response to (1a). Then, please consider this: The concept of a musical composition that exists entirely in software is, as far as real-time computer music is concerned, a natural development of the live electronic music notion of a "hardware composition," or a piece whose "score" is a circuit diagram. Among others, the composers David Behrman and Gordon Mumma, utilizing complex synthesizer patches or employing electronic circuitry of their own design ("homemade" electronics), made pieces that exhibited a kind of "behavior," as distinct from so-called live synthesizer pieces of the period that basically were "performed," running through sequences of precomposed events in essentially traditional fashion.

Greg White: All the above are part of the picture. Some of my programming is interface—provides access to parameters on different machines in a central location [and] . . . visual feedback of ongoing processes. Some is transductive—like the typing display in *Silence of Eyes*—"converting" from one form to another. Most is comprovisational. I am drawn to generative rather than exploratory (as referenced above).

(8) Why do you make computer-interactive work?

Phil Burk: I think that complex mathematical and technical systems can be beautiful and that the best way to experience that beauty is through sound. Not everyone can read the code and say, "Wow, that's gorgeous!"

Sidney Fels: To explore intimacy and embodiment.

Jim Franklin: Because I got sick of human performers who often couldn't figure out (or to whom I couldn't effectively communicate) what I was after.

Greyworld: It gives us the ability to create powerful spaces that react meaningfully to the public. It allows us to "democratize" the process of making art [and] . . . sound.

Joseph Hyde: I believe it opens up new models for human interaction in a performance situation and new modes of performance.

George Lewis: My interactive computer pieces, along with my work in free improvisation and various African American musical traditions, have long been directly concerned with exploring the nature, practice, and functions of sound as discourse, and as history/memory. In *Voyager,* the fluency and variety of the computer's performance, often flawed but in many ways compatible with that of a trained musician, obliged both performers and audiences to come to grips with their idea of creativity and its role in their lives.

Inviting the listener, through improvisation, to speculate upon the epistemological and ontological aspects of musical interaction, is part of the discourse embedded in *Voyager* as a musical experience. I view the performance practice that I have developed for *Voyager* as part of a process of teaching people how to find order in improvised music, without necessarily transforming the performance space into a classroom. This is consistent with the instrumental dimension or tendency in African musical organization, or what Robert Farris Thompson calls "songs and dances of social allusion." I feel completely free to work intuitively while programming computers to create improvisations; the necessary combination of the utterly logical and the completely intuitive is what attracts me to this kind of work.

For me computer music can be a powerful symbolic way of doing philosophy or sociology, manifesting resistance, and presenting alternative solutions to both musical and social problems. Charlie Parker told an interviewer, "Music is your own experience, your thoughts, your wisdom. If you don't live it, it won't come out of your horn." The clear implication is that what you do live does come out of your horn. Far from being nonreferential, pure, or abstract, I see my music as taking a direct part in the dialogue about our planetary situation.

Greg White: [I'm] drawn to the modeling of ideas in a real-time environment at once suitable for exploration, performance, and development of objects (compositions, recordings).

Mitchell Whitelaw: In regard to the Omnivore [an ensemble]-live interactive improvisation stuff, a fascination with the sonic possibilities and the possibilities of a particularly restricted approach (live sampling). So it's exploring the idea of a kind of electroacoustic music that is as spontaneous and ephemeral as possible, tied to the smallest possible number of preexisting structures and decisions. So it's a kind of music that tries to work very much in its own present—the ongoing moment of its own creation. More generally, in regard to this work and other solo experiments (not all of which use live sampling): interactive computer processes allow me to create music, in real time, which other processes simply would not. For example a current project involves a system which rapidly switches, in real time, between four concurrent stereo audio streams. "Playing" the music is in fact simply making decisions about the patterns of this switching. It's a simple premise but relies on real-time programmable DSP.

(9) Can computer interaction provide unique opportunities/outputs? If so, could you elaborate?

Curtis Bahn: One thing I see as being very new is the notion of the "composed instrument" an interface whose potentials and scope are dynamic; a compositional structure of musical possibilities with the agency of their realization given to the performer. This presents a view of personal creativity and expression in performance as being primary over technological structures, and is antithetical to the traditional "tape-and" performance with the poor human struggling to overcome the "tyranny" of the unyielding tape while attempting to present a smooth and polished performance.

Roger Dannenberg: I think I have had many musical opportunities working in this way that would not arise otherwise.

Gerhard Eckel: It may allow a musically untrained audience to explore music on a structural level.

Sidney Fels: The main point I feel that computer interaction provides is a separation of sound and the physical cause of that sound. This provides new directions for improvisation, musical expression, and collaborative sound production.

Jim Franklin: Yes. I treat it, rather egoistically, as a sort of self-multiplication/replication—allows me to perform with myself in an interactive fashion, not possible with works for recorded medium and instrument.

Joseph Hyde: Yes—specifically in a multiuser situation, which can offer a sophisticated and complex way to control a performative entity.

George Lewis: I'm taking this to be a version of the FAQ "What do you get out of improvising with computers that you don't get from improvising with people?" I invert this question to maintain that the most important formal issues in this sort of music concern how a program operating in a conceptual space compatible with group improvisation might have the *same* set of problems as a human musician—namely, how sonic behavior, communication, personal narrative, and intersubjectivity affect musical form. These are the issues that I am addressing, and they don't go away simply by adding megabytes or megahertz to the host system's capabilities. These deeper issues are the interesting ones for me—finding similarity and difference at the same time.

Eric Lyon: This remains to be proved with respect to live improvisation. It seems that it should, but real time imposes two important limitations: processing CPU cycles and thus depth of DSP processing, and operator attention and physical-control bandwidth limitations. That has to be weighed against the "feel factor" of direct control inaccessible in batch mode.

Eric Singer: As far as uniqueness [goes], the hyperinstrument concept is important here. Computers are able to generate certain types of output that are physically impossible for humans to do in a manual way.

Martin Wesley-Smith: It allows, partly through chance, new processes, sound masses, visual shapes, color combinations, etc., as well as combinations of sound and image, to be discovered. It stimulates the imagination in ways other processes cannot do so practicably. It allows rich timbral (sound and image) possibilities within a fluid, nonfixed creative process. It allows a performer to be a co-composer (with the "composer"/programmer), allowing her to use her performance and improvisation skills to control the direction and large-scale form of a piece. It will enliven the live concert scene. It allows audience participation in a meaningful way, particularly over the Net. It is poised to take advantage of new convergent media. It allows effective instruction in many fields as well as in music, where it can improve hand-eye coordination, listening skills, etc., and promote the ability to see abstractions (in sound, image, ideas, etc.)....

Greg White: Unique advantages:
- the extensible nature of the computer (to LAN to Internet)
- simultaneous access to multiple physical spaces
- multidisciplinary with transference of processes between media

Mitchell Whitelaw: Yes, see [earlier quotations]. But also more.... It has the potential to radically transform established conventions for sound [and] music making; e.g., potential for distributed control (either local or networked) and multiplayer instruments ... interaction with nonhuman processes (deterministic, stochastic, algorithmic, or responsive artificial agencies), etc....

(10) Are there any aspects of computer interaction you would like to point out as important to sound improvisation? Please elaborate.

Curtis Bahn: I understand the notion of unexpected results in computer-interactive performance as presenting a soundscape that may draw solo improvisers outside themselves in performance, challenging them, urging them to new areas. However, in a group performance especially, the integration of an autonomous technological voice has most often seemed to me to hinder the rapid exchange of human interaction. It also questions the meaning of human communication in improvisation.... I am interested in structures extending the personal creative and interactive potentials of the participants in a musical situation, assigning the agency for their realization completely with the performer in a way that will maximize the direct human contact of the moment. I think that this is actually an important image of our projected human relationships within an increasingly technological society.

Gerhard Eckel: Any other interaction would be better than computer interaction, but the sound processing capabilities of computers are important for my work.

Joseph Hyde: For me, live sampling is very important as a way of working with aural memory and integrated sound worlds.

Jonathan Impett: Looking at Adorno, Boulez, Eco, Ligeti, and Xenakis c. 1957–65, what seems to have emerged in post-high-modernist theory (i.e., after the collapse of the integral serialism experiment) was a new sense of the "spatialization" of what had previously been considered naturally temporal structures in "out-of-time" spaces. The tension . . . between these is then what drives/informs the actual sequence of events. One might say that the situated, interactive context is the only one in which this tension can be resolved in a nonarbitrary way, in a juggling act maintaining a critical balance of closure and openness, in the generation of linked "hyper-times," as it were. We might justly say that all music works this way, but as Eco points out, we can only say that because this is the natural way of looking at such things for our time.

Philip Johnson-Laird: My only real thought is that the best programs for improvising seem, at present, to depend on procedures that strike me as psychologically implausible. There's a parallel with speech synthesis: the best programs are engineering kludges, and not psychologically plausible.

George Lewis [in response to a follow-up query from me as to whether computer programs inevitably involve Eurologic]: You could also look at this article—my part of it has the nascent version of my concerns: R. Rowe, B. Garton, P. Desain, H. Honing, G. Lewis, et al., "Putting Max In Perspective," *Computer Music Journal* 17, no. 2 (Summer 1993): 3–11. There my main complaint about MAX was not about the program's structure, but about how its users tended not to notice how their use of the program constructed not merely Eurological, but frankly Eurocentric approaches to musical form. As the program developed through community contributions, both the Eurocentricity of that community and its reliance on high-culture notions of musical aesthetics started to embed itself in the contributed code.

In contrast, my idea is that that one should be able to transform the platform based upon one's own way of looking at the world, perhaps in the manner that African American musical practice transformed European-based instruments to the point that one of them, the saxophone, was essentially disowned by its parent tribe. Jon Rose's work on bringing together the multiplicity of cultures that use the violin (as I encountered it at the DAAD show in Berlin) emphasized this notion of transformation. I believe that Steve Coleman (now at UC Berkeley, <mbase@cnmat.berkeley.edu>) has been able to do this with MAX; you might want to query him about his recent Ircam premiere.

Computer program code need not become the ultimate site of Eurological essence. I would agree with the import of Georgina Born's work on Ircam, namely that music technology tends to reflect the uses for which it is envisioned, and that ethnographic study of the field needs to take musical vision into account. Certainly Ron Kuivila's catholicity of musical vision (with code examples from Conlon Nancarrow to Sonny Rollins) informed the structure of the FORMULA platform.

[I e-mailed George Lewis the following question in the context of the possibility implied by his writings that Afrological musicality emphasizes "narrative."]

Roger Dean: How do you see this relating to the version of analysis of the postmodern that emphasizes its defiance of meta-narrative?

George Lewis: Seems to fit in rather well with the idea that instead of the defining grand narrative, what we have with improvisers today is a multiplicity (or, using Gilroy's term, "polyphony") of narratives.

Eric Lyon: Controllers with higher resolution, lower latency and [that are] more physically and tactilely attractive. More-nuanced software mediation.

Jeff Pressing: Physicality is essential to get engagement. Without it there is no stage projection.

Martin Wesley-Smith: Composers, performers, and composer/performers can explore and exploit, in real time, densities; sonic shapes; sounds that move in 360 degree space with specific directions, velocities, accelerations, etc.; spoken and sung texts that can change according to directions given (played) by the performer; and concrete sounds—of, say, recognizable objects—that can be transformed and placed anywhere on the recognizability-unrecognizability scale. . . .

(11) If convenient, please send me a list (or give me a Web address) of your relevant work. . . .

(12) Please indicate whether you have software that might be suitable and available for inclusion in a CD-ROM accompanying the book. I have in mind algorithmic patches in MAX, MSP, or other platforms, including audiovisual work. There will be scope for some relevant sound examples also. I am also interested in any material you might suggest beyond t

Phil Burk: Examples on my Web site at <http://www.softsynth.com/jsyn>, and "Yuppies in the Jungle," in which a custom 56,000 DSP board is controlled by HMSL running on an Amiga. Various live DSP sounds are triggered by a MIDI keyboard to accompany a spoken text. My TransJam/WebDrum **is** a drum pattern editor, melody editor, and envelope editor are controlled from a Java Applet running in a Web browser. Multiple performers can share and edit the same musical material using a central custom server. See my article "Jammin on the Web," in Proceedings of the International Computer Music Conference 2000, International Computer Music Association, page 117.

(13) Please list a few of your musical peers relevant to the field of computer-interactive sound improvisation whom you think of interest yet unlikely to be known already to a British Australian musician living in Sydney.

[It would be invidious to specify the sources of the suggestions below, and few of the names put forward were unfamiliar to me. The nominees are listed here if they are not mentioned significantly in the book, as pointers to interesting creators in the field; I of course followed up the work of all the nominated people with great pleasure.]

Extractor, led by Andrew Deakin
Toshio Iwai (interactive artworks)

Ron Kuivila
Jonatas Manzolli (interactive composition systems)
Alzek Misheff (sound painting using a Lightning)
Dafna Naphtali
K. Nishimoto (working on general multimedia instruments)
Ake Parmerud
Matt Rogalsky
Joel Ryan
Sten Sandell
Daniel Scheidt
Satosi Simura, shakuhachi/electronics
S. Takahashi (improvisation with sound and movement)

Eric Lyon: They're all famous already.

APPENDIX 2

The CD-ROM

The material on the CD-ROM is by the author unless otherwise stated. All performance rights are reserved. All material remains the copyright of its author(s) and is only released here to be used in conjunction with the book and for educational (non-commercial) purposes. In all cases, the authors are delighted to have their work presented and used, but please seek permission for public use. Authors' contacts are given on the readme of the CD-ROM and may also be readily obtained from the Web.

■ COMPACT DISC AUDIO

Compact Disc Audio
Audio Recordings of Interactive Software Performance
(use in a CD player or with Mac CD or DVD drives)

Sizing the Tools *Drum and bass machine, alias Dr. Metagroove (MAX) mastered by Greg White, 1998*

LowHz: An Excerpt from an Immersive Soundevent Using MSP and GRM Tools *Martin Ng and Roger Dean, 2000*

Sbass *Curtis Bahn, 2001* (interactive performance using the Rig, from the album of the same name, Electronic Music Foundation CD 030)

■ CD-ROM MATERIAL

Software Modules (Mac only):
Recombine (MAX)

Transposer (MAX)
MidiController Controller (MAX) Greg White

Software Patches (Mac only)

Rhythm Engine (MAX) austraLYSIS Rhythm Machine
Ostinato (MAX)

Where/Samples (MSP) (DSP modification patch)
Twittering Drum Machine (MSP) Eric Lyon

ChaosBand (MAX) Per-Anders Nilsson

StepTrance (MSP) Mitchell Whitelaw

Web and CD-ROM Pieces (Cross-platform)

Wordstuffs (MIDI) Hazel Smith, Roger Dean, and Greg White, 1998 (interactive web sound, image, animation, text for Netscape)
Sympathetic Strings Roger Dean and Darani Lewers, 2000 (interactive Flash piece, image and sound; n.b.: use the FlashPlayer with plenty of memory allocated)
The Centre Series: Sites in Sound Roger Dean and Darani Lewers, 2000 (interactive sound field with independent [noninteractive] animation)

Compressed Audio (Cross-platform)

AI-Generated Performance *Virtual Bird* (Quicktime) Paul Hodgson, software created 1995

Compressed Audio/Image (Cross-platform)

Documentation of Evolutionary Audio/Image *Listening Sky* (Quicktime) Rod Berry and Colleagues, 2000

Other Items (Mac only)

MAXMSPPlayPPC3.5.9 (freely distributable "player" application for MAX and MSP with which the MAX/MSP patches provided can be played on a Macintosh computer)
Image of the Rig Setup Curtis Bahn (bahnrig.tif: cross-platform)

■ README

For the CD/CD-ROM as a text and as a PDF file

References, Selected Bibliography, and Discography

This list contains all the materials cited in the body of the text, together with some additional relevant bibliography and discography. Some of the citations are to Web locations, which are sometimes given here, sometimes a movable feast. However, note that there is a separate appendix of useful Web sites, and that advice on efficiently locating removed, new, and additional relevant sites is provided there.

Alparova, N. 1994. "'Sound Finds Me': Improvisation on the Theme of 'The Composer in the World of Electronics'." *Muzykal'naja akademija* 4: 31–33.

———. 1995. "Who is Sergej Zagnij?" *Muzykal'naja akademija* 2: 53–57

Ames, C. 1987. "Automated Composition in Retrospect: 1956–1986." *Leonardo* 20, no. 2: 169–85.

Ames, R. 1996. "Morton Subotnick's Making Music." *Computer Music Journal* 20, no. 4: 60.

Anonymous. "Clara Rockmore, 1911–1998." 1998. *Computer Music Journal* 22, no. 4: 14.

Appleton, J. H., and R. C. Perera, eds. 1975. *The Development and Practice of Electronic Music*. Englewood Cliffs, N.J.: Prentice-Hall.

Assayag, G., S. Dubnov, and O. Deleru. 1999. "Guessing the Composer's Mind: Applying Universal Prediction to Musical Style." Paper presented at the International Computer Music Conference of the International Computer Music Association, Beijing 1999.

austraLYSIS Electroband. 1997. *Present Tense*. Tall Poppies CD TP 109.

———. 2000. *Lysis Lives: Resounding in the Mirror*. Future Music Records CD 73-0900

Bahn, C. 2000. *The Rig: Solo Improvisations for Sensor Bass And Live Electronics*. Electronic Music Foundation (EMF) CD 030.

Bailey, D. 1992. *Improvisation: Its Nature and Practice in Music.* Rev. ed. London: British Library. Bartlett, M. 1985. "Software for a Microcomputer-Controlled Synthesizer for Live Performance." In *Foundations of Computer Music,* edited by C. Roads and J. Strawn. Cambridge: MIT Press.

Bel, B., and J. Kippen. 1992. "Identifying Improvisation Schemata with QAVAID." *Computing in Musicology* 8: 115–19.

Bell, K., L. Connellan, and D. Toop, eds/curators. 2000. *Sonic Boom: The Art of Sound.* London: South Bank Centre. (book and CD).

Benedikt, M., ed. 1991. *Cyberspace: First Steps.* Cambridge: MIT Press.

Berry, M. 1999. "An Introduction to Grainwave." *Computer Music Journal* 23, no. 1: 57–61.

Bievre, G. 1991. "The Improvisation Moderator: An Interview with Nicolas Collins." *Musicworks* 49: 28–36.

Biles, J. A. "Interactive GenJam: Integrating Real-Time Performance with a Genetic Algorithm." See Biles's Web site: www.it.rit.edu/~jab.

———."Life with GenJam: Interacting with a Musical IGA (interactive genetic algorithm)." Web site.

Bischoff, J., R. Gold, and J. Horton. 1985. "Music for an Interactive Network of Microcomputers." In *Foundations of Computer Music,* edited by C. Roads and J. Strawn. Cambridge: MIT Press.

Boden, M. 1991. *The Creative Mind: Myths and Mechanisms.* New York: Basic Books.

Bongers, B. 1998. "An Interview with Sensorband." *Computer Music Journal* 22, no. 1: 13–24.

Boon, J.-P., and O. Decroly. 1995. "Dynamical Systems Theory for Music Dynamics." *Chaos* 5: 501–8.

Borchers, J., and M. Mühlhäuser. 1998. "Design Patterns for Interactive Musical Systems." *IEEE Multimedia* 5, no. 3: 36–46.

Born, G. 1995. *Rationalizing Culture: IRCAM, Boulez, and the Institutionalization of the Musical Avant-Garde.* Berkeley and Los Angeles: University of California Press.

Braxton, A. 1985. *Tri-Axium Writings.* Dartmouth, N.H.: Synthesis Music and Frog Peak.

Bregman Studio, Dartmouth College, USA. 2000. *Electro-Acoustic Music at Dartmouth.* Dartmouth College, NH. CD-ROM [no catalog number].

Brown, C. 1989. *Snakecharmer.* Artifact Recordings CD ART 1001.

———. 1996. *Duets.* Artifact Recordings CD ART 1016.

Brown, C., J. Bischoff, and T. Perkis. 1996. "Bringing Digital Music to Life." *Computer Music Journal* 20, no. 2: 28–32.

Brown, R., and M. Griese. 2000. *Electronica Dance Music Programming Secrets.* 2d ed. Harlow, UK: Pearson Education.

Burt, W. 1988. "The 3DIS System: A New Computer Control System." *Sounds Australian* 19: 28–33.

———. 2000. "A Happy Glut of Windows Music Shareware and Software: Some Personal Selections." EMF Worldwide Guide, at <www.emf.org>.

Burtner, M. 1998. *Portals of Distortion.* Innova CD 526.

Burton, A. R., and T. Vladimirova. 1999. "Generation of Musical Sequences with Genetic Techniques." *Computer Music Journal* 23, no. 4: 59–73.

Carroll, J. M. 1997. "Human-Computer Interaction: Psychology as a Science of Design." *Annual Review of Psychology* 48: 61–83.

Chadabe, J. 1989. "Interactive Composing: An Overview." In *The Music Machine: Selected Readings from "Computer Music Journal,"* edited by C. Roads. Cambridge: MIT Press.

———. 1992. "Flying through a Musical Space: About Real-Time Composition." In *Companion to Contemporary Musical Thought,* vol. 1, edited by J. Paynter, T. Howell, R. Orton, and P. Seymour. London: Routledge.

———. 1997. *Electric Sound: The Past and Promise of Electronic Music.* Upper Saddle River, N.J.: Prentice-Hall.

Chion, M. 1994. *Audio Vision.* New York: Columbia University Press.

CNMAT. www.cnmat.berkeley.edu.

Collier, G. L., and J. L. Collier. 1996. Microrhythms in Jazz: A Review of Papers. *Annual Review of Jazz Studies* 8: 117–39.

Cook, P. R., ed. 1999. *Music, Cognition, and Computerized Sound: An Introduction to Psychoacoustics.* Cambridge: MIT Press.

Cope, D. {N.d } *Classical Music Composed by Computer: Experiments in Musical Intelligence.* Centaur Records CD 2329.

Cope, D. 1991. *Computers and Musical Style.* Oxford: Oxford University Press.

———. 1997. "The Composer's Underscoring Environment, CUE." *Computer Music Journal* 21, no. 3: 20–37.

Corcoran, M. 1999. "Life and Death in the Digital World of the Plaintext Players (Online Improvisation)." *Leonardo* 32: 359–64.

Cross, I. 1998a. "Music Analysis and Music Perception." *Music Analysis* 17: 3–20.

———. 1998b. "Music and Science: Three Views." *Revue belge de musicologie* 52: 207–14.

Cutler, C. 1995. *p53.* London, ReR Megacorp, CD {no catalog number}.

Dannenberg, R. 1989. "A Composed Improvisation." On CD in *Current Directions in Computer Music Research,* edited by M. V. Mathews and J. Pierce. Cambridge: MIT Press.

Dannenberg, R. B. 1993. "Software support for interactive multimedia." *Journal of New Music Research* 22: 213–28.

Davies, H. 1992. "New Musical Instruments in the Computer Age: Amplified Performance Systems and Related Examples of Low-Level Technology." In *Companion to Contemporary Musical Thought,* vol. 1, edited by J. Paynter, T. Howell, R. Orton, and P. Seymour. London: Routledge.

———, ed. 1967. *A Bibliography of Electronic Music.* Cambridge: MIT Press.

Dean, R. T. 1989. *Creative Improvisation: Jazz, Contemporary Music, and Beyond.* Milton Keynes: Open University Press.

———. 1992. *New Structures in Jazz and Improvised Music since 1960.* Milton Keynes: Open University Press.

———. 1997a. "Jazz, Improvisation, and Brass." In *The Cambridge Companion to Brass,* edited by J. Wallace and T. Herbert. Cambridge: Cambridge University Press.

———. 1997b. "Polyphonies of Pulse: On the Control of Pulse and Meter in Computer-Interactive Improvisation." *MikroPolyphonie,* <http://farben.latrobe.edu.au/mikropol>.

———. 1998. "Computer Modelling of Swing." Paper read at the Australasian Computer Music Association Annual Conference, Canberra, Australia, 1998.

Desain, P., and H. Honing. 1999. Computational Models of Beat Induction: The Rule Based Approach. *Journal of New Music Research* 28: 29–42.

Deutsch, D., ed. 1999. *The Psychology of Music.* 2d ed. San Diego: Academic Press.

Dodge, C., and T. A. Jerse. 1997. *Computer Music: Synthesis, Composition, and Performance.* 2d ed. New York: Schirmer Books.

Dolby, T., T. Dougherty, J. Eichenseer, W. Martens, M. Mills, and J. S. Mountford. 1999. Interactive Music Generation System Making Use of Global Feature Control by Non-Musicians. Patent Application, available on IBM Intellectual Property Network. (see Table 11.1 on p. 154 of the present book).

Duesenberg, J. 1999. M. *Electronic Musician.* East, Z. 1995. Review of *Voyager. Computer Music Journal* 19, no. 1: 109–10.

Eckel, G., and V. Royer. 2000. "Traverse." International Computer Music Conference of the International Computer Music Association, 2000, Berlin [track on CD].

Emmerson, S. 1991. "Live Electronic Music in Britain: Three Case Studies." *Contemporary Music Review* 6: 179–95.

———. 1996. " 'Live' versus 'Real-Time'." *Contemporary Music Review* 10: 95–101.

Ernst, D. 1977. *The Evolution of Electronic Music.* New York: Schirmer.

Fels, S., K. Nishimoto, and K. Mase. 1998. "MusiKalscope: A Graphical Musical Instrument." *IEEE Multimedia* 5, no. 3: 26–35.

Fiske, J. 1994. *Media Matters: Everyday Culture and Political Change.* Minneapolis: University of Minnesota Press.

Forum, E. 1993. "Putting Max in Perspective." *Computer Music Journal* 17, no. 2: 3–11.

Fry, C. 1989. "Flavor Band: A Language for Specifying Musical Style." In *The Music Machine: Selected Readings from "Computer Music Journal,"* ed. C. Roads. Cambridge: MIT Press.

Fryer, T. 1999. "When Is a Guitar Not a Guitar?" *Chroma: Journal of the Australasian Computer Music Association* 25 [online] Garrigus, S. R. 1999. "Interactive Web Music." *Electronic Music* (October).

Gehlhaar, R. 1991. "Sound ↔ Space An Interactive Musical Environment." *Contemporary Music Review* 6, no. 1: 59–72.

Gervas, P. 2000. "WASP: Evaluation of Different Strategies for the Automatic Generation of Spanish Verse." In *Proceedings of the AISB 2000 Symposium on Creative and Cultural Aspects and Applications of AI and Cognitive Science.* Birmingham, England: Society for the Study of Artificial Intelligence and the Simulation of Behaviour.

Giomi, F., and M. Ligabue. 1991. "Computational Generation and Study of Jazz Music." *Interface: Journal of New Music Research* 20, no. 1: 47–63.

Griffiths, P. 1979. *A Guide to Electronic Music.* London: Thames and Hudson.

Grime, T. 2000. Untitled presentation in Symposium on Sound and Image, February 14, 2000, Sydney.

Gruppo di Improvisazione Nuova Consonanza Milan. {Eponymous.} Audio recording RCA Italiana MILDS 20273; DGG 643541.

Hajdu, G. 1990. "The Domestication of Chance: Klarenz Barlow's Computer Program AUTOBUSK." *Neue Zeitschrift für Musick* 151, no. 7–8: 8–14.

Haken, L., E. Tellman, and P. Wolfe. 1998. "An Indiscrete Music Keyboard." *Computer Music Journal* 22, no. 1: 30–48.

Hamman, M. 1999. "From Symbol to Semiotic: Representation, Signification, and the Composition of Music Interaction." *Journal of New Music Research* 28, no. 2: 90–104.

Hiller, L. A., and L. M. Isaacson. 1959. *Experimental Music: Composition with an Electronic Computer.* New York: McGraw-Hill.

Hodeir, A. 1995. "Two Times for Research." *Musurgia: Analyse et pratique musicales* 2, no. 3: 35–42.

Hodgson, P. 1990. "Understanding Computing, Cognition, and Creativity." MSc thesis, University of the West of England.

———. 1994. "Modelling Cognition in Creative Musical Improvisation: 'The Improviser Program'." Conference Presentation, England.

———. 2000 *Modelling Cognition in Creative Musical Improvisation.* University of Sussex, UK, PhD thesis.

Holmes, T. 1985. *Electronic and Experimental Music.* New York: Charles Scribner's Sons.

Hub. 1989. *Computer Network Music.* Artifact Recordings CD ART 1002.

———. 1994. *Wreckin' Ball.* Artifact Recordings CD ART 1008.

Hunt, A., R. Kirk, and R. Orton. 1990. "MidiGrid: An Innovative Computer-Based Performance and Composition System." Presented at the International Computer Music Conference, of the International Computer Music Association. Glasgow, UK.

Hunt, A., R. Kirk, R. Orton, and B. Merrison. 1998. "A Generic Model for Compositional Approaches to Audiovisual Media." *Organised Sound* 3: 199–209.

Impett, J. 1994a. *Ladder of Escape 7.* Attacca, Babel 9476.

———. 1994b. "A Meta-Trumpet(-er)." Presented at the International Computer Music Conference, International Computer Music Association. Aarhus, Denmark

———. 1996. "Projection and Interactivity of Musical Structures in *Mirror-Rite*." *Organised Sound* 1: 203–11.

———. 1998a. "The Identification and Transposition of Authentic Instruments: Musical Practice and Technology." *Leonardo* 8: 21–26.

———. 1998b. "Modelling the Dynamics of Musical Engagement." In *Emotional and Intelligent: The Tangled Knot of Cognition,* edited by D. Canamero. Menlo Park, Calif.: AAAI Press.

———. In press. "Situating the *Invention* in Interactive Music." *Organised Sound.*

International MIDI Association, 1983. *MIDI 1.0 Specification.* Los Angeles: International MIDI Association.

Jaffe, D. A., and W. A. Schloss. 1994. "The Computer-Extended Ensemble." *Computer Music Journal* 18, no. 2: 78–86.

Johnson-Laird, P. N. 1991. "Jazz Improvisation: A Theory at the Computational Level." In *Representing Musical Structure,* edited by P. Howell, R. West, and I. Cross. London: Academic Press.

Kager, R. 1998. "Poetry of the Moment: Interactive Compositions of the Austrian Composer Karlheinz Essl." *Neue Zeitschrift für Musik* 159: 10–11.

Kahn, D. 1999. *Noise Water Meat: A History of Sound in the Arts.* Boston: MIT Press.

Keller, P. 1999. "Attending in Complex Musical Interactions: The Adaptive Dual Role of Meter." *Australian Journal of Psychology* 51: 166–175.

Kershaw, D. 1992. "Music and Image on Film and Video: An Absolute Alternative." In *Companion to Contemporary Musical Thought,* vol. 1, edited by J. Paynter, T. Howell, R. Orton, and P. Seymour. London: Routledge.

Kimura, M. 1995. "Performance Practice in Computer Music." *Computer Music Journal* 19, no. 1: 64–75.

Kippen, J. 1992. "Tabla Drumming and the Human-Computer Interaction." *World of Music: Journal of the International Institute for Traditional Music* 34, no. 3: 72–98.

Kirk, R., and A. Hunt. 1998. *Digital Sound Processing for Music And Multimedia.* Oxford: Butterworth-Heinemann.

Krefeld, V. 1990. "The Hand in the Web: An Interview with Michel Waisvisz." *Computer Music Journal* 14, no. 1: 28–33.

Kurzweil, R. 1999. *The Age of Spiritual Machines: When Computers Exceed Human Intelligence.* Sydney: Allen and Unwin.

Large, E. W., C. Palmer, and J. B. Pollack. 1995. "Reduced Memory Representations for Music. *Cognitive Science* 19: 53–96.

Laubier, S. D. 1998. "The Meta-Instrument." *Computer Music Journal* 22, no. 1: 25–29.

Laurel, B. 1993. *Computers as Theatre.* Reading, Mass.: Addison-Wesley.

League of Automatic Composers [John Bischoff, Paul DeMarinis, Phil Harmonic, Frankie Mann, Maggie Payne and Blue Jean Tyranny]. Audio LP released by Lovely Music VR-101-06.

Leonard, N. 1996a. "'Legacy: San Lazaro': The Integration of Composition, Performance, and Computer Programming." *Computers and Mathematics with Applications* 32: 89–92.

———. 1996b. "A Personal Approach to Contemporary Jazz: Works for Saxophone and Computer-Controlled Electronics." *Leonardo Music Journal* 6: 15–20.

Levitt, D. 1984. "Machine Tongues X: Constraint Languages." *Computer Music Journal* 8: 9–21.

Lewis, G. 1993. *Voyager.* Disk Union, CD AVAN 014.

———. 1995. Singing the alternative interactivity blues. *Front* 7: 18–22; reprinted in Grantmakers in the Arts, 8 No 1 (1997).

———. 1996. Improvised Music since 1950: Afrological and Eurological Perspectives. *Black Music Research Journal* 16: 91–122.

———. 1999b. Interacting with Latter-Day Musical Automata. *Contemporary Music Review* 18: 99–112.

———. 2000. *Endless Shout.* Tzadik.

Löthe, M. 2000. "Knowledge-Based Composition of Classical Minuets by a Computer." *Proceedings of the AISB 2000 Symposium on Creative and Cultural Aspects and Applications of AI and Cognitive Science.* Birmingham, England: Society for the Study of Artifical Intelligence and the Simulation of Behaviour.

Lunenfeld, P., ed. 1999. *The Digital Dialectic.* Cambridge: MIT Press.

Manning, P. 1985. *Electronic and Computer Music.* Oxford: Clarendon Press.

Manowski, W. 2000. Untitled presentation in Symposium on Sound and Image, February 14, 2000, Sydney.

Marty, E. 1998. "Events: San Francisco Contemporary Music Payers and CNMAT in Concert." *Computer Music Journal* 22, no. 4: 76–79.

Mathews, M. V. 1969. *Technology of Computer Music.* Cambridge: MIT Press.

Mathews, M. V., F. R. Moore, and J. C. Risset. 1974. "Computers and Future Music." *Science* 183: 263–68

Mazolli, J. 1996. CD Review. *Computer Music Journal* 20, no. 1: 113–15.

McCullough, M. 1996. *Abstracting Craft: The Practiced Digital Hand.* Cambridge: MIT Press.

Minsky, M. 1987. *The Society of Mind.* New York: Simon and Schuster.

Miranda, E. R. 1998. "Parallel Computing for Musicians." Paper presented at the Fifth Brazilian Symposium on Computer Music, Belo Horizonte, 1998, available on the web.

Modler, P., and R. Kirk. 1999. "Evaluation of Architectures for Sound Generation Systems with Respect to Interactive Gestural Control and Realtime Performance." Paper presented at the International Computer Music Conference of the International Computer Music Association, Beijing, 1999.

Morrill, D., and P. R. Cook. 1989. "Hardware, Software, and Compositional Tools for a Real Time Improvised Solo Trumpet Work." Paper presented at the International Computer Music Conference of the International Computer Music Association.

Morris, A., ed. 1997. *Sound States: Innovative Poetics and Acoustical Technologies.* Chapel Hill: University of North Carolina Press.

Mumma, G. 1975. "Live-Electronic Music." In *The Development and Practice of Electronic Music,* edited by J. H. Appleton and R. C. Perera. Englewood Cliffs, N.J.: Prentice-Hall.

Musica Elettronica Viva, *Live Electronic Music Improvised.* Audio LP Mainstream MS 5002.

———. {N.d.} Audio LP *The Sound Pool.* BYG 529 326 (actuel 26).

Narmour, E. 1977. *Beyond Schenkerism.* Chicago: University of Chicago Press.

———. 1989. *The Analysis and Cognition of Basic Melodic Structures.* Chicago: University of Chicago Press.

———. 1992. *The Analysis and Cognition of Melodic Complexity*. Chicago: University of Chicago Press.

Nettl, B., and M. Russell, eds. 1998. *In the Course of Performance: Studies in the World of Musical Improvisation*. Chicago: University of Chicago Press.

Neumark, N. 2000. "Making Contact with Artful CD-ROMS." *IEEE Multimedia* 7, no. 1: 4–6.

Orton, R. 1992. "From Improvisation to Composition." In *Companion to Contemporary Musical Thought*, vol. 2, edited by J. Paynter, T. Howell, R. Orton, and P. Seymour. London: Routledge.

———. 1996. "Design Strategies for Algorithmic Composition." *Contemporary Music Review* 15, no. 3–4: 39–48.

Ostertag, B. 2000. "All the rage." In *Arcana: Musicians on Music*, edited by J. Zorn. New York: Granary Books.

Pachet, F., G. Ramalho, and J. Carrive. 1996. "Representing Temporal Musical Objects and Reasoning in the MusES System." *Journal of New Music Research* 25, no. 3: 252–75.

Palmer, C. 1997. Music Performance. *Annual Review of Psychology* 48: 115–38.

Paradiso, J., and N. Gershenfeld. 1997. "Musical Applications of Electric Field Sensing." *Computer Music Journal* 21, no. 2: 69–89.

Paradiso, J. A. 1999. "The Brain Opera Technology: New Instrument and Gesture Sensors for Musical Interaction and Performance." *Journal of New Music Research* 28: 130–49.

Parker, E. 1999. *Drawn Inward*. ECM 1693.

Parker, E., and L. Casserley. 1997. *Solar Wind*. Touch Records, CD TO 35.

Peebles, S. 1996. "High-Tech versus My-Tech: Developing Systems for Electroacoustic Improvisation and Composition." *Musicworks* 66: 4–13.

Pennycook, B., D. R. Stammen, and D. Reynolds. 1993. "Toward a Computer Model of a Jazz Improviser." Paper presented at the International Computer Music Conference, 1993 of the International Computer Music Association.

Penrose, C., and E. Lyon. 2000. "FFTease: A Collection of Signal Processors for Max/MSP." Paper presented at the International Computer Music Conference 2000, Berlin, of the International Computer Music Association.

Perkis, T. 1993. "The Impact of Computer Technology on the Artistic Process." Paper presented at the Conference on Computers, Freedom, and Privacy, San Francisco, 1993, available on the web.

———. 1998. "Complexity in the American Experimental Music Tradition." Present in the conference "Complexity and Art," (Abisko, Sweden; unpublished; available on the Web at the Artifact site.

———. 1999. "Digital Music under the Stars." *Computer Music Journal* 23, no. 1: 78–79.

Polansky, L. 1989. "Interview with David Rosenboom." In *The Music Machine: Selected Readings from "Computer Music Journal,"* edited by C. Roads. Cambridge: MIT Press.

———. 1994. "Live Interactive Computer Music in HMSL, 1984–1992." *Computer Music Journal* 18, no. 2: 59–77.

Polli, A. 1999. Active Vision: Controlling Sound with Eye Movements. *Leonardo* 32: 405–411.

Poole, S. 1998. "Bird by Mouse." *Guardian Weekly,* April 12, p. 26.

Pope, S. T. 1996. "A Taxonomy of Computer Music." *Contemporary Music Review* 13, no. 2: 137–45.

Povall, R. 1995. "Compositional Methods in Interactive Performance Environments." *Journal of New Music Research* 24: 109–20.

———. 1996. "Adding Video into the (Real)Time Domain." *Organised Sound* 1, no. 2: 93–106.

———. 1997. "Sociological, Artistic, and Pedagogical Frameworks for Electronic Art." *Computer Music Journal* 21, no. 1: 18–25.

Pressing, J. 1988. "Improvisation: Methods and Models." In *Generative Processes in Music: The Psychology of Performance, Improvisation, and Composition,* edited by J. Sloboda. Oxford: Clarendon Press.

———. 1990. Cybernetic Issues in Interactive Performance Systems. *Computer Music Journal* 14, no. 1: 12–25.

———. 1992. *Synthesiser Performance and Real-Time Techniques.* Madison, Wis.: A-R Editions.

———. 1997. Some Perspectives on Performed Sound and Music in Virtual Environments. *Presence* 6: 1–22.

———. 1998. Psychological Constraints on Improvisational Expertise and Communication. In *In the course of performance,* edited by B. Nettl and M. Russell. Chicago: University of Chicago Press.

Ramalho, G. L., P.-Y. Rolland, and J.-G. Ganascia. 1999. "An Artificially Intelligent Jazz Performer (IMPACT)." *Journal of New Music Research* 28: 105–29.

Riddell, A. M. 1989. *A Perspective on the Acoustic Piano as a Performance Medium under Machine Control.* La Trobe University, Melbourne, Australia, MA Thesis.

———. 1990. "A Meta-Action for the Grand Piano." Paper presented at the International Computer Music Conference, Glasgow, UK, of the International Computer Music Association.

Roads, C., ed. 1985. *Composers and the Computers.* Los Altos, Calif.: William Kaufmann.

———. 1989. *The Music Machine: Selected Readings from "Computer Music Journal."* Cambridge: MIT Press.

Roads, C., and J. Strawn, eds. 1985. *Foundations of Computer Music.* Cambridge: MIT Press.

Rose, J. 1996. "Improvisation and Interactive Technology." *London Music Collective Magazine* [available at Jon Rose's Web site].

Rose, T. 1994. *Black Noise: Rap Music and Black Culture in Contemporary America.* Hanover, N.H.: University Press of New England.

Rosenboom, D. 1989. *Extended Musical Interface with the Human Nervous System: Assessment and Prospectus.* New York: Leonardo Monographs.

———. 1990. The Performing Brain. *Computer Music Journal* 14, no. 1: 48–66.

———. 2000. "Propositional Music: On Emergent Properties in Morphogenesis and the Evolution of Music: Essays, Propositions, Commentaries, Imponderable Forms, and Compositional Methods." In *Arcana: Musicians on Music,* edited by J. Zorn. New York: Granary Books.

Rothenberg, A. 1990. *Creativity and Madness: New Findings and Old Stereotypes.* Baltimore: Johns Hopkins University Press.

Rothenberg, D. 1996. "Sudden Music: Improvising across the Electronic Abyss." *Contemporary Music Review* 13, no. 2: 23–46.

Rowe, R. 1993. *Interactive Music Systems: Machine Listening and Composing.* Cambridge: MIT Press.

Rudi, J. 1998. Computer Music Animations. *Organised Sound* 3: 193–98.

Rule, G. 1999. *Electro shock! Groundbreakers of Synth Music.* San Francisco: Miller Freeman Books.

Rush, M. 1999. *New Media in Late Twentieth-Century Art.* London: Thames and Hudson.

Sarath, E. W. 1996. "A New Look at Improvisation." *Journal of Music Theory* 40: 1–38.

Sawyer, K. 1992. "Improvisational Creativity: An Analysis of Jazz Performance." *Creativity Research Journal* 67: 1–55.

Schellenberg, E. G. 1996. "Expectancy in Melody: Tests of the Implication-Realization Model." *Cognition* 58: 75–125.

Schiemer, G. 1999. "Improvising Machines: Spectral Dance and Token Objects." In *Predictions and Inaccuracies: Collisions of Musical Histories and Futures Approaching the Millennium,* edited by P. Platt. Sydney: Sydney Chapter of the Musicological Society of Australia.

Schiemer, G., and G. Leak. 1987–88. "Polyphonic Variations," on CD *Wattever.* Tall Poppies, TP 074.

Schloss, W. A., and D. A. Jaffe. 1991–92 As for Schiemer. *Wildlife.* Centaur Records on CD *The Virtuoso in the Computer Age* {CDCM Computer Music Series Volume 15.}.

———. 1993. "Intelligent Musical Instruments: the Future of Musical Performance or the Demise of the Performer?" *Journal of New Music Research* 22: 183–93.

Schuller, G. 1968. *Early Jazz.* Oxford: Oxford University Press.

Schwanauer, S. M., and D. A. Levitt, eds. 1993. *Machine Models of Music.* Cambridge: MIT Press.

Shams, L., Y. Kamitani, and S. Shimojo. 2000. "What You See Is What You Hear." *Nature* 408: 788.

Shapiro, P. 1999. *Drum 'n' Bass: The Rough Guide.* London: Rough Guides.

Siegel, W. 1998. The Challenges of Interactive Dance: An Overview and Case Study. *Computer Music Journal* 22, no. 4: 29–43.

Sirota, W. 1991. "Review: The Hub—Hub Computer Network Music CD Art 1002." *Computer Music Journal* 15, no. 2: 76–77.

Sloboda, J. A. 1988. *Generative Processes in Music: The Cognitive Psychology of Music.* Oxford: Clarendon.

Smith, C. 1998. "A Sense of the Possible: Miles Davis and the Semiotics of Improvised Performance." In *In the course of performance,* edited by B. Nettl and M. Russell. Chicago: University of Chicago Press.

Smith, H., and R. T. Dean. 1997. *Improvisation, Hypermedia, and the Arts since 1945.* London: Harwood Academic.

Smith, H. A., and R. T. Dean. 2001. *Returning the Angles.* Soma 787 [sound and image technodrama, released on CD with interactive CD-ROM].

Spiegel, L. 1986. *Music Mouse: An Intelligent Instrument for the Macintosh.* New York: Retiary.org.

———. 1992. *Unseen Worlds.* New York, Compact disc, Aesthetic Engineering AE-11001-2.

———. 1996. "That Was Then—This Is Now." *Computer Music Journal* 20, no. 1: 42–45.

———. 1998. "Graphical Groove: A Memorial for the Vampire, a Visual Music System." *Organised Sound* 3: 187–91.

Subotnick, M. 1995. *Making Music.* Voyager Educational CD-ROM. [No catalog number].

Subotnick, M., and T. Machover. 1996. "Interview with Mort Subotnick." *Contemporary Music Review* 13, no. 2: 3–11.

Tagg, P. N.d. From Refrain to Rave: The Decline of Figure and the Rise of Ground. *ReR/Recommended Sourcebook 0402:* 20–30.

Talking Heads Experiment. 2000. <talkingheads.csl.sony.fr/>.

Taylor, G. 1999. "David Wessel Interview." On the *Cycling '74.* Web site.

Teitelbaum, R. 1976. "In Tune: Some Early Experiments in Biofeedback music (1966–1974)." In *Biofeedback and the Arts: Results of*

Early Experiments, 2d ed., edited by D. Rosenboom. Banff, Aesthetic Research Centre of Canada.

———. 1984. "The Digital Piano and the Patch Control Language System." Paper presented at the International Computer Music Conference of the International Computer Music Association, Paris. 1984. 1985. Concerto Grosso, Hat Hut Compact Disc Hat Art CD 6004.

———. 1993. *Cyberband.* Moers Music CD 0300. Thaemlitz, T. 2000. Talk given at Lux Centre, London, April 6.

Thayer, J. F., and R. A. Levenson. 1983. Effects of Music on Psychophysiological Responses to a Stressful Film. *Psychomusicology* 3: 44–52.

Theberge, P. 1997. *Any Sound You Can Imagine: Making Music/Consuming Technology.* Music/Culture Series. Hanover, N.H.: Wesleyan University Press.

Toiviainen, P. 1995a. "Modeling the Target-Note Technique of Bebop-Style Jazz Improvisation: An Artificial Neural Network Approach." *Music Perception* 12: 399–413.

———. 1995b. "Tonal Hierarchies in Jazz Improvisation." *Music Perception* 15: 415–37.

Toop, D. 1995. *Ocean of Sound: Aether Talk, Ambient Sound, and Imaginary Worlds.* London: Serpent's Tail.

———. 2000. "Just Look at That Sound." *Guardian,* April 25.

VanHandel, L., and G. Nauck. 1994. "From Gost Scores to CD-ROM: The Interactive Music of Morton Subotnick." *Positionen: Beiträge zur Neuen Musik* 21: 12–15.

Van Noorden, L., and D. Moelants. 1999. "Resonance in the Perception of Musical Pulse." *Journal of New Music Research* 28, no. 1: 43–66.

Various. 2000. *Digital Space.* Lovebytes, CD and CDRom DSP1.

Various (2000a). Ohm: the early gurus of electronic music 1948–1980. Compact Disc, Roslyn, New York, Ellipsis Arts.

Walker, W., K. Hebel, S. Martirano, and Scaletti, C. 1992. "ImprovisationBuilder: Improvisation as Conversation." Paper presented at the International Computer Music Conference of the International Computer Music Association, San Jose, California, 1992.

Walker, W. F. 1994. "A Conversation-Based Framework for Musical Improvisation." Ph.D. diss., University of Illinois.

Wanderley, M. M., and M. Battier, eds. 2000. *Trends in Gestural Control of Music.* Paris: IRCAM.

Wellcome Trust. 2000. Noise: An Exhibition about Information and Transformation. London: Wellcome Trust.

Wessel, D. L. 1991. "Improvisation with Highly Interactive Real-Time Performance Systems." Paper presented at the International Computer Music Conference of the International Music Association, Montreal, 1991.

Whitney, J. 1980. *Digital Harmony: On the Complementarity of Music and Visual Art.* Peterborough, N.H.: McGraw-Hill.

Wilson, P. N. 1996. "Remix of Reality: Current Thoughts on Composing/Improvising with the Aid of Electronic Technology." *Neue Zeitschrift für Musik* 157, no. 5: 14–17.

Winkler, T. 1998. *Composing Interactive Music: Techniques and Ideas Using Max.* Cambridge: MIT Press.

Winterfeldt, S. 1992. "Richard L. Teitelbaum: The Golem." *Positionen: Beiträge zur neuen musik* 2: 12–16.

Wishart, T. 1985. *On Sonic Art.* York: Imagineering Press.

———. 1994. *Audible Design: A Plain and Easy Introduction to Practical Sound Composition.* York: Orpheus the Pantomime.

Xenakis, I. 1971. *Formalized Music.* Bloomington: Indiana University Press.

Yavelow, C. 1989. "Music and Microprocessors: MIDI and the State of the Art." In *The Music Machine: Selected Readings from "Computer Music Journal,"* edited by C. Roads. Cambridge: MIT Press.

———. 1992. *Macworld Music and Sound Bible.* San Mateo, Calif.: IDG Books Worldwide.

———. 1997–98. *Music Is the Message.* Zandvoort, Netherlands: Yav Interactive Media.

Youngblood, G. 1970. *Expanded Cinema.* London: Studio Vista.

Zicarelli, D. 1987. "M and Jam Factory." *Computer Music Journal* 11, no. 4: 13–29.

Zicarelli, D., and M. Puckette. 1990–. Max. A software platform originally published by Opcode and IRCAM; and currently by Cycling74'.

Zorn, J. 2000a. "Treatment for a Film in Fifteen Scenes." In *Arcana: Musicians on Music,* edited by J. Zorn. New York: Granary Books.

———, ed. 2000b. *Arcana: Musicians on Music.* New York: Granary Books.

Web and Software Resources

This selective list is intended to give key pointers to sources of information on the Web and of software relevant to the topic of this book. The Web addresses are the home pages of sites from which much other information can be gathered, checked at the time of production of this book (2002). Such addresses change frequently, and the reader is advised that they can usually be quickly refound using search engines such as Google, Lycos, or Yahoo. Google also supplies some archived pages from older versions or locales of sites. Abbreviations are listed in the preface to this book.

■ SELECTED WEB SITES

Artifact Recordings (information on the Hub, Tim Perkis, and other relevant artists): www.artifact.com

austraLYSIS: http://www.australysis.com

Phil Burk's links list: at the softsynth site, http://www.softsynth.com/

CNMAT: http://www.cnmat.berkeley.edu

Cycling '74: http://www.cycling74.com

Digital Music Archives (electroacoustic recordings supplier): http://www.digital-music-archives.com/

EMF: http://www.emf.org (includes Warren Burt's synopsis of PC software for computer music)

International Computer Music Association: http://www.computermusic.org/

IRCAM: http://www.ircam.fr

MikroPolyphonie (an online journal of electronic music): http://farben.latrobe.edu.au/mikropol

STEIM: (Studio for Electro-Instrumental Music) http://www.steim.nl/
ARiADA (University of East Anglia electroacoustic research and journal) : http://www.ariada.uea.ac.uk/

■ SELECTED SOFTWARE SOURCES

Cycling '74: http://www.cycling74.com
International Computer Music Association: http://www.computermusic.org/
IRCAM: http://www.ircam.fr
jMusic: http://jmusic.ci.qut.edu.au
Opcode: www.opcode.com/
Softsynth: http://www.softsynth.com/
Supercollider: www.audiosynth.com/

Index

A
Accentuation, 75
Acoustic piano, 43
Afrological, 82–83
AI, 6, 7, 73, 100, 133, 142, 146, 156
aLEb, 88, 93, 97, 99
Algorithms
    Cell, 31
    Generator, 135
    Player, 31
    Scan, 31
    Synopsis, 49
    Token, 31
a-life, 5, 151
ALMC, 113
Analog synthesizer, 12
Analysis, 52–53
    Natural, 16
    Shenkerian, 16
    SPEAC, 16
Anamnesis, 143
Antecedents, 11–22
Applied improvisation, 7
Artifact albums, 113, 114
Artificial intelligence, 6, 7, 73, 100
Artificial life, 5, 151
ARTIST, 155
Asynchronous cinema, 133
ATN, 16
Audio exchange, 134
Audio generation and modification, 68
Augmented transition network, 16
AustraLYSIS, 58, 88, 93, 97, 119
Autocatalyst, 92
Avatars, 134
Averaging, 81

B
Bandwidth, 73, 135, 141
Beatnik, 73–74, 135, 137
Beat tracking, 75
Black Box, 12, 145
Bodily action, 38
Bop, 148
Breakbeats, 71

BubbaBall, 39, 43
Buffer, 56

C
Cassette tape, 131
CD-ROM, 28, 131–33, 152–53
Chained, 53
Chain exchange, 131
Champ d'action, 85
Chromosomes, 149
CNMAT, 29, 69, 74, 98
Cognition, 147
Cognitive-based, 147, 148
Common clock, 90
Compositional ideas, 15–18
Compositional method, 49
    Algorithmic, 51
    Cognitive model, 50
    Pragmatics, 50
Comprovisation, 87, 95, 132
Computer, 3–10
    Antecedents, 121–27
    Artists, 5
    Digital, 12
    Use by women, 4
    Use in cultural arts, 4
Computer algorithmic composition, 16, 76
Computer based samples, 80
Computer Music Instrument (CMI), 13
Control-stochastic axis, 135
Conversation, 90
Core pitch, 52
Cyborg, 4, 7
Cyclic code generator, 30–31
Cypher, 66–67, 149, 152

D
Dance floor, 39
Data flow language, 65
Dedicated sampler, 68
Delay step, 53
Digital cinema, 133, 137
Digital electronic technology, 16

Digital performance instruments, 27
    Microprocessor, 27
    MIDI, 27
    Sample-based, 28
    Synthesizer, 27
    Yamaha DX7 keyboard, 27
Digital Sound Processing (DSP), 29, 31
Displayed motion, 49
Drum and bass idiom, 70, 76–77, 86
DSP, 29, 31, 68, 77, 86, 95, 104, 108, 110, 133, 134
DVD, 132

E
Easy Beat, 71, 72
Electroband, 95
Electronic instruments, 11–13, 15
    Chamberlain, 13
    Hypercello, 12
    Interactive, 11, 19–22
    Moosak machine, 12
    Ordes martenot, 12
    Telharmonium, 12
    Theremin, 11, 15
Electronic manipulation, 107
Electronics, 104–5
Emergence, 141, 142–43
Emergent behaviors, 142
EMF, 62
Ether, 131
Eurocentric, 171
Eurological, 82–83
Evaluation, 145
Evolutionary algorithms, 98
Evolutionary computation, 145, 156
Experience-in-music intelligence, 17
Exploitation, 152
Exploratory, 133
Extraction, 52

F
Feeping Creatures, 150
Flexibility, 143
Fractals, 115
Fragments, 144, 148

G

Generation, 56, 72
Generative algorithm, 73
Generative programming, 98, 100
Genetic programming, 150–51
Gestural control, 28, 41, 42, 43, 166
Gestural display, 88
Gestural interface, 98
Gesture, 42, 49
GinJam, 149–50
Giuppo Nuova Cinsonanza (GNC), 19
Global features, 49
    Pitch contour shape, 49
    Rhythm pattern, 49
    Volume contour, 49
Gloves, 38
GNC, 19
Grainwave, 69
GROOVE, 13, 62, 117, 119

H

Hard bop, 148
Hardware, 27–35
HMSL, 64
Home key, 147
Hub, 22, 84, 86, 88–89, 90–94, 95, 97, 99, 107, 113
Human-computer interaction, 99
Hybridization, 53
Hypergroove, 86–87
Hyperinstrument, 31, 173
    "Brain Opera" project, 35
    Celletto, 32
    Guitar, 32
    Perkophone, 31, 34
    Trumpet, 31, 34
    Violin, 32–33
Hysteresis, 171

I

IB, 18
ICMA, 132
I-cube, 38
Identification, 52
Idiomatic improvisation, 18
IMA, 132
Immersion, 137
IMPACT, 148–49
Implication-realization model, 146–47
Improvisation, 83–86
    Applied, 7
    Computer-interactive, 152–53, 173
    Computer-mediated, 136
    Idiomatic, 18
    Looping, 70
    Networked sound, 113
    Pure, 7
    Real-time, 109, 152
Improvisation Builder (IB), 18
Improvisor, 147
    Computer as, 151
Indeterminacy, 82–83
Instruments, electronic, 11–13
    Chamberlain, 13
    Hypercello, 12
    Interactive, 11
    Moosak machine, 12
    Ordes martenot, 12
    Telharmonium, 12
    Theremin, 11, 15
Intelligent Computer Music Systems, 63
Interactive sound improvisation, 79, 87–88, 94, 96–100, 117, 133
Interface, 37–44
    Properties, 41
    Semiotic, 44
Intermedia work, 15, 101
Interpenetration, 4
InterSpace, 134
IRCAM, 61, 70, 76, 80, 98, 104

J

Javascript, 135
Jazz, 64, 75, 109, 147

K

Koan, 73–74, 135, 137

L

LAMC, *see* League of Automatic Music Composers
League of Automatic Music Composers (LAMC), 21–22, 89, 96–97
Lexical power, 152
Limitations, emergence, 141
    Access speed, 141
    Bandwidth, 141
    Hardware, 141
    Memory, 141
LiSa, 68, 69, 70
Looped beat, 71
Looping, 68, 70
Loop manipulation, 71

M

Manipulation, 53–56
Mapping, 41, 53
    Convergent, 41
    Cross-disciplinary, 109
    Divergent, 41
    Multiparametric, 42
    One-to-one, 41
    Sensor, 166
MAX, 13, 29, 31, 38, 51, 58, 64–67, 70, 72, 73, 74, 76, 77, 81, 83, 94, 97, 98, 104, 107, 108, 110, 113, 115, 116, 117, 118, 132–33, 135, 137, 145, 179, 180
Meta-composition, 84, 86
Meta-idiom, 117
Meta-instrument, 79–80
Meta-orchestra, 80
Meta-sound, 51, 52, 69, 134, 145
Meter and pulse, 74
MEV, 19
MIDI, 7, 14, 15, 19, 27, 28, 29, 30, 31, 32, 33, 36, 38, 40, 51, 52, 53, 54, 55, 58, 61, 63, 65, 67, 68, 69, 71, 72, 73, 74, 75, 77, 80, 81, 85, 90–91, 94, 95, 96, 97, 98, 107, 108, 110, 114, 117, 120, 124, 134, 147, 152, 169, 170
    Toolbox, 30
MIDI-Conductor, 95
MIDIGRID, 64
MIDI-stream generator, 64–67
Mind map, 81
Mixing sounds, 103
Modeling, 146
Morphing, 104
MSP, 69–70, 72, 77, 104, 108, 110, 117, 119, 180
Multiple meters and pulses, 57
Musica Elettronica Viva (MEV), 19
Musical segment global features, 49
Music is the Message, 110–11
MusicMouse, 62
MusiKalscope, 109

N

NATO, 108, 110
Natural analysis, 16

Network band, 90
Neural activity, 38
Neural net, 73, 145, 148
Normalization, 64

O
Onset gaps, 81
Opcode Studio 5 MIDI, 114
Open network configuration, 55
Overlays, 58

P
PACTS, 148
Patch, 74, 76, 95
Patch Control Language, 65, 97
Patch memory, 132
Patents, 153–55
PCL, 65, 97
Percussion controller, 38
Performance layout, 121
Phrase recording, 98
Pitch contour, 49
Pitch identification, 52–53
Pitch insets, 52
Pitch pattern, 147
Pitch register, 81
PMIS (Performer/Machine Interactive System), 43–44
Polyrhythms, 57
Postmodernism, 9
Programming, emergence, 142
ProTools, 68, 69, 72, 74
Pure improvisation, 7

Q
Qualia, 5
Quicktime, 132, 135
Quicktime Musical Instrument, 72

R
Random Rhapsody, 115
RealAudio, 132, 135
Real time, 13
Real-time improvisation, 152
Real-time synthesis, 152

ReCycle, 69, 74
Remote, 136–37
Resynthesis, 143
Rhythm engines, 74, 76
Rhythmic pattern, 147
Rose, John, 97

S
Sample, 51, 68, 103
Sampler instrument, 68
Schenker, Heinrich, 16
Sensorband, 95–96
Sensor mapping, 166
Sensors, 38
Set response, 170
Signatures, 17, 147
Sonic artifact, 114
Sonic Arts Union, 19, 20
Sonic texture, 114–15
Sound, 5, 43, 51
    Asymmetrical, 6
    Computer-interactive, 141
    Inputs, 52
    Mixing, 103
    Modification, 117
    Natural, 104
    Samples, 55, 103
    Shapes, 103
    Source, 43
    Streams, 56
    Symmetrical, 6
    Synthesis, 117
SoundNet, 95–96
Spacialization, 178
SPEAC analysis, 16
Special distribution, 103
Speaking wands, 39
STEIM, 32, 39, 40, 68, 95, 108
Stochastic computer approaches, 16
Stochastic process, 166
Streaming, 42, 51, 132, 135
Strung net, 89
Supercollider, 69, 72, 73–74, 95
Swing, 75–76

Synthesis, 41, 106, 152

T
Tactile inputs, 40
Techno, 69, 70, 86
Tele-improvisation, 134
Teleportation, 151
Text-based referents, 16
Texture, 90, 104, 114–15
Timbral variation, 103
Thunder, 38
Thunder pads, 38
Transformation, 98

U
Universality, 146
User input device, 49
Utility, 152

V
Variables, 55, 89
Variation, 144
Verbal specification, 153
Viables, 80
    Foot pedals, 80
    Pressure-sensitive keys, 80
Video, 39
Virtual Bird, 147–48
Virtual chaos band, 116
Virtuality, 4
Virtual reality, 5
Virtual subject, 4
Volume contour, 49
Voyager, 81, 84, 124–25, 162, 165, 167, 169–71, 172, 173, 174–75
VR, 5

W
Web hypermedia, 133
Web interaction, 134
Web interface, 152
WELL, 107
WorldBeat, 153

ML 74 .D43 2003
Dean, R. T.
Hyperimprovisation